Introduction to the Psychology of Ageing for Non-Specialists

Ian Stuart-Hamilton

Jessica Kingsley *Publishers*
London and Philadelphia

First published in 2014
by Jessica Kingsley Publishers
73 Collier Street
London N1 9BE, UK
and
400 Market Street, Suite 400
Philadelphia, PA 19106, USA

www.jkp.com

Library of Congress Cataloging in Publication Data
A CIP catalog record for this book is available from the Library of Congress

British Library Cataloguing in Publication Data
A CIP catalogue record for this book is available from the British Library

ISBN 978 1 84905 363 1
eISBN 978 0 85700 715 5

Printed and bound in Great Britain

To the memory of Michael Hornigold (1946–2012),
who deserved to experience a lot more of it

Contents

Preface

This book is derived from a much larger work of mine called *The Psychology of Ageing: An Introduction*. The first edition of the book was released on an unsuspecting world in 1991 and was gratifyingly successful. I would not presume to claim it was a best seller amongst the general public. I once calculated that J.K. Rowling sold more copies of *Harry Potter and the Deadly Hallows* in the first thousandth of a second it was on sale than I have sold in a lifetime.[1] However, within its field it sold well enough and has been sufficiently well regarded to be translated into 18 or more languages and go through five editions. A few years ago, the British Medical Association named it as one of their books of the year, *and* it has topped Amazon's gerontological nursing bestsellers list.[2] This is all very agreeable and the critics have been uniformly nice about the book.[3]

However, there was a rich man's problem with the book as it went into later editions. When I wrote the first edition, I obviously had to do preparatory reading, and I was recommended to try the then new-fangled method of performing an electronic database search. Incredible as it now seems, this involved making an appointment with a specialist librarian, who performed the task for me (I supplied

---

1 But equally, try finding anything meaningful on the disuse hypothesis of ageing and intelligence in any of J.K.R.'s work. Whilst on the subject, given the impressive sales of *Cuckoo's Calling* once the true authorship was revealed, if anyone wants to spread the rumour that Ian Stuart-Hamilton is another of her pen names, I wouldn't object.

2 Another thing that J.K. Rowling hasn't done. I doubt she loses much sleep over it.

3 Apart from the anonymous letter writer who said that reading it had made his testicles fall off. Given the content of the rest of his letter I feel he had a number of issues.

the keywords). The resulting print-out (on tractor feed paper, a term that will have anyone under 40 scratching their heads) ran to under 100 pages. Today, a computer search of PsycINFO or Medline[4] will produce a larger print-out for just a single specialist topic within the psychology of ageing. The subject has mushroomed in size, and in order for the book to reflect the full diversity of the research literature, it has likewise increased in size in each successive edition. To give one illustration – the fifth edition's references section alone has a word count that is not far off the whole of the first edition. This increased coverage is fine and dandy if the reader wants coverage of not only the key topics, but also the side arguments, the discussions of research methodology, etc. And given sales and critical reception, clearly a lot of people do.

However, there are many potential readers who have been alienated by all this added detail. In writing this book, I had three groups particularly in mind:

1. social workers and care workers

2. nursing and medical workers

3. non-specialists with an interest in their own ageing or the ageing of a relative or clients.

People in these groups might want to know about key aspects of psychological ageing, such as changes in intelligence, memory, personality, etc., and are likely to have an especial interest in changing lifestyles and mental illness of older adults. What they do *not* want or need is lengthy discussion of the minutiae of differences in test methodologies or in-depth discussions of relatively esoteric psychological processes. The latter are very important (indeed, essential) if you are taking geropsychology as a specialisation, but they are unnecessary for readers in many cognate fields. The present book has therefore taken the fifth edition of *The Psychology of Ageing: An Introduction* and trimmed it down. Drastically.

For starters, three chapters have been removed. Two of these are concerned with research methodologies. If you find you need these,

---

4   Two of the key computer databases containing records of hundreds of thousands of research papers and books on Psychology and Medicine respectively.

then you probably should be reading the fifth edition and not this.[5] The other chapter is on death and dying, which is not strictly speaking part of the study of ageing anyway.[6] The remaining chapters have been shorn of detailed discussions of methodological issues and laboratory studies that are largely or solely of theoretical interest to psychologists. All the chapters have then been rewritten to some extent. In part this is to cope with the removed text, but I have also tried to make the text more practically meaningful, rather than demonstrating that a particular finding is a useful test of a particular theory, for example. Chapters 1 and 2 have been particularly heavily revised. The end result of these changes is a book that is about a quarter of the size of the fifth edition. However, this book is not a 'simplified' text. What remains has, I hope, the same gravitas as the book it is derived from. The important distinction is that in this book, the reader gets the plain story without the additional information that is unlikely to be of great use to them.

This book should have been published a year ago. Unfortunately, in late 2011 my mother developed very florid vascular dementia along with delirium.[7] My father had died earlier in the year, and as the only child, I had the experience alas all too many people have had of trying to keep a job and look after my mother and spend time with my own family. Eventually my mother's condition deteriorated so much that she spent her final year alternating between hospital and nursing home, before finally dying in November 2012. I am not writing any of this to elicit sympathy, but rather to make a confession. If you have to experience caring for someone with dementia yourself, you suddenly get a radical new view of what are important psychological questions in dementia research. Being woken repeatedly at 4.00 a.m. to be asked 'Is it morning or night?' or being called in to the residential home because Mum had punched one of the carers were two of many unwelcome new experiences for me. Thus, I began to wonder if studies that addressed such burning topics as whether demented participants

---

5   Unless you are reading this as a primer and have the fifth edition as well, which is fine by me. I have two children's university fees to pay and the royalties are welcome.
6   On a worldwide scale, death is likely to be before a person reaches old age, as you will see in Chapter 1.
7   The terms are explained in Chapter 6.

could remember lists of nonsense syllables were really addressing what was needed. Therefore, I have tried as far as possible to restrict mention of any of the more theoretical research to where it underpins more applied concerns. However, there are limits – thus, I have not discussed issues such as where to get help for caring for relatives, the ins and outs of patients' rights, etc. These are very important topics, but they are not within Psychology's ambit.

I would like to thank Jessica Kingsley and her staff and my wife and children for being incredibly supportive and putting up with even more of my lunacy than usual whilst I wrote this book.

Ian Stuart-Hamilton
Professor of Developmental Psychology
University of South Wales

CHAPTER 1

Some Basic Information About Ageing

Defining old age

A person's age is typically measured in terms of how many years old they are; or in other words, how many times the Earth has been round the sun since they were born. This is known as *chronological age*. We tend to treat age as if it is a precise and accurate marker. In part this is because we use it as a legally binding guide to the age at which certain things become permissible. But these are essentially arbitrary measures, devised by countries according to their particular value systems. Thus, there are considerable national differences in the age at which it is legal to have sex or to drink alcohol. In the case of retirement, pensionable age varies widely between countries, from the mid-50s to the late 60s, and in many countries there is no compulsory retirement age.

Thus, retirement ages, although because they are official have an appearance of objectivity about them, in reality are fairly arbitrary (if they were not, then every country would have the same retirement age). Exactly the same argument applies to deciding the chronological age at which old age begins. It is possible to devote *very* lengthy discussions to this topic (and academics have been prolix on this matter), but to cut to the chase, we generally argue that old age begins when a person reaches the chronological age of 60 years. There is nothing particularly important or significant about the age of 60.[1] Over the centuries, there had been an informal consensus that it was a reasonable rule-of-thumb measure of the onset of old age, but it was not until the 19th century that opinion became a more formal belief. In part this was because of the work of a Belgian statistician called Quetelet, who wrote a highly influential book on how humans could be statistically analysed (he also, incidentally, invented the body mass index). In one of his key pieces of writing, Quetelet asserted that from 'sixty to sixty-five years of age viability loses much of its energy, that is to say, the probability of life then becomes very small' (Quetelet, 1836, p.178). We now know this argument is utterly wrong, but because the rest of the book was well received, by the 1840s the 'fact' that old age begins around the ages of 60 to 65 was widely believed (Mullan, 2002), and current researchers also tend to use these same ages as indicating the onset of old age.

It must be stressed that the age of 60 is these days only intended as a useful guide. Because we have to have some sort of figure for the purposes of classification, etc., 60 is generally used. But it must also be stressed that nobody actually believes that on a person's 60th birthday they 'become' old so that the day before they were a hale and hearty person and the day after they are devoid of teeth, hair, senses and mobility. Nor does anybody seriously think that everybody who is the same chronological age is also identical in other respects as well. It is perfectly obvious that people change and become 'old' at different rates, to the extent that we can say that some people look 'young for their age' whilst others of the same chronological age look 'right for their age' or 'old for their age'. Researchers know perfectly well that this figure is arbitrary, but it is better than saying 'old age sort of begins in the 60s or later or sooner in some people'.

Changes in life expectancy

Presented with the words 'life expectancy' an intelligent person might reasonably interpret it as meaning how long a person can expect to

---

1   Humans tend to give greater significance to ages or anniversaries ending in zero. Conversely, they tend to find numbers ending in zero contrived in real-life data – hence the old adage never to hand in an expenses claim that ends in zero (e.g. a claim for £103.34 looks more plausible than one for £100.00).

live. This is accurate in one sense, but in another far more important way, it is totally misleading. Consider the following example, taken from Stuart-Hamilton (2011). In 1400, it is estimated that the life expectancy in Europe was 35 years; by 1841, this had risen to 40 years, but by 1981, it had skyrocketed to 71 years (i.e. over double the 1400 figure). To the unwary, these figures seem to indicate that in 1400 it was almost impossible to grow old since most people died before they reached 35. Indeed, the irresistible mental image for some is that in 1400 'old age' must have been in the 40s. This is wrong. The reason for the lower life expectancy in 1400 is because a lot more people died in infancy and childhood than they do today. If a lot of people die at a very young age in a sample, then this drags down the group's mean or median score very dramatically; but this does not mean that if you survived childhood, your *remaining* life expectancy would be as bad. To illustrate this point, consider the life expectancy figures for people who have already reached the age of 60. In 1400 their life expectancy was 69, in 1841 it was 73, and in 1981 it was 76. The difference between the 1400 and the 1981 figures has shrunk from 36 years at birth to seven years at age 60. This clearly illustrates the prime reason for differences in life expectancy figures over historical time – namely, fewer people die in childhood, not that people who reach adulthood live vastly longer lives.

However, it can be argued that nonetheless, even allowing for infant mortality, people still live longer these days than in the past. For example, even if one of our ancestors reached the age of 60, they were still likely to be in the grave years before someone of the same age today. Can this trend continue? At this point the argument gets quite technical. Some researchers (e.g. Oeppen and Vaupel, 2002) argue that the only way is up, and that life expectancy is going to continue to rise year upon year. Others (e.g. Post and Binstock, 2004) claim that the rise is attributable to infant mortality statistics exerting an influence, and that once infant mortality is reduced to as close to zero as possible, the life expectancy figures will stop rising. Others have argued that future health trends are uncertain and that whilst health care has lowered death rates, increased obesity coupled with lower levels of exercise might increase death rates again, leading to an uncertain future in which numerous mortality rates and hence life expectancy figures could be possible (Continuous Mortality Investigation, 2006a, 2006b). Thus, whether the trend will continue is uncertain.

The above is about the future – what about the present? In Britain today, about 11 million (c. 16%) of the population is aged 65 or older. There are similar figures for other industrialised nations (OECD, 2004).[2] The study of ageing is the study of a significant proportion of the population; and moreover, it is the study of a time of life that the majority of us can expect to experience.

Differences in life expectancy

Where people live can have a big effect on how long they will live. For example, North America has a life expectancy of 78, Latin America 74, Europe 76, Asia 70 – and Africa 55 (Population Reference Bureau, 2010). This largely reflects the level of technological development in the countries concerned (e.g. in Europe, if the EU countries are considered separately, their life expectancy is 79). A better infrastructure means not only better care, but better housing and public sanitation create an environment in which infectious disease is harder to spread. Death by communicable disease is ten times higher in developing countries, whereas in industrialised nations, death is far more likely to be due to chronic (i.e. long-lasting) conditions such as heart disease and cancer (Leader and Corfield, 2007).

However, even within the same country, some places confer better life expectancy than others. For example, within the UK, people in the north east of England have a life expectancy two and a half years less than people living in the south west of England. Many reasons can be suggested for this – differences in climate, local health care, level of stress in daily life, etc., can all be proposed with some justification. Ultimately, however, wealth seems to be the single most dominant factor. If we consider smaller areas of the country, the differences become more startling, with Kensington and Chelsea (a very prosperous area of London) recording the highest male at-birth figure of 84.4 years, compared with, at the other end of the scale, Glasgow City (71.1 years) (Office for National Statistics, 2010a, 2010b). This accords with reports from other countries that found

---

2   Throughout I will tend to use UK figures. However, all the arguments raised from them are generally applicable to other industrialised countries.

similar regional differences, where they also are largely associated with socio-economic status (see Griffiths and Fitzpatrick, 2001). It is worth noting that the differences between groups need not be very pronounced for there to be a difference in life expectancy. Marmot and Feeney (1997) studied UK civil servants and found that even within this occupational group (where nearly all could be described as at least financially comfortable), life expectancy significantly rose the higher the income of the sub-group being considered.

It would be misleading to attribute all differences in life expectancy to wealth. Other lifestyle factors that are not particularly wealth-dependent also play a role. A striking illustration of this is the *Roseto effect* (see Egolf *et al.*, 1992). This is named after an Italian-American community in Roseto, Pennsylvania, whose members' susceptibility to heart disease increased as it became more 'Americanised'. The instinctive reaction is to assume this was a dietary issue as Italian food is often seen as adhering to the 'Mediterranean diet' ideal of few saturated fats. Nothing could be further from the truth – the regional variant favoured by the Roseto community included seemingly artery-clogging quantities of saturated fats (the people also drank and smoked). The reason for the greater resistance to heart disease was ascribed to the Roseto community itself: wealth was not flaunted, people supported each other and social life was family-centred. However, as time progressed, members of the community moved away from this communal view to a more individualistic one. A study of Roseto at the point when this transition was becoming apparent predicted that there would be a concomitant rise in heart disease (Lynn *et al.*, 1967) – alas, this prediction proved all too accurate. However, it should be noted that the effect on the inhabitants of Roseto was not a uniform one – younger men and older women were disproportionately more badly affected (Egolf *et al.*, 1992).

Roseto is not quite unique – several other immigrant communities have been found that also have longer life expectancies (see Leader and Corfield, 2007). There is no doubt that cohesive supportive societies can in some instances improve life expectancy. However, it is improbable that this is the total explanation. For every supportive community resembling the town in *It's a Wonderful Life* there are arguably many more close-knit places that are snooping, judgemental and, accordingly, stressful. Presumably, sometimes the right balance of support and interference is attained, but this seems to be a hard thing to achieve, given the rarity of places like Roseto (the town was originally selected for study precisely because it was so unusual). And whether a longer life spent in a town where individuality is repressed and everyone knows their place is a blessing or a curse is a debatable point. This is not to deny the principal findings from Roseto *et al.* – undoubtedly community support can prolong life expectancy under certain circumstances (similarly, Giles *et al.*, 2005 found that having five or more friends at the start of a ten-year study gave people a quarter less chance of dying by the end of the research). But nor can the findings be accepted uncritically.

How to increase life expectancy

It is understandable that throughout recorded history, people have been searching for ways to prolong life, and these are woven deeply into our ideas and attitudes. In past centuries, the *antediluvian ageing myth* (the belief that in ancient times, people lived far longer because they led more virtuous lives) was widely promulgated. A variant on this is the *hyperborean ageing myth* (the belief that there is a far-distant land where people live to incredible ages). An example of this is the belief in Prester John, which preoccupied many people in medieval Europe. Prester John was (supposedly) a Christian king who ruled over a land of fabulous wealth and great piety somewhere far away (reports generally place the kingdom as either in central Africa or China). Expeditions were even sent to find him (part of Marco Polo's brief was to find the kingdom if possible). We might smile at the naivety of the idea now, but science fiction writers often play on it – think how many science fiction films and TV series present races of wise and serene space aliens as being very old in human terms.

Yet another myth is that of the *fountain of youth* – the idea that there is an elixir or magic food that will confer immortality. This is the stuff of many a legend and popular work of fiction. It is also a keystone of the cosmetics and health and fitness industries. However, making someone *appear* younger is not the same as actually slowing down or stopping ageing. So, assuming that you cannot find the land of Prester John or a fountain of youth, what options are open to you to increase life expectancy?

Choosing the correct lifestyle is a good start. For example, it is estimated that the root causes of 35 per cent of all deaths in the USA in this century are attributable to indolence, poor diet and smoking (National Center for Injury Prevention and Control, 2006). Increasing the level of exercise, eating sensibly, cutting out smoking and excessive drinking are all good things to do and supported by ample research evidence (Ostwald and Dyer, 2011). For those who reject the idea of exercise and a limited-calorie diet of lettuce leaves and tofu, and hope instead that medical science will provide anti-ageing treatments, there might be a long wait. Ageing involves changes in multiple biochemical processes, and treating one without the others is unlikely to be particularly beneficial (an analogy might be replacing the window frames of an old house whilst the unusable floor boards, wiring and utility supplies are left untouched). Thus, even if there is a breakthrough tomorrow in one area of anti-ageing research, researchers are still likely to have to wait for other areas to catch up before an effective treatment can be created (see Rose, 1999, for an excellent review of the issues involved). And if a 'cure' for ageing is found, this may create more problems than it solves, not least of which is that if everyone can avoid ageing, overpopulation to an unprecedented degree seems inevitable. In which case, anti-ageing treatments will be either rationed or banned, both of which in turn create serious ethical and political dilemmas.

In addition to their lifestyle and where they live, a person seeking a long life also needs the right sort of genetic inheritance. This is the most probable explanation of the *Winston Churchill argument* – namely, that there are some people who can do all the wrong things (over-eat, over-drink, smoke like a chimney, have a highly stressful life) and yet live to an extreme old age. Put simply, regardless of other factors, long-lived people tend to produce long-lived offspring (Murphy, 1978). Which genes promote longer life is not fully known, and a lot of research has concentrated on fruit flies (which although they have about 70 per cent of genes in common with humans, clearly are not identical). So far, over 500 genes have been found that are associated with longevity (de Magalhaes, 2011). It is very unlikely that a simple single gene will be found that guarantees long life.

Another aspect of genetic inheritance is gender. Put simply, women live longer than men. In peaceful societies (i.e. where heavy war casualties do not distort the figures), the balance of men and women is roughly equal until about 45 years. Thereafter, men die at a faster rate, so that by 70, there are approximately six women for every five men, and by 80, this ratio has moved to 4:1. Many reasons for the earlier deaths of men have been suggested. A popular conception is that it is because men have traditionally led physically more strenuous lives. However, this seems at best a marginal explanation, since comparisons of men and women matched for levels of physical industriousness still show a strong sex difference in mortality rates. It is also unlikely that there is a hormonal or other biological explanation (Austad, 2006). The most feasible explanation is that men are slightly more prone to risk-taking behaviours than women. Thus, they are more likely to drive a bit faster, be less fussy about healthy eating, and so forth. These differences might seem to be minor, and at any one point in time they probably are. However, over the years, the cumulative effects of these behaviours begin to mount up, leading to men dying earlier (see Zhang, Sasaki and Kesteloot, 1995).

The cost of living longer

The Ancient Greeks had a tale of Tithonus, a mortal man who asked for immortality, but forgot to add the important caveat that he wanted to remain eternally youthful. The Greek gods, with their typical twisted sense of humour, allowed Tithonus to become immortal, and for all eternity he grew older and older and older. The point of this cheerful tale is that people want to live long, but not at any price. One of the abiding worries of many individuals is the (false) belief that the medical profession wants to keep older people alive, no matter what the pain or suffering or indignity, simply because they have the means to do. Not surprisingly, this mistaken belief is called the *Tithonus myth*. The reality is that the medical profession is not trying to make people suffer, but they are bound by a professional and ethical code to prolong life. But nonetheless, old age is not necessarily a time of unbridled joy.

One of the prices of living longer is that a person is more likely to contract painful but not necessarily fatal conditions such as arthritis, as well as other conditions that might ultimately be fatal but can be kept under control albeit with some discomfort (e.g. heart disease causing angina, pulmonary disease causing breathlessness). From birth, the average citizen of an industrialised country can expect to spend at least the final 10 per cent of their life suffering an appreciable disability (World Health Organization, 2004). And if this is not depressing enough, serious chronic illness (i.e. enough to impinge significantly on quality of life, if not immediately to disable) will probably appear several years prior to this (World Health Organization, 2004). What this means is that although life expectancy has increased over the past couple of centuries, *active life expectancy* (the predicted remaining years of mobility and freedom from pain and/or disability) has not increased at the same impressive rate.

This looks like a version of the Tithonus myth is correct – namely, that medical science has increased our lifespans but we pay for it with pain. However, this is arguably too gloomy a picture. Many conditions, although in themselves painful, can be successfully kept under control through drug therapy and palliative treatment (e.g. painkillers). And furthermore, although this sounds likes a cliché, there are improvements in medical care all the time. Thus, many commentators have argued that the future will be a time of *compression of morbidity* – in other words, in the future, the time spent in discomfort in later life will be diminished (see Fries, 2000). Indeed, there is already evidence that active life expectancy has increased over recent decades (Manton, Gu and Lowrimore, 2008), although the actual size of the improvement depends upon how exacting a scale of measurement is used (Unger, 2006).

There is another cost to growing older, and that is financial. The proportion of the population who are aged over 60 is growing. This currently stands at about one fifth for most industrialised nations, but is expected to rise to one third or more by 2040. In the case of the UK, the current figure is circa 27 per cent and is expected to rise to circa 50 per cent by 2050 (OECD, 2004). This is potentially economically disastrous news. Older people are by far the biggest consumers of health care, and also of course are the largest recipients of pensions, but in the main, older people do not pay for these. Pensions and health care are funded from taxation, and the bulk of that is paid by younger adults in employment. However, whilst the proportion of older adults is increasing, by definition the proportion of younger adults is *decreasing*. Thus, just when more people are needed in employment, the means for paying pensions and health care is diminishing. This change in the old-age dependency ratio leads to what has been termed the *demographic time bomb* – the major and potentially catastrophic financial burden on the economies of the coming decades created by a greying population.

How this problem is to be dealt with is currently a key preoccupation of most governments. The full story is too lengthy to be dealt with here and in any case falls well outside the scope of this book, and at the time of writing it is changing so rapidly that a detailed account would be almost instantly out of date. However, in essence, governments need to deal with a huge increase in pensions and health and welfare provision. One way to do this is to increase the state pensionable age. This is being done in many countries (e.g. UK from 65 to 68 by 2044; Germany 65 to 67 by 2031, USA to 67 by 2027), though not always without protest. For example, in France in 2010, it was proposed that the pensionable age for state workers should be raised from 60 to 62, and the age for receiving a full state pension from 65 to 67, resulting in nationwide protests and strikes.

Another method of dealing with the problem is to make current pension schemes less generous (e.g. by no longer linking them to final salary levels) – financially sound, but morally reprehensible for those workers who have already invested in a pension scheme in good faith and are now nearing retirement. A further method is to make new pension schemes less generous. This is potentially a good solution. Those who want a spendthrift early life can do so knowing they will only have a subsistence pension later on, whilst the more prudent have time through additional pension contributions to bolster their savings. However, this scheme will only have its full effect decades from now when these workers retire. A further method is to increase current pension contributions; but then this is asking employees to pay more at a time when wage rises are being kept low and prices are nonetheless rising. And the final and possibly worst problem of all is the at times perilous state of the stock market. Pension funds rely very heavily on investments in stocks and bonds. Poor returns on these mean in turn there is less money for pensions. The financial crisis resulting from the collapse of several important banks from 2008 onwards resulted in appallingly poor investment conditions at the very time when a financial boom was needed.

However, it is also possible to over-egg the pudding. There has never yet been an economic downturn that has not been met with expert predictions that catastrophe and universal poverty lay round the corner, and yet, here we all are, and in the main enjoying a far better standard of living. There are also good grounds for arguing that the costs of health care of older adults may be exaggerated by current accounting methods, and the real cost may turn out to be significantly lower (see Sanderson and Scherbov, 2010). At the time of writing, there is an over-used slogan resurrected from a World War II poster, which simply says 'Keep calm and carry on'.[3] In many respects this is the sanest advice for dealing with media doom-mongering about the future of pensions and pensioner care. To put things into perspective: in a pre-industrial society, a person has barely an even chance of reaching their fifth birthday.

***

So far in this chapter we have examined how we measure ageing and life expectancy, and some of the pitfalls that these measurements can create. In addition, we have examined how increasing life expectancy is not without potential problems in terms of both personal and financial cost. However, these issues beg the question of *why* we age at all. What are the processes that determine this, why do they exist, and what are their physical effects? The remainder of this chapter will be spent addressing these issues.

The ageing body

A full description of what happens to the body in later life would take a sizeable text, and in any case would be over-detailed for the purposes of this book. However, the fundamental message is this – as people grow older, they lose cells. This means that many parts of the body lose bulk and their functionality is lowered. For example, there is less muscle and skin, which get less elastic. If a fold of skin on the back of a person's hand is (gently!) pinched, the skin will go back to its original shape when the fingers let go. In younger adults, this happens almost instantly, because the skin is still very elastic. However, in an

---

3   On a note of historical accuracy, the poster was never actually publically used in World War II, merely prepared for distribution. It was a chance find of one of the few surviving copies that led to its reprinting a few years ago as a piece of decorative art.

older adult, the skin will revert to its previous shape more slowly. In a very old person with thinning wrinkling skin, the fold of skin might not totally revert to its previous shape, because the skin has lost a high proportion of its elasticity. Given that this pattern of decline is taking place throughout the body, it can be readily appreciated that this will have a profound effect upon older people's physical state and capabilities. In a word, the body becomes less *efficient*.

Loss of physical efficiency can have far-reaching psychological consequences. The changes might alter people's images of themselves and others. That this is seen overwhelmingly in negative terms is witnessed by the billions of pounds spent on cosmetic treatments each year in an attempt to hide or remove the signs of ageing. But even for those not concerned with their appearance, a less efficient body has direct effects on how well the brain functions. Less efficient respiratory and cardiovascular systems mean that the brain is less well supplied with oxygen and nutrients carried in the blood. This is akin to a car engine being expected to run on a low-octane fuel. The brain thus begins to run slower and tires more easily. One of the main reasons older adults tend to fall asleep after a meal is that the body requires so much oxygen and energy to digest the food that there is not enough in reserve to keep the brain fully active and alert.

The above applies to healthy, disease-free bodies. The situation of course only becomes worse if the body parts are damaged further. As we grow older, all the parts of our body get worn through use. This would be bad enough in itself, but on top of that, the longer we live, the greater the chances that we will develop chronic conditions such as arthritis, rheumatism, or one of a host of cardiovascular or respiratory diseases. Therefore, it is small wonder that the ageing body is an increasingly inefficient support mechanism for the brain and thus the mind. Furthermore, all the senses, responsible for directly providing the brain with information about the world, show deterioration (see Jackson and Owsley, 2003).

What of the brain itself? It has long been known that the brain decreases in volume in later life, even in healthy, well-functioning individuals. Recent brain-scan studies have found that in old age, we lose between 0.5 and 1 per cent of our brain tissue each year (Fjell and Walhovd, 2010). This loss is probably not uniform across the brain. For example, there is greater loss in the frontal and temporal regions of the cortex. For the uninitiated, the cortex is the wrinkly outer surface of the brain, and is responsible for a very high proportion of what is termed higher-order functioning – in other words, what might be termed intellectual processes (as opposed to more basic mechanisms such as controlling hunger and body movements, which although of course important are not 'intellectual'). The frontal cortex (roughly speaking, the bit behind the forehead) and the temporal cortex (the bit behind the temples) are heavily involved in planning and memory. In general (though note there are exceptions), the more brain tissue that is lost, the greater the intellectual decline in old age (Fjell and Walhovd, 2010).

In addition to loss of brain tissue, the surviving brain cells also change in function. Generally, older nerve cells send signals more slowly and with greater *neural noise*. The concept of noise in the system is an important one in some psychological theories and is best explained by analogy. In the brain, millions of nerve cells are carrying messages all the time. In an ideal world, each neural signal would be transmitted without any leakage of that signal (rather like lots of people talking in the same room at once, but each whispering into the recipient's ear, so nobody else is distracted). In reality, these signals often 'leak' so that signals form background noise to each other (extending our analogy, this is like everyone whispering a bit too loudly, so that unintended listeners get to hear other people's whispers as background distraction). The end result of this is that neural noise interferes with brain processing and makes mental activity less efficient.

A further ageing effect on the brain is that many activities in the brain become less localised. We will return to this in a later chapter, but in essence what happens is this: in younger adults, many mental tasks seem to be performed by very specifically defined and relatively small areas of the brain, whereas in older adults, more of the brain (and often in two or more different areas) are required to do the same task. The reason for this is still being debated, but it seems likely that older people have to compensate for the decline in brain cell numbers and efficiency by using more of the brain to do the same mental tasks.

Thus, both mind and body are physically less efficient in later life, both in terms of the lowered number of cells and the poorer abilities of the cells that are left. However, this begs the question of why this should occur at all, and that is addressed below in the final section of this chapter.

Causes of biological ageing

'Biological ageing' is generally used loosely to refer to the physical state of the body and how it changes over time. This typically involves cataloguing what the state of the body is at different chronological ages, and thus can be used to measure whether an individual is physically ageing faster or slower than the norm. There is no escaping the fact that no matter how many skin creams are bought and trips to the gym are made, the body declines with advanced chronological age. In the hands of many biologists and medics, this can be expressed in unnecessarily depressing terms. For example, there is a famous description of later life as being *post-developmental*: 'all the latent capacities for development have been actualized, leaving only late-acting potentialities for harm' (Bromley, 1988, p.30). Physical ageing does indeed seem to be one of nature's cruellest jokes. Understandably, people have questioned why it should happen, as the numerous works of art and literature on the subject amply demonstrate. The scientific explanation is not yet fully known, but research over the past few decades has given us insights into at least the broad set of reasons, even if all the details have yet to be worked out.

The first point to establish is that the body's cells are not immortal – over a period of about seven years most of them die and are replaced by new cells or are lost. Cell loss becomes a notable feature from early adulthood onwards, with most bodily systems showing a decline of 0.8–1 per cent per annum after the age of 30 (Hayflick, 1997). The course of this loss is very slow and, as most bodily systems have over-capacity built into them, it is only in about the sixth decade of life that the change is first apparent to the casual observer. This explains why a lot of bodily ageing changes occur (quite simply, cells are lost and not replaced) and why they occur in later life (because over-capacity makes the loss unnoticeable for decades). This explains why we get thinning hair, weaker muscles, thinner and less elastic skin, and so forth. However, it immediately begs the question – why don't cells carry on replacing themselves? Why do they eventually die off after so many duplications?

There are two explanations as to why cells do not replicate themselves ad infinitum. The first is that the cells seem to have a limited 'shelf life' built in. The *Hayflick phenomenon* (named after its discoverer: see Hayflick, 1997) states that living cells taken from the body and raised *in vitro* will only reduplicate themselves a limited number of times before dying (the *Hayflick limit*). In other words, cells seem to be pre-programmed to die. Why this happens is open to debate. One plausible explanation currently in great favour concerns the *telomere*, a sequence of DNA located at either end of all chromosomes. Each time the cell duplicates, the telomere shortens a bit, until eventually it disappears, and the genetic information disintegrates, preventing further duplication. The analogy frequently made is to imagine the chromosome as a shoelace, with the telomere as the plastic bit at either end that prevents the shoelace fraying. The analogy is an appropriate one, because it is felt that telomeres are a key component in maintaining the structural integrity of chromosomes (see Cong, Wright and Shay, 2002; de Megalhaes, 2011).

But this begs the question – why does the telomere do this? This leads to the second explanation of why cells don't replicate themselves ad infinitum. If the telomere did not shorten after each duplication, then the cell could in effect become immortal.[4] The problem is that although this sounds desirable, it is the last thing that one would want to happen. The reason for this is because each time the cell copies itself, errors occur. Up to a point, the cell copies are sufficiently similar to the original to be workable, but after a few copying processes, the cumulative errors make the cell in effect unusable for purpose.[5] The Hayflick limit is therefore a useful device – it kills off cells before they can be more of a hindrance than a use. Indeed, if damaged cells are accidentally revived and given longer and unbreakable telomeres, then they can and do result in cancerous growths (see Holliday, 2007).

This still begs the question as to why nature has given us such an appalling method of replicating cells. Why have we not got a better way of replicating cells that avoids the problems of poor duplication, the Hayflick limit, etc., so that we have no cellular decline in later life?

---

4   That is, only physically destroying it would kill it, but otherwise it could replicate itself time after time.
5   If you have the time, money, and inclination, try photocopying a black and white photograph on a photocopier. Then copying the copy. Then copying the copy of the copy, and so forth, ad infinitum. You will find that after a few copies, the original photograph is nigh-on unrecognisable. Clearly all that copying of copies does not preserve the original. Would you want one of these very poor copies to be preserved as an example of the original photograph? Of course not – the copy is in effect useless. A similar problem besets cell copies.

One argument occasionally raised is that the debilitation caused by ageing is planned. This states that bodies have an inbuilt programme to decay and die in order to make way for younger members of the species, and thus prevent the problem of overcrowding. Other versions include the concept that individuals grow weaker so that they become easier targets for predators, thereby preventing younger species members (still capable of breeding) from being chosen as targets. Such arguments are still accepted uncritically by a few commentators, but they are undermined by one simple fact: very few animals in their natural habitat reach old age. Accordingly, because older animals are so rare 'in the wild', it is unlikely that evolutionary pressure has created a method of 'self-culling' a species – predators, disease and accident do a satisfactory job in themselves (see Medawar, 1952).

For the majority of the time life has existed on this planet, nearly all multi-cellular organisms died long before they could show signs of ageing. Therefore, there has never been an evolutionary drive for better cell replication in later life. Incredible as it seems, the only time a large number of older animals can be seen is when they are family pets or in zoos. In the wild, old animals are scarce. What this means is that inefficient cell replication and the ageing changes resulting from this are something that nature never planned for: the effects of old age are extremely unusual in the natural world because old age is so rarely reached.

Thus, when we consider an older person, it is difficult to argue that a particular change in behaviour or bodily function is 'designed' to happen. Wrinkled skin, more brittle bones, lowered memory span or lowered response speeds may never have been 'planned'[6] by evolutionary forces – they have arisen because of one of several reasons. First, there was no evolutionary pressure to prevent them so they just happened (this is the basis of the *mutation accumulation theory*). Another theory argues that some bodily processes have beneficial effects in early life and only have bad effects in later life. But because people usually died of other causes before they reached old age and

---

6   Note that 'planned' is a metaphor: evolutionary change is essentially random even if the end result appears to be the result of intentional planning. People with some interpretations of religious belief may take exception to this argument and they are welcome to place their own explanation on the phenomenon, based on providential design.

the bad things happened, the downside of these processes was never controlled for by evolutionary forces. For example, high levels of male hormones might confer more strength and virility in early life, but if males are going to be dead before they reach old age, there is no reason to worry about the late life downside of baldness and heart disease (this is the essence of the *antagonistic pleiotropy theory*). Another theory (the *disposable soma theory*) argues that we spend early adult life optimising our reproductive success and keeping our reproductive systems in top condition so we can breed and spread our genes. If this maintenance means that other bodily systems decline in relative terms because they do not get maintained to the same level, then once again, there is no reason for concern, because death will occur before there are noticeable effects of ageing. These arguments might sound fanciful, but it must be stressed once again that most individual members of species in 'natural' surroundings are dead before these characteristics can ever manifest themselves (see Zwaan, 1999). It is both the curse and the privilege of modern life to see evolution cheated in this way.

Hayflick (1994) makes the useful analogy of the life course being, in evolutionary terms, like a satellite sent on a mission to survey a distant planet. Once a satellite has done its mission and sent back pictures of its target, it carries on into space, continuing to send back useful and informative signals until eventually accident or simple decay terminates its activities. In a similar way, individuals, once they have accomplished their target of producing viable offspring, continue to live until accident or illness kills them. However, the life of the satellite after sending back the photos of the target, or of the individual after breeding, is coincidental. Enough 'over-engineering' has to be built into the system to ensure that the job can be accomplished with something to spare. We interpret this extra life afforded by the over-engineering as a 'natural' part of the lifespan, but in fact in evolutionary terms it is an accidental gift, not a right. However, in another sense the argument that old age 'defeats' evolution is inaccurate – what is being shown in effect is what evolutionary pressure thinks of old age. Namely, it is a time when in evolutionary terms the usefulness to species survival is low, and thus it can act as a repository for all types of decay that will strike those who have 'failed' to die having successfully reproduced their genes.

Suggested further reading

An excellent text on ageing populations and the ageing body is *Brocklehurst's Textbook of Geriatric Medicine and Gerontology* (Tallis and Fillit, 2003). It should be noted that at the time of writing, the current hardback edition retails at circa £130 (thus, for many this may be a book for borrowing from a library). If you are not already fed up with the author's writing, then *An Introduction to Gerontology* (Stuart-Hamilton, 2011) is quite readable and indeed is excellent if you skip the author's own chapters. Fjell and Walhovd (2010) provide a solid review of brain anatomy changes in later life. For those interested in the history of ageing, then Thane (2000) is warmly recommended. In addition to being scholarly and informative, it is also an engrossing read. Although the book concentrates on the history of ageing and later life in England, many of the findings will be applicable to other cultures. For discussions of population change and its effects on policy, it is difficult to recommend a particular source for fear of it being immediately out of date. Government websites such as National Statistics Online (www.statistics.gov.uk) and the Population Reference Bureau (www.prb.org) are useful for basic up-to-date figures and often produce (surprisingly readable) summary reports. Wait (2011) gives an excellent review of the basics of policies on ageing and the issues facing policy-makers.

CHAPTER 2

Intelligence

What is intelligence?

One way of defining intelligence is to say that it is the efficiency with which mental problems can be solved. The simplest way of measuring intelligence is to argue that our abilities at all mental skills are shaped by a single mental force, called *general intelligence* (or *g*). However, a lot of researchers have argued that *g* is in fact made up of two related skills called *crystallised intelligence* and *fluid intelligence*. Crystallised intelligence is the knowledge that we have already acquired. It is impossible to answer a crystallised intelligence question unless we already have the answer stored in our memory. For example, consider the following questions:

- What is the colour of a Manchester United shirt?

- How many members of parliament are there in the UK House of Commons?

- How many white squares are on a chessboard?

- Name five types of cheese.

- What is the first verse of *The Star-Spangled Banner*?

In a room with no access to books or the internet, the only way we could answer these questions correctly would be if we already had the knowledge in our heads. In contrast, fluid intelligence measures the ability to solve novel problems. Thus, obviously enough, it is tested by giving people a set of problems they have never encountered before and measuring how many questions people get correct. There are various types of fluid intelligence questions, depending upon the specific test. One of the commonest questions is to ask which number or letter comes next in a series (e.g. M, T, W, T, __?). Another is to show people a set of shapes and ask them to judge which from a set of alternatives belongs with the other shapes. And so on and so forth. Anyone who has ever done a 'test your own IQ' type puzzle in a book or a magazine will be familiar with the general concepts involved.[1]

One final point needs to be made before we examine the effect of ageing on intelligence. Typically, test performance is measured straightforwardly enough in terms of how many questions a person gets right on the test. This is known as the *raw score*. However, sometimes psychologists use a different measure, called the *intelligence quotient*, or IQ. This measures how well a person performs relative to their age group. This is done by mathematically adjusting the score into a different format. Many readers will be familiar with the traditional IQ scoring system where 100 indicates average, and a score below 100 indicates below average and a score above 100 indicates above average. Another method in common use is the *percentile* method, where people's scores are represented in terms of the percentage of the population who get lower scores on the same test (e.g. a score on the 90th percentile indicates that 90 per cent of the general population will get a lower score than the person being tested). The concept of the intelligence quotient is an important one, as we shall see. However, for the moment we will concentrate on research that has been conducted on raw scores.

The classic ageing curve

The earliest studies of ageing and intelligence largely concentrated on the *classic ageing curve*. Measuring a basic ageing curve is a simple task,

---

1   Some researchers have made a further division, and argued that different types of intelligence are used depending upon the modality of the problem. Thus, they argue, solving problems that use verbal materials requires verbal intelligence, solving problems involving visual shapes requires visuo-spatial intelligence, and so forth.

provided one has the money and resources to hand. We need to find a good-sized sample of children and adults of all ages, with lots of individuals in each year of age. We then calculate the mean raw score for each age group, from children through to older adults (e.g. mean score for 6-year-olds, mean score for 7-year-olds, etc. through to mean score for 80-year-olds, 81-year-olds, etc.). Then, we plot the figures on a graph. Now unless our study defies over a hundred years of research experience, we should find that we have created a classic ageing curve. Basically, the mean raw score rises each year through childhood and adolescence, hits a plateau in the late teens, and then at some point in later adulthood, the score starts to drop again, and declines a little bit, year by year.

The general principle of the classic ageing curve is not disputed – everyone accepts that raw scores rise through childhood and adolescence, peak in early adulthood, and then decline in later adulthood. The devil is in the details. Although geropsychologists (psychologists who specialise in research on ageing) agree on the idea of the classic ageing curve, seemingly no two of them can agree on how it is best measured, and what it means. We shall spend a lot of this chapter examining this debate.

Measuring age changes in intelligence

Let us suppose that we want to compare the intelligence levels of people aged 20 and people aged 80. There are two basic ways of doing this:

1. Take a group of people aged 20, another group aged 80, and test them at the same time (the *cross-sectional study*).

2. Take a group of people aged 20, test them, wait 60 years, and then retest them when they reach 80, and then compare their test results with their scores on the same test when they were 20 (the *longitudinal study*).

Both these approaches have their benefits and pitfalls. The cross-sectional study looks at first to be the clear winner, since the testing can be done very quickly. The problem is that the cross-sectional study is prone to what are called *cohort effects*. A cohort is a group of people with a shared characteristic, but in the psychology of ageing, it almost invariably is shorthand for *birth cohort*, or a group of people born in the same historical period of time (e.g. born in the same calendar year). Cohorts of people born decades apart have generally been raised in radically different ways. For example, people now in their 80s would have had an early childhood where food rationing was universal, medical care primitive (by today's standards) and access to higher education very limited. In comparison, a person now in their 20s has been raised in a society where food is plentiful (or even over-plentiful), medical care considerably superior, and access to higher education is far more widely available. It follows from this that if we compare people aged 20 and 80 in a cross-sectional study, we are not comparing people who are basically the same except for their difference in age – the two groups have also been brought up differently and have hugely different experiences of the world. This is the essence of the cohort effect – namely, that at least some of the difference between age groups is due to differences in upbringing rather than being purely due to age.

Researchers have been well aware of the cohort effect for decades, and have looked at ways of combating it so that they can identify how much of the difference between age groups is due to ageing alone, rather than anything else. One common way of doing this is to find the difference in scores between age groups, and then mathematically adjust the size of this difference based on calculations of how much of the difference found is 'really' due to confounding variables rather than ageing. Studies have been doing this for over five decades (e.g. Ghiselli, 1957; Latimer, 1963) and have generally found that when confounding variables are controlled for in cross-sectional studies, the age difference is typically diminished but not removed. What this essentially means is that if historical and societal forces acted the same on everyone, there would still be an ageing change in intelligence. Returning to the classic ageing curve, cross-sectional studies, after adjustment, generally argue that intelligence rises until about 18 years where it reaches a plateau before declining again in the 30s.

However, for all the talk of adjusting scores in cross-sectional study to account for confounding variables, there is always a lingering suspicion that the analysis did not take account of *all* the possible confounding variables, and that part of the old–young difference might still be illusory. One way of getting round this problem is the aforementioned longitudinal study, where the same people are tested at different ages and their scores compared. If there is a difference in scores, then this cannot possibly be due to differences in the way the groups were brought up, because people are being compared with themselves at different ages. Thus, at a stroke, the longitudinal study removes the cohort effect problems that beset cross-sectional studies. Interestingly, when longitudinal studies were first run, they found that the decline in the classic ageing curve did not occur until the 50s or even 60s, implying that cross-sectional studies, even after being supposedly adjusted for cohort effects, were still exaggerating age differences.

However, there are problems with longitudinal studies. The first is that in their simplest form they are not very informative at all. If you choose to follow one group of people, all born in the same year, you will learn a lot about what happens to the intelligence of people born in that particular year. But what about people born, for example, 20 years later? Are they bound to show the same pattern of change? In order to be truly informative, longitudinal studies need to follow people born in several different cohorts born some years apart. The method for doing this is called an *overlapping longitudinal study*. Basically, it tests several age cohorts on one occasion, then retests them at regular intervals thereafter. To take a simplified[2] example, suppose that at the first test session there are groups of people who are 50, 57, 64 and 71 years old. They are tested, and their performances at Session 1 can be compared in the manner of a traditional cross-sectional study. At regular intervals thereafter (for the sake of argument, let us say every seven years), the participants are retested. Thus, at Session 2, the 50-year-old group is now 57, the 57-year-old group is now 64, and so forth. The age groups at Session 2 can once again be compared in a cross-sectional manner, but in addition, the members of each group can be compared with their younger selves, as in a longitudinal study (e.g. the people who are 71 at Session 2 can be compared with their 64-year-old selves at Session 1).

There are considerable advantages to this measurement technique. Consider Table 2.1, which conceptually represents this imaginary study. As can be seen, as the study progresses, the younger cohorts will become the ages the older cohorts were earlier in the study. For

---

2   Real-life studies of this kind generally take on new recruits over the different test sessions and will sometimes do one-off studies at individual test sessions, etc. But the underlying structure of the main study is very much as described here.

example, at Session 4, Cohort 1 will become the age Cohort 4 was at Session 1. Armed with such information, it is possible to gauge and control for cohort effects. Take the following (intentionally simplified) example. Suppose that at Session 4, it is found that Cohort 1 has scores 20 per cent higher than Cohort 4. Does this mean that ageing from 71 to 92 will result in a 20 per cent loss in ability, or is this change due to a cohort difference? To answer this, we can consult Cohort 4's scores on Session 1, when they were the same age as Cohort 1 is at Session 4. Suppose we find that Cohort 4 when aged 71 had scores only 5 per cent lower than when aged 92. We now have two measures of ageing decline – the longitudinal method says the change is 5 per cent, the cross-sectional method says the change is 20 per cent. Armed with such information, it is possible to tease apart how much of ageing change is due to ageing *per se*, and how much is due to cohort effects.

Table 2.1 A conceptual table illustrating the overlapping longitudinal study

	Session 1	Session 2	Session 3	Session 4	Session 5
Cohort 1	50	57	64	71	78
Cohort 2	57	64	71	78	85
Cohort 3	64	71	78	85	92
Cohort 4	71	78	85	92	99

Using this technique, Schaie and colleagues conducted the *Seattle Longitudinal Aging Study* (e.g. Schaie, 2005). In 1956, a group of people aged between 20 and 70 were tested and then retested at seven-yearly intervals thereafter (i.e. in 1963, 1970, 1977, and so forth). Periodically new participants have been added. By cross-checking the figures in a manner conceptually similar to the above example, Schaie has demonstrated that part of the difference between age groups is due to cohort effects. For example, the earlier born participants have significantly lower scores when matched for age with people born later (e.g. people who were tested when aged 60 in 1970 will have lower scores than a group of 60-year-olds tested in 2000). Thus, some of the lowered scores in later life might simply be because older people were born at a time that did not favour intellectual skills as well as later times did.

However, this does not mean that the longitudinal study is necessarily any more accurate than the cross-sectional study. Although (at considerable effort and expense) the longitudinal study can circumvent some of the issues created by cohort effects, it adds other distortions all of its own making. One of these is the *practice effect*. If people are given the same test on each occasion they are re-tested, then it is highly likely that they will get better at the test each time they take it. In general, researchers do not give exactly the same test on each occasion[3] to avoid this very problem. However, the test has to be compatible with the test used on the previous test session, otherwise performances on the different test sessions cannot be compared. Thus, researchers often use *parallel forms* of the same test. This means that the same test format is used on each occasion, but the specific questions are different. However, before testing has begun, it has been established that the score that a person gets on one version of the test will be more or less identical to the score they get on its parallel form. In theory, this means that there should not be a practice effect, since the participants are faced with brand-new questions each time they are tested. Although this is plausible in theory, in reality a practice effect still takes place. This is because the parallel forms of the test, although they use different questions, still have the same format and often the questions follow the same lines of logic in the different versions of the test. For example, suppose that in the first test there is a question asking for the next number in the sequence 3, 5, 7, 9, __. If the participant encounters a similar question at the second test session, asking for the next number in the sequence 2, 4, 6, 8, __, this should be easier to solve because the participant will remember from the first test session the general principle of how these problems are worked out. Researchers have repeatedly found that even when using parallel forms and with gaps as long as seven years between test sessions, practice effects still take place (e.g. Rabbitt *et al.*, 2004).

A further significant cause of distortion in longitudinal study results is the *drop-out effect*. A surprisingly high percentage of participants who attend the first session of a longitudinal study subsequently

---

3   Though some have. This is often because no parallel form of the test is available.

refuse to come back to further test sessions. Salthouse (2010, p.173) in a review of percentage attrition from longitudinal studies, found figures varying from 26 to 92 per cent. This might not be of too much concern if these drop-outs were random. However, in general they are not, and significantly more of the people who drop out are those with lower intelligence test scores. This is mainly for motivational reasons. Quite simply, if people think they did badly on the tests, they don't come back for more. No matter how hard researchers try to explain to the contrary, most participants in experiments seem to regard psychological tests as a competition. Therefore, volunteers who perceive themselves to be worsening in intellectual performance will be less willing to be retested. This means that as a longitudinal study progresses, the 'declining' participants drop out, leaving a rump of 'well-preserved' volunteers. This is a well-established finding in the research literature (e.g. Riegel and Riegel, 1972; Singer *et al.*, 2003).

The upshot of this is that neither cross-sectional nor longitudinal methods nor overlapping longitudinal methods can, in their basic forms, provide a reliable answer to the apparently simple question of when the ageing decline in intelligence begins. Recent research into this question has tended to concentrate on the findings of longitudinal studies, which are then mathematically adjusted to take account of practice effects, drop-out effects, etc. When this is done, the consensus opinion is that there is a decline in some intellectual skills across most of the adult lifespan (Verhaeghen, 2011). This means that the plateau of the classic ageing curve is relatively short, with a decline starting in the late 20s (Salthouse, 2009). We have thus come full circle, back to the findings of the earliest studies, which argued the same thing nearly a century ago.

However, a word of caution is needed here. Recent research using mathematical adjustments of data is generally very complex indeed. But it should be remembered that nobody can see this age-related decline is there if the raw data are looked at – we have to assume that the actual figures in front of us are distorted and that the statistical adjustments that are made to the data produce a more accurate result. The problem is that in the main there is no objectively reliable measure to gauge whether these adjustments are correct – often it is the fact that the adjustments to the data produce demonstrable changes in the direction the researchers expected that is taken as the acid test. This is not to belittle this research at all, but some caution is required. Part of the reason for arguing this is that the declines that this new method of analysis claim are there just do not tally with real-life experiences. For example, a reasonable consensus figure for a mean age change over adult life is that by the age of 75, the mean test score on a measure of intelligence such as the Wechsler Adult Intelligence Scale[4] is approximately 1 standard deviation lower than the young adult mean (Miller *et al.*, 2009). The *standard deviation* is a measure of variability in the data. In most instances, the mean tells us what a typical member of a group is like. However, we know from everyday experience that not everyone is average, and most people vary a little, being either a bit above or below average, be it height, weight, intelligence, or whatever other attribute can be measured on a measurement scale. This variability is measured in standard deviations. Roughly 95 per cent of people are within 2 standard deviations of the mean. For example, if the mean score on a test is 100 and the standard deviation is 10, then circa 95 per cent of people will have a score on that test that is between 80 and 120.

The finding by Miller *et al.* that by the age of 75, people have dropped 1 standard deviation at first does not seem all that remarkable, since anything within 2 standard deviations of the mean is considered reasonably normal. However, there is more to it than this. What the Miller *et al.* finding means is that the *average* 75-year-old person has dropped 1 standard deviation. But what about the people who were below an average score to begin with? To cut to the chase, a significant proportion of older people who had lower than average intelligence test scores when they were young will now have scores that are more than two standard deviations below the average. This is a very meaningful figure, because in children and younger adults, having an intelligence test score more than 2 standard deviations below the mean is a key diagnostic sign of learning disability. Seen in this light, findings of a large drop in intelligence test scores indicates that many older adults now have an intelligence level on or below the level of a child with learning disabilities.

However, this palpably cannot be the case. Although some older adults develop dementia in later life (as we shall see in a later chapter),

---

4   A widely used and accepted test of intelligence.

common sense and everyday experience tells us that non-dementing older people do not act or behave or think like children with a learning disability. Nobody would deny that there might be *some* changes in *some* older people, but nothing on a par with what a literal interpretation of the intelligence test score data are apparently suggesting. Therefore, although studies of general intellectual change are important, we should be careful before assuming that the classic ageing curve can be applied uncritically and automatically to everyday life.

Before leaving this section, we need to return to the raw score and intelligence quotient (IQ) distinction mentioned earlier in this chapter. The classic ageing curve is based solely on raw scores (i.e. how many questions a person gets right). As already mentioned, IQ is how well or badly a person performs on the test relative to the other people in their age group. Although raw score rises and falls across the lifespan, in the absence of dementia, IQ remains relatively constant (Deary *et al.*, 2000). Thus, if a person begins life with a test score better than 75 per cent of their age group, they will still be more or less on the same 75th percentile in their age group if they live to their 90s. In some ways, IQ is a fairer and more egalitarian measure of ability than raw score, and it is encouraging to know that even if raw scores fluctuate and their applicability to everyday functioning can be questioned, a person's ability relative to their age peers is likely to remain relatively unchanged.

Changes in types of intelligence

The discussion in the previous section of this chapter was devoted to general intelligence. However, it is known that intelligence can also be viewed as a collection of sub-skills, each dealing with a different facet of mental skills. One of the commonest ways of looking at this is to consider fluid and crystallised intelligence, as noted at the start of the chapter. These skills do not change with age in the same way, with fluid intelligence declining far more than crystallised intelligence. Indeed, it is largely the change in fluid intelligence that accounts for the decline in the classic ageing curve.

Numerous studies have found fluid intelligence test performance declines in later life (e.g. Salthouse, 1991), and researchers are uniformly agreed that this is true. However, although *test performance* gets worse, it is unclear how well this measures older people's actual fluid intelligence. Most fluid intelligence tests are against the clock – participants have a limited time in which to answer as many questions as possible. Thus, the tests require quick responses. But older adults are more likely to have physical ailments such as arthritis and rheumatism that slow their movements, and thus they might perform less well on intelligence tests, not because they lack the mental skills, but, for example, because they cannot write quickly enough. Researchers have found that when speed of response is taken into account, the difference in scores between older and younger adults can be halved (Storandt, 1977). Similarly, a lot of intelligence tests use quite small print, which older adults might struggle to see. If print size is increased, then older adult test scores improve (Storandt, 1976). Thus, fluid intelligence test design might exaggerate age differences.

In contrast, crystallised test design arguably often artificially reduces the true size of the age difference. In contrast to most fluid intelligence tests, crystallised measures are rarely against the clock, and participants can take as long as they like. If crystallised tests have a time limit imposed, then older people, with slower responses, perform significantly less well (Core, unpublished, cited in Rabbitt, 1984). Again, the marking criteria for many crystallised tests are arguably lax. For example, a common measure of crystallised intelligence is to ask people to provide definitions for words. The marking criteria for such tests often allow for very vague or inexact answers to be marked correct. Introducing stricter marking criteria again results in an age difference being found (e.g. Kaufman and Horn, 1996).

Although test methods might exaggerate fluid intelligence decline whilst making crystallised intelligence seem better than it is, there are still definite differences between fluid and crystallised intelligence. Even allowing for the distortions produced by test methods, fluid intelligence still declines with age, whilst crystallised intelligence remains at worst relatively unaffected by ageing (e.g. Salthouse, 2009; Verhaeghen, 2011). Further proof of differences comes from Blelak et al. (2010), who tested a group of older adults (aged 64–92 years) four times over three years. When people re-do tests, they rarely score exactly the same each time. The researchers found in their study that within individuals, the scores on fluid intelligence tasks varied significantly more over this time period than did crystallised task scores.

These findings echo the stereotype of older adults as being reasonably sound on matters of general knowledge, but nonetheless being slow on the uptake when it comes to new ideas. However, the applicability of laboratory studies to everyday life in this instance is not without question. As noted earlier in the chapter, general intelligence decline observed in laboratory tests seems to be far greater than is reflected in everyday functioning. The same argument applies here. Studies of fluid intelligence have found declines of up to 5 or more standard deviations below the young adult mean (e.g. Salthouse, 1992b) and this appears to be far in excess of the changes observed in real life.

However, intelligence can be regarded in other ways than crystallised and fluid. Another method in common use is to consider intelligence in terms of the type of information that is being processed. Schaie (e.g. Schaie, 2005) divided intellectual tasks into six sub-skills: *inductive reasoning* (ability to work out rules governing newly encountered data), *spatial reasoning, perceptual speed* (essentially, speed to respond to basic stimuli such as flashes of light), *numeric ability, verbal ability* and *verbal memory* (in effect, ability to remember words). If we consider the performance of a group of older adults as they get older, then verbal ability shows little or no age-related decline,[5] but the other measures all decline (see Verhaeghen, 2011). However, if *individual* participants are considered, then a different picture emerges, with each individual showing their own unique pattern of change as they get older. For example, one person might show a decline in skills A, B and C, whilst showing preservation of skills D, E and F. For another individual, the reverse might be true. Another individual might show a relative decline in A, C and E but not in the other skills, and so on. In a six-year longitudinal study by Wilson *et al.* (2002), a group of older participants were tested annually. It was found that there was considerable variation between individuals in the pattern of decline they showed. Although decline in one sub-skill was likely to be met with a decline in another, this was not inevitable, and level of performance at the start of the study was not an indicator of the rate of decline in skills as the study progressed.

---

5   This is unsurprising, since many of the verbal ability tasks used in studies are also used to assess crystallised intelligence.

The upshot of this is that everyone's intellect has its own unique way of ageing, and when it gets down to the details of what skills are preserved and what skills are lost, group averages are uninformative beyond giving a broad-brush idea of what is going on. There are limits to this uniqueness, however. The fact that people's IQs stay relatively constant throughout life means that relative to the rest of their age group, they will not stray too far from their youthful intellectual status. But equally, it would be foolhardy to assume that every older person will think in the same way and show the same levels of deterioration.

Wisdom

Before finishing the discussion on types of intelligence, it is important to note the closely related topic of *wisdom*. It is tempting to see wisdom as being synonymous with crystallised intelligence, since both are concerned with knowing about the world around us, and some researchers treat it largely in this manner. However, the term can also be used in a more specialised sense, where it is seen as the ability to produce a pragmatic, as opposed to a logical, solution. In other words, a pragmatic solution might not be logically watertight, but it is more likely, by integrating emotional considerations into the equation, to appease people and/or maintain a sense of social order. It thus allows for a bending of the rules that a purely logical solution could never do. Measures of wisdom are usually based on realistic moral dilemmas (e.g. a terminally ill friend wants to commit suicide – what would you say?); accordingly, this tends to favour producing pragmatic responses. An example of this is a research technique used by Baltes and colleagues (e.g. Baltes and Staudinger, 2000). Participants are asked a realistic problem akin to the suicide example given above, and then have to think out loud about the problem. This is then graded on various measures, such as how factually accurate the response is, how much attention is paid to social considerations, etc. To score well on such a test, participants must be aware of social considerations, and indeed it can be argued that wisdom is to some considerable extent a social skill rather than 'intellectual' in the conventional sense (see Staudinger, Kessler and Dorner, 2006).

Empirical evidence on wisdom generally finds a reasonably strong correlation with intelligence, tempered by personality traits, but with a significant proportion of measurement independence (e.g. Staudinger, Lopez and Baltes, 1997). In other words, although wisdom is in part a product of a person's personality and intelligence, it is also in part independent of these factors (i.e. it is not just another way of describing general intelligence). Predictably, researchers have also found that wisdom is a beneficial ability, and is strongly related to, *inter alia*, life satisfaction in older people (Ardelt, 1998; Ardelt and Jacobs, 2009) and preparation for death (Ardelt, 2010). But, interestingly, wisdom is *not* found to be a preserve of old age. Adults of any age can score highly (or badly) on measures of wisdom. Most studies have found no evidence that older people are significantly wiser than other adult age groups (see Ardelt and Jacobs, 2009; Baltes and Staudinger, 2000). However, more recent research by Ardelt (2010) suggests that older adults score more highly on affective (pertaining to emotion) and reflective aspects of considering problems. Therefore, although the basic skill of wisdom might not be particularly age-dependent, older adults might nonetheless show greater skill in some aspects of wisdom-related issues.

Causes of intellectual change

So far, discussion of intellectual change in later life has centred on what happens to intelligence test scores as people grow older. However, an equally pertinent point is *why* these changes occur. We shall consider some of the key theories that have been advanced.

Physical health and exercise

It is generally agreed that one cause is a person's physical health. For example, it has been demonstrated that improving a person's health and fitness through regular exercise also improves intelligence test scores (e.g. Hawkins, Kramer and Capaldi, 1992). Again, people who maintain a reasonable level of physical fitness appear in general to change less over time on indices of intellectual performance, particularly fluid intelligence (Bunce, Barrowclough and Morris, 1996).

There are many reasons why physical exercise might have a beneficial effect on the intellect. For example, exercise is beneficial to the cardiovascular system and it is known that cardiovascular health is correlated with cognitive skills in older adults (e.g. Elwood *et al.*, 2002).

Again, a sensible exercise and diet regime are useful in staving off old-age diabetes, which is associated with a lowering of intellectual skills (Bent, Rabbitt and Metcalfe, 2000). Keeping physically healthy is therefore almost certainly beneficial for the ageing mind. However, there are caveats. First, there is evidence that the intelligence–health relationship is a two-way process – in other words, being intelligent makes a person more likely to lead a healthy lifestyle. For example, Starr et al. (2000) demonstrated that a child's intelligence level is a strong predictor of their health in later life. Again, nearly all studies of health and intelligence in older adults have found strong effects of socio-economic status (e.g. Elwood et al., 1999; Starr et al., 2000); in other words, healthy people with higher levels of intelligence also tend to be of a higher socio-economic status. We cannot therefore assume that higher intelligence is automatically caused by physical health – there could be other factors involved (e.g. socio-economic status) and level of physical health might in part be caused by intelligence. However, none of these caveats denies the findings of studies where people who have been given an exercise regime show a rise in intellectual skills (e.g. Hawkins et al., 1992; Powell, 1974). A sensible exercise programme and diet are undoubtedly good things.

Terminal drop

Longitudinal studies have found that many individuals show a steep decline in test scores in the months before they die. This has the moribund title of *terminal drop* (Kleemeier, 1962; Riegel and Riegel, 1972). The finding has been replicated in sufficient studies that the phenomenon is not in serious doubt. However, what has been disputed is which test scores have to change for death to be imminent. For example, some studies have argued that many intellectual skills can change without it being a harbinger of death, but a decline in fluid intelligence greater than 10 per cent is serious news (Rabbitt et al., 2008). Other studies (e.g. Siegler, McCarty and Logue, 1982) have said that it is a decline in verbal skills that is of crucial importance. Practically every study published on this area has a different explanation, and although, at the time of writing, more studies identify a decline in some type of verbal skill as the key cause, there is no overall consensus of opinion.

Disuse theory

A commonly used expression is 'use it or lose it'. The more refined psychological term is *disuse theory* – the belief that age-related declines are attributable to a failure to use skills, so that eventually they fall into a decline (see Milne, 1956). The upshot of this theory is that we should be able to demonstrate that if older people practise a skill, they will maintain a youthful level of performance at it. Several studies have found evidence for this. Perhaps the best known of these is by Charness (1981), who studied older chess players who regularly played the game, and found that they were able to play chess as well as younger adults. However, what was remarkable was that the older players often showed quite serious declines in skills that we might intuitively suppose were essential to playing the game well. For example, a key facet of chess playing is the ability to plan several moves ahead, and this requires a great deal of memory. However, the older chess players in Charness's study had significantly poorer memories than the younger players, and the same applied to other basic cognitive skills that one would suppose are essential to playing chess well. So how were the older players able to play chess as well as they did?

Charness found that the older players compensated for this loss by having a greater fund of experience. Because they had played (literally) thousands more games than younger opponents, they were able to tap a greater store of knowledge. Thus, when faced with practically any sort of game, they had probably been in the same situation many times more often than younger players. Greater experience thus compensated for loss of more basic skills. Similar findings have been found for older players of other games, such as bridge (Charness, 1979) and the Japanese game *go* (Masunaga and Horn, 2001). Compensation can also be effective in other situations. For example, Salthouse (1985) found that the older typists generally had slower finger movements and reaction times, but showed no difference in typing speed. This was because the older typists planned longer sequences of finger movements than younger typists (with less experience) could manage. Thus, although it took an older typist longer to move a finger to a key, the move towards that key started earlier because they looked further ahead (in essence, younger typists were starting later in their sequences of finger movements and then catching up with the older typists). In another study of compensatory strategies, Hoyer and Ingolfsdottir (2003) conducted an ingenious experiment on medical laboratory technicians. They showed the participants microscope slides with the task of identifying what was on them. Anyone other than a biologist who has seen slides of cells and similar will readily appreciate that the difference between such slides and random blobs of ink can seem fairly minimal, and the task is a demanding one. Hoyer and Ingolfsdottir found that the older technicians (in their late 40s) took significantly longer over the task than younger technicians (in their 20s) if just presented with the slide images. However, if they were given contextual information (i.e. orienting them to what was expected) before they started, then the age difference disappeared. In other words, given the capacity to use a compensatory strategy (20 years' greater experience of looking at slides) the age decline in basic visual search skills could be overcome.

Thus, there is evidence that compensation can have its uses (see Hertzog and Jopp, 2010; Vahia, Cain and Depp, 2010 for recent reviews). However, even in its full flowering, it might not be totally effective. For example, Charness et al. (2001) conducted a study in which young, middle-aged and older typists who were either novices or experienced were given the task of learning a new word-processing application. In the case of the novices, the younger participants were faster to learn and retained more information at the end of the training course. In the case of the experienced participants, the older group differed only minimally from the younger groups in what was learnt and retained. Thus, there is evidence that experience acts to compensate for age-related decline. However, the older group had a significantly slower learning rate. Lindenberger et al. (2008) found that older graphic designers given training in a memory-improvement technique showed a significantly greater *relative* improvement in memory scores than age-matched controls or younger graphic designers. However, in absolute terms, the older graphic designers still had poorer memory scores than the younger participants, even after training.

Therefore, compensation through practice has its limits. However, even if it cannot fully compensate for cognitive changes in later life, that does not mean in practical terms that it is a bad thing. Even one of the sternest critics of disuse theory has argued that there are considerable personal benefits to keeping up mentally demanding exercise and having faith in the idea that it staves off at least the worst of the decline (see Salthouse, 2006). Compensation can also be seen in the broader, whole lifespan terms of the *SOC model* (e.g. Baltes and Baltes, 1990; Freund and Baltes, 2007). 'SOC' stands for selection, optimisation and compensation. The theory argues that we develop in adulthood by first selecting what to specialise in doing, then optimising by practice, and in later life, protecting against decay of skills through compensatory strategies.

Recent research has considered how compensation works at a neurological level. This work is in its relative infancy, and some commentators have argued that the area is not yet as clear-cut as some advocates would like to suppose (see Mast, Zimmerman and Rowe, 2009). Various models have been proposed, many of which argue that as specific areas of the brain decline in later life, other areas of the brain take over some of the declining areas' functions. For example, one model argues that as many neural mechanisms decline, these are offset by increased use of the prefrontal cortex. This leads to the *scaffolding theory of ageing and cognition* (STAC), which in effect argues that declining mental mechanisms are 'propped up' by greater reliance on the workings of the prefrontal cortex (Park and Reuter-Lorenz, 2009). This reflects a similar proposal by Cabeza (2002), who argued that the prefrontal cortex in older adults tends to be less lateralised (i.e. the left and right sides of the brain are more equally involved). This leads to the *HAROLD* (hemispheric asymmetry reduction in older adults) model. For those readers interested in how these changes might occur at the level of the individual neuron, Kumar and Foster (2007) provide a useful review.

The concept of neurological compensation thus looks fruitful. It also points to the possibility of computerised cognitive intervention that could directly stimulate the appropriate areas of the brain, thus further enhancing neurological compensatory mechanisms (Cruz-Jentoft *et al.*, 2008). However, it is not the only neurological explanation of intellectual change in later life. Of the alternatives, one of the most prominent is often set up as the opposite of the traditional 'use it or lose it' disuse theory. In its strongest form, it argues that practising skills is a largely fruitless exercise: ageing decline is due to an inexorable biological process of the slowing of bodily functions that in turn leads to a slowing and lowering efficiency of mental processes. This argument is considered in the next section.

The general slowing hypothesis

The *reaction time* (RT) is the time taken to respond to a stimulus. It is measured as the time between the stimulus first appearing and the person making a response. In the most commonly used measure, the stimulus is an image on a computer screen, which is responded to by pressing a particular key on the computer keyboard. RT studies come in two basic flavours:

- *Simple reaction time* (SRT) measures speed of response when there is only one stimulus and only one response allowed (e.g. pressing a button every time a light flashes).

- *Choice reaction time* (CRT) measures speed of response when there are different stimuli requiring different responses (e.g. press button *A* if a red light flashes, *B* if a green light, or *C* if a blue light).

Because CRT experiments require more decision making than SRT experiments, response times on CRT are longer and as the number of stimuli that have to be chosen between increase, so does the mean response time.

It is very well established that reaction times get slower as people get older. According to a review by Birren and Fisher (1995, p.329), it is 'one of the most reliable features of human life'. Furthermore, the age difference gets proportionately larger the more choices that must be discriminated between in a choice reaction time task (see Deary and Der, 2005). The simple explanation for these phenomena is that older people's nervous systems are slower and less efficient at conducting signals, and the disadvantage imposed by the extra choices is a manifestation of the *age × complexity effect*, which argues that the more complex a task becomes, the disproportionately worse older people are at it relative to younger people.

Why is the study of reaction times relevant to intelligence? The simple answer is that it is well established that reaction times correlate with measures of intellectual performance (e.g. Ferraro and Moody, 1996). For example, Rabbitt and Goward (1986) found that if groups of older and younger adults are matched for intelligence test scores, then there is no difference in their choice reaction times. Hertzog (1991) similarly reported that when the effect of speed of response is statistically controlled for, differences between age groups on intellectual tasks are significantly lowered, or disappear altogether. The reason for this link between RTs and intelligence is straightforward:

1. RTs are in effect measuring how efficiently a person's nervous system is working.

2. How intelligent a person is depends upon how well their brains can process information.

3. How well a brain processes information depends upon how efficiently a person's nervous system is working.

4. And how well a person's nervous system is working is measured by RTs.

It follows from this that if RTs slow down, then a person's intellectual skills are also likely to decline. This is because a slowed down RT means the nervous system is working less efficiently, and that means that mental information is being processed less efficiently. As noted in Chapter 1, the ageing body is characterised by cell loss and a decline in efficiency. Therefore, the physical decline in the elderly nervous system could directly lead to lowered intellectual skills. This argument is called the *general slowing hypothesis*.[6] At a general level, this argument is not greatly disputed: low speed typically equals low test scores and changes in speed of processing correlate significantly with changes in fluid intelligence (Zimprich and Martin, 2002). Instead, the debate is principally about the degree to which general slowing alone predicts intellectual performance.

A central issue has concerned the degree to which general slowing can account for the age × complexity effect (to reiterate: as the task gets harder, so older adults become disproportionately more disadvantaged). This is a topic that has fascinated many key researchers in the field, but anyone outside the area might be forgiven for wondering why such a

---

6   Rather confusingly, some researchers also call it the *speed hypothesis*.

fuss has been made about it. What follows is a *very* truncated version of the debate.

A key idea behind the general slowing hypothesis is that age-related declines in intellectual skills can be described by a simple equation. In effect, if we know by how much an older person's nervous system has slowed down, we can then predict with reasonable certainty by how much intellectual skills will have declined. Ultimately, this would be very useful information to have, if, for example, a 'nerve tonic' could be developed that speeded up neural transmission – speed up the nervous signals by the right amount, and a youthful level of intellect could be restored. But this depends upon finding a simple link between slowing and intellectual performance. And at first sight, the age × complexity effect is spoiling the party. This is because as the task gets more complicated, the difference between older and younger adults gets bigger and bigger. Unfortunately, there is no easy mathematical equation that will describe this. That means that the link between speed of processing and intelligence is not a straightforward one, and that undermines the claim that speed of processing is the prime mover of intellectual change in later life.

However, this problem resolves itself if the data are approached in another way. Traditionally, age-group differences are measured by considering how young people's RTs increase as the task is made harder and then comparing this with how older people's RTs change on the same task. For example, let us assume that a task has ten levels of difficulty – we would look at how, over tasks 1–10, the younger people's RTs got slower, and then compare this rate of increase with older people's RTs on the same ten tasks. This will give us the standard age × complexity finding. However, there is another way of looking at these data. What we can also do is plot on a graph the times taken by each age group on each task. Thus, in our example, we would have a graph with two axes – one giving the RTs for young adults, the other giving the RTs for older adults. We then take the RT for the first task, and plot the younger and older groups' average RT for that task. We then repeat the exercise for all the remaining tasks. What we will find is (allowing for measurement error) a straight line. This is illustrated in Figures 2.1 and 2.2.

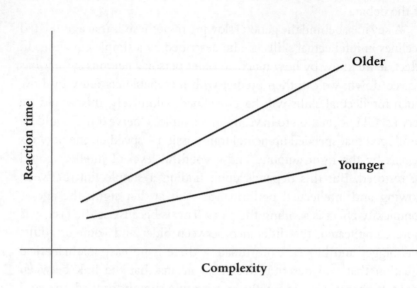

Figure 2.1 Illustration of the age × complexity effect

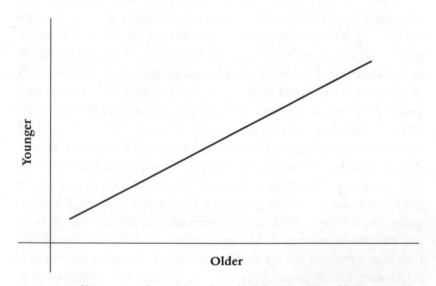

Figure 2.2 Illustration of a Brinley Plot, plotting younger v. older means on same data as Figure 2.1

This straight line is known as a *Brinley plot*, and was promoted by various researchers (notably Cerella, 1985, 1990, following earlier research by Brinley, 1965) as demonstrating that the general slowing model worked. The reason this claim was made was relatively straightforward. By showing that old and young groups' performances could be plotted on a straight line, mathematically it was easy to demonstrate that the ageing RTs were following a simple, easy to predict pattern. There was no longer any mathematical awkwardness about trying to explain how age differences got disproportionately bigger the more complex the task became. Instead, by examining the same data in a different way, this apparent contradiction had been removed. At a stroke, intellectual decline could be explained in terms of a simple slowing down of the nervous system.[7]

It is true that a lot of studies have found Brinley plots that uphold this argument (e.g. Cerella, 1990; Lindenberger, Mayr and Kliegl, 1993; Maylor and Rabbitt, 1994; Verhaeghen, 2006), and nobody disputes that the phenomenon exists. However, whether it measures what it claims is not as clear-cut. For example, researchers noted that although individual studies showed evidence of slowing, the rate of slowing varied between tasks, with some showing more slowing than others (e.g. Lindenberger *et al.*, 1993). This means that there is not necessarily one general slowing that affects all processes equally, but rather, several different types of slowing. This does not undermine the theory (since different types of neural mechanisms might slow in different ways), but it negates the idea of a single general slowing in neural processing undermining every aspect of ageing change.

A more serious criticism concerns the mathematical means of identifying the straight line in the Brinley plot. As already hinted at, when the old and young RTs are plotted against each other in real-life experiments, they do not form a straight line. Instead, if the points on the graph were joined by a line, it would be a zig-zag. This is normal in most real-life studies, and is usually attributed to measurement error and other minor experimental flaws. To find out what the 'true' line

---

7   If non-mathematical readers are having problems with this explanation, the key message is simply that the Brinley plot allowed researchers to claim that the slowing down of the nervous system in old age was the prime cause of ageing decline in intelligence. The theory thus set itself up to be judged by how well the Brinley plot argument stood up to criticism.

would look like with these errors ironed out, a statistical technique called *regression* is used. And when the early researchers used a regression analysis on the data, a straight line was found.

However, the regression techniques used were not as reliable as they first appeared. For example, Perfect (1994) suggested that similar linear relationships[8] can be generated using essentially random data. Again, Rabbitt (1996) notes that when data increase in variability with task complexity, a linear relationship can still be obtained. This is a mathematically difficult argument, but in essence it means that the regression equation is probably quite accurate when it claims that the first few points on the graph (representing the more basic tasks) fall on a straight line. However, the final few points on the graph (representing the more complex tasks) probably are not best represented by a straight line, and that in effect the regression equation is making more and more false assumptions about a linear relationship the more complex the tasks the groups are doing. Finally, a study by Sliwinski and Hall (1998) found that many of the early studies had used the wrong form of regression analysis (the *ordinary least squares multiple regression* or OLS) and that another form (the *hierarchical linear model* or HLM) was more appropriate. When the two techniques were compared on the same sets of data, the OLS produced Brinley plots, whilst HLM identified rather greater variability (i.e. not nice, neat straight lines).

The evidence thus seems to pull in two directions. On the one hand there are a lot of studies that demonstrate the validity of Brinley plots, and yet there are others that say Brinley plots can be flawed. The most parsimonious explanation of these findings is that Brinley plots apply in some situations and not others. Thus, there are some processes that genuinely do show a linear pattern of slowing, whilst in other instances, this model simply cannot apply. Even within studies where Brinley plots have been shown to be sound measures, it now appears that slowing can be at two broad rates – in some instances older people are slower than younger adults by about 20 per cent, whilst in other studies, they are slower by circa 80 per cent (Verhaeghen, 2011). Findings such as these do not mean that the general slowing

---

8   A linear relationship simply means that if you plot it on a graph, it forms a straight line. This generally means that the relationship between the variables involved is fairly uncomplicated.

hypothesis is 'wrong' – simply that it is not quite as universal an explanation as might have been first assumed.

However, general slowing is not just about Brinley plots. If we consider the argument that, regardless of what shape the line on the graph is, speed of processing is strongly related to many aspects of ageing change in intelligence, then there is a lot of evidence in favour. For example, in an impressive meta-analysis of the research literature (172 studies, with a total of over 53,000 participants), Sheppard and Vernon (2008) demonstrated a reliable, significant correlation between speed of processing measures and cognitive ability. So general slowing almost certainly *does* play a role. The follow-up question concerning the *size* of this role is less easy to answer. As we have just seen, there seem to be many exceptions where speed of processing is not central to an ageing change. And when it is, the size of the effect can at first sight seem surprisingly small. For example, Salthouse (1985) found an average correlation of 0.28 between age and simple reaction times and 0.43 between age and choice reaction times. For those unfamiliar with statistics, this means that ageing can only account for about 8 per cent of the variability in simple reaction times and about 19 per cent in choice reaction times. This seems to indicate that the interest in reaction times is unmerited given that they have a relatively peripheral role to play. However, this would be an inaccurate conclusion. Salthouse has provided an ingenious, if mathematically complex, rejoinder, which demonstrates that changes in intellectual skills are *mediated* by the decline in processing speeds (Salthouse, 1985, 1991, 1992a). In a similar manner, the chains connecting the carriages of a railway train are relatively unimportant in comparison with the power of the engine – but try pulling a train without the chains.

The frontal lobe hypothesis

Different parts of the brain control different functions. Much of the brain does the necessary but unglamorous work of controlling bodily functions such as digestion, temperature regulation, etc., and these largely lie beyond conscious control. Other areas of the brain are responsible for what are sometimes called 'higher mental functions', such as thinking, reading, language and remembering. A key area of the brain in this regard is the *frontal lobes*, which are heavily involved in many forms of complex thought processes, particularly those involving planning sequences or remembering the order in which events occurred. The frontal lobes do this in a variety of ways, but a key method is to inhibit unwanted responses. Typically our thought processes generate not just one, but several alternative responses to any question, and the frontal lobes suppress the answers that are less plausible, and only allow the most probable answer to be given. For example, if asked 'Who is the President of the USA?', the correct answer (at the time of writing) is 'President Obama'; in generating this answer, the brain probably produced other answers that are connected to the question but are incorrect, such as 'David Cameron' (current Prime Minister of the UK) or 'Ronald Reagan' (previous President of the USA). For this reason frontal-lobe activity is often referred to as *inhibitory functioning* or similar. When the frontal lobes decline in performance, people produce more false answers, cannot plan in sequence as efficiently and/or confuse the sequence in which a set of items appeared. Evidence that older people show a decline in skills known to involve the frontal lobes is considerable (e.g. Persad *et al.*, 2002; Sanchez-Benavides *et al.*, 2010). This in turn leads to the *frontal lobe hypothesis*, which argues that ageing intellectual changes are largely the result of changes in the frontal lobe.

At issue is not that frontal-lobe skills decline in later life (nobody really disputes this), but the extent to which changes in the frontal lobes are *uniquely* responsible for age-related changes in intelligence. The evidence for this is far from convincing. For example, some younger adults suffer damage specifically to the frontal lobes through accident or a stroke, and their intellectual problems are qualitatively different from those of older people (Phillips, 1999). In addition, research has shown that although frontal-lobe problems play a key role in age differences on many cognitive tasks, they are rarely the sole area of the brain that is significantly involved (Robbins *et al.*, 1998; Whelihan *et al.*, 1997). Salthouse, Fristoe and Rhee (1996) studied age changes in skills associated with the frontal, parietal and temporal lobes, and found that an average of '58 per cent of the age-related variance in a given variable was shared with that in other variables' (p.272). In other words, although different areas of the brain may each contribute something unique to the pattern of age-related decline, a great deal of what they do is in tandem with other ageing changes.

However, these findings must be put in perspective. Arguing that frontal lobes do not have the overwhelming influence that researchers initially supposed does not deny the existence of frontal-lobe problems. There are still many research papers being produced that identify frontal-lobe dysfunction as being a prime cause of age differences in cognitive functioning. The distinction is that identifying an *important* cause does not mean that it is the *sole* cause. To make an analogy, a naturally clumsy man might break his leg. Seeing him struggling to get around on crutches may be ultimately part of the manifestation of his clumsiness, but that does not mean that the specific problems associated with a broken leg have gone away. In other words, whether frontal-lobe problems are a cause of age-related decline, an effect, or a bit of both, does not stop them being a significant factor in considerations of ageing decline in intellectual skills.

Causes of intellectual change – a summary
It would appear that there are several causes of intellectual change in later life, and although a case can be made for each of them, no single factor accounts for all of the decline. This should not be surprising, since ageing effects are, by definition, the cumulative effects of a lifetime of experience. There are therefore likely to be a variety of causes. Although some changes probably are the product of unavoidable physical ageing, the effects of experience and exercise (both mental and physical) are likely to be more malleable.

Other types of intellectual change
The research cited so far in this chapter has largely centred on changes in performance on traditional intelligence tests. However, there are other aspects of intellectual performance beyond paper-and-pencil tests. In the final section of this chapter, we shall consider some of these skills.

Conceptual organisation
The ability to treat items at an abstract level, in order to uncover basic rules and principles, is called *conceptual organisation*. One way of measuring this is the '20 questions' type of task. This is a version of the parlour game in which the participant is told that the experimenter

is thinking of an object, and by a series of questions to which the experimenter can only answer 'yes' or 'no', the participant tries to elicit the name of the object. Denney and Denney (1974) found that older people are far less efficient at this, because they tend to ask too few constraint-seeking questions[9] before they start guessing at specific answers.

Another measure of conceptual organisation uses shapes and symbols, where the rules that classify the groupings have been experimenter-decided and it is the task of the participant to uncover these rules (e.g. 'shapes are grouped by colour irrespective of size and shape' or 'all shapes are grouped by colour and by shape'). Researchers have shown that, in many instances, older people have difficulty in doing these sorts of tasks (see Filoteo and Maddox, 2004). It might be argued that the decline in categorisation skills is due to an artefact of declining memory (i.e. older adults cannot simultaneously keep in mind everything they need to sort through). However, varying the memory load by varying the number of items to be categorised has no appreciable effects on performance (see Rebok, 1987). Nor can differences in education level provide a total explanation (Lawrence and Arrowood, 1982). Nor again can a cohort difference in knowledge of how to deal with this sort of task, since even after being shown the best strategy, older adults failed to use it as extensively as younger controls (Hybertson, Perdue and Hybertson, 1982). Maddox *et al.* (2010) found that where older adults could learn the formal rules of a categorisation task, they nonetheless were worse than younger adults at integrating the information necessary to use the rules (i.e. they knew what to do in principle but in practice were less adept). These processes are underpinned by working memory (see Chapter 3) skills, which are known to be especially ageing-sensitive.

Some of the categorisation errors made by older adults can be qualitatively different. For example, Lawrence and Arrowood (1982) found that in a sample of older hospitalised (but not dementing) older adults, 42 per cent of them used *sentential grouping* to place items in the same category. For example, it might be assumed that 'rabbit' belongs in the category of 'animals' and 'carrot' in 'vegetables', but in sentential grouping, rabbit and carrot can belong together because

---

9   Questions that progressively constrict the choice of alternatives (e.g. 'Is it an animal?', 'Is it a mammal?', 'Is it a household pet?').

they can be used in the same phrase ('the rabbit ate the carrot'). This seems like a failure to think in abstract terms, and not seeing rabbits and carrots at a more abstract level of belonging to different semantic categories. Arguably a similar problem besets understanding many colloquial phrases such as proverbs. Taken at face value, the adage that people in glass houses shouldn't throw stones implies rather obvious advice to greenhouse owners. However, it might be intuitively assumed that knowledge of what proverbs mean is part and parcel of crystallised intelligence and thus relatively resistant to ageing decline. However, Albert, Duffy and Naeser (1987) found that older people were worse at interpreting the meaning of proverbs. This applied whether participants were left to provide their own answers unaided, or were given a multiple-choice test. Furthermore, Arenberg (1982), in a longitudinal study, showed that younger participants' performance on a conceptual-formation task improved on subsequent test sessions, whilst the older participants got worse.

It may be observed that when people make 'errors' in a classification task, they are only 'wrong' because their classifications do not conform with what the experimenter wanted. Grouping a carrot with a rabbit is perfectly sensible; although, in a wider scheme of things, it is not the most elegant solution, it is perhaps more fun.[10] Denney (1974) argues that older people make grouping mistakes, not because of any 'decline' but because they forget the accepted 'correct' way of grouping things as defined by educational practice, and instead adopt an arguably more 'natural' method of grouping. This may be coincidentally related to education level and intelligence, because higher-educated and higher-intelligence people tend to enter professions and have leisure activities more demanding of formal grouping practices, and thus maintain these methods longer than other people.

Creativity in later life

Running in tandem with general intelligence is *creativity*. Researchers are divided on how best to describe the skill, but most would agree that for an act to be creative, it must be novel, and it must be appropriate to the situation. The best way to demonstrate this is to consider a typical

---

10 That participants might seek amusing solutions does not seem to occur to many experimenters. Running the same test day after day for several weeks does tend to blunt a researcher's sense of humour.

creativity test. The participant is presented with a house brick and is asked to think of as many uses for it as possible. There are two types of response that are classified as being 'uncreative'. The first is appropriate but conventional (e.g. 'Use it in building a house'). The second is novel but inappropriate (e.g. 'Use it to cure insomnia by knocking yourself out with it'). A creative answer would be something like 'Scrape the surface of the brick to make a powder paint' (i.e. something both novel and feasible). People who produce a lot of creative answers are said to be good at divergent thinking (i.e. given a simple situation they can produce answers that diverge from mainstream thought).

Studies have found that older people are poorer at divergent-thinking tasks, producing fewer answers and/or at a lower rate (Foos and Boone, 2008), peaking in their scores about the age of 40 (McCrae, Arenberg and Costa, 1987). It might be argued that this is because the older also have depleted intellectual skills in general. However, the age difference persists even when older and younger participants are matched for intelligence and education level (McCrae *et al.*, 1987). However, as several researchers (e.g. Hendricks, 1999; Simonton, 1990) have argued, divergent-thinking scores are not very reliable indicators of 'real-life' creative abilities in all cases.

Another way to consider creativity is the biographical approach. By this method, the lives of acknowledged leaders in fields of activity where originality of thought is highly prized are examined, to see what made or makes them 'better' than others. Some generalisations can be gleaned from such studies. Artists and musicians tend to display their talents early in life (e.g. Mozart), whilst scientists are usually in their 20s before they show signs of outstanding ability. In addition, scientists are often competent, but not outstanding students, until the area of specialisation in which they will become pre-eminent grips their imagination (Hudson, 1987). Charles Darwin was a classic example of this. Thereafter, most eminent persons make their major contributions to their field before the onset of old age. Most have a peak of creative output before they are 40. This applies to disciplines as diverse as mathematics, chemistry and musical composition. It is important to note that 'great' and 'routine' pieces of work tend to be produced in tandem. In other words, in a prolific period, a creative person will produce the same ratio of good to indifferent work as he or she will during relatively unproductive periods – thus, the *quality ratio* stays fairly constant (Simonton, 1990). Creativity has for *most* people relatively declined by their 60s (see Rebok, 1987). Although there have been several studies claiming that creativity continues to rise throughout life (e.g. Reed, 2005), it is notable that these often rely on self-report and self-perception, not on more objective measures. However, this is not *universally* true, and Butler (1967) made a spirited counterattack to this view, citing numerous masterpieces produced late in their creators' lives. Titian, for example, continued to paint into his 90s, and most critics agree that his later work far surpasses his earlier output. However, Butler cited notable *exceptions*. For the majority of creative people, ageing is associated with a decline.

It can be argued that the sensory and physical declines of ageing will affect creative people especially badly, because above all others they need a precise, accurate and untiring view of the world (Rebok, 1987). Undoubtedly in some creative fields, where physical fitness is *de rigueur*, this is true. Opera singers and ballet dancers are never at their peak in old age (but equally, there are few ballet dancers over 35 who still perform on the stage). However, for the majority of creative persons, another explanation must be sought, since there is a long list of innovative people who have succeeded in spite of, or even because of, physical incapacity (e.g. Beethoven was deaf when he wrote many of his greatest works). Similarly, attribution for the effects of ageing cannot be laid upon a general intellectual decline, for two main reasons. First, because as was seen from Alpaugh and Birren (1977), age differences in creativity exist even when intelligence levels are matched. Second, intelligence is in any case a poor predictor of creativity (Hudson, 1987). Therefore, another explanation must be sought.

One possibility is that creative people are victims of their own success. Scientists who achieve pre-eminence in their field are likely to find themselves quickly elevated to headships of departments or research groups. Once in this position, much of the running of experiments and 'hands-on' experience is passed on to research assistants, whilst the head of department finds him- or herself embroiled in an increasing quantity of administrative duties. Thus, the eminent scientist's reward for success at a particular endeavour may be to have his or her future activities in the field restricted, thus causing a decline in creative output. A different set of values probably applies to people pre-eminent in the arts. First, far more than scientists, artists (of any type) rely for their success on critical and public opinion. Accordingly, the worth of an artist depends upon what is fashionable at the time; and to be considered creative, the artist must be seen as a leading interpreter of the fashion and/or to have been the creator of that fashion. A second consideration is that few artists are able to support themselves if their craft does not pay. Accordingly, if they do not achieve success in early life, they are likely to withdraw from full-time creative activity and seek other employment. It follows from these two premises that the creative person usually becomes noticed for being a skilled exponent of a current fashion at an early stage in his or her career. Obviously, the artist seeks to capitalise on this, and accordingly becomes increasingly identifiable with that fashion. However, opinions change, and almost inevitably the artist becomes a representative of a movement that is now unfashionable. The more successful he or she was, the more strongly he or she is now identified as being unfashionable. In short, successful artists are hoist by their own petard (for a brilliant fictional account of this, see the shamefully under-regarded novel *Angel* by Taylor, 1957). The only solution for most artists is to move with the fashion. Since this probably involves a radical change of style, their output is likely to suffer. The speed at which these changes occur vary from discipline to discipline. Anyone with any knowledge of pop music will know that a cycle such as the one described occurs every three or four years. However, in any field, there are very few artists who produce 'timeless' works that rise above the mercurial changes of fashionable opinion. For example, a quick perusal through a second-hand bookshop or a musical dictionary will readily reveal how many 'geniuses' of literature and music from previous generations are now completely forgotten. Thus, the reasons behind the changes in creative output across the lifespan may be due far more to the lifestyles and job demands of the gifted than to ageing *per se*. Older people may have 'lost' their creativity because they were too good at their job earlier in life.

The above arguments apply to people who are outstanding in their field, but they do not deny a role for creativity in everyday life. It is important to note that even where studies have found creativity scores to be lower in later life, nobody has argued that creativity is non-existent. This argument is not just a simple justification for older adults to pick up their paint brushes. It also counteracts the claims of some creativity advocates that mainstream psychology has claimed older adults are over the hill and lack creative powers. This is not the case – on objective measures, creative acts usually *decline* in later life. Nobody has said that they *stop*, nor that older adults should be barred from creative acts. In fact, there is considerable evidence that engaging in creative activity (e.g. painting, writing, and so on) is of considerable value to older participants, and is reported as enhancing feelings of well-being and general self-esteem (e.g. Hickson and Housley, 1997; Weisberg and Wilder, 2001).

Piagetian tasks

The developmental psychologist Jean Piaget created a series of ingenious experiments to demonstrate that young children often think in radically different ways from adults. One of the best known of these concerns *conservation*, which in this instance means the knowledge that an item can retain the same quantity of material even if its outward appearance changes. In Piaget's experiment, the participant is shown two balls of modelling clay of equal size and shape, and agrees that each is composed of the same amount of clay. The experimenter then rolls one of the balls into a sausage shape, and asks the participant if the two pieces have the same amount of clay in them, to which of course the answer is 'yes'.[11] Up to about the age of 7, children get this task wrong – they typically believe that the quantity of clay in the sausage shape has changed. There are various explanations for this, but one of the most straightforward is that the children have not been attending to all of the dimensions of the ball of clay as it is rolled out. Thus, a child who has only been concentrating on the height of the piece of clay thinks it has got smaller, as the clay lowers in height as the ball is rolled out into the sausage shape. By the same reasoning, a child who has been concentrating on width will think that the shape has got bigger. The correct thinking is of course to realise that the decrease in one dimension is offset by an increase in the other dimension.[12]

Whether Piaget is really testing what children think has been debated at (very) great length. Some critics have argued that the test

---

11 Pedants note that one ignores the minuscule amount lost on the hands and table surface during rolling.

12 Or, for example, to realise that as none of the clay has been taken away or added to, the same quantity must still be present.

method he used confuses young children rather than tests their genuine abilities. Whether this criticism and others like it are valid is not in question here. What is certain is that the established research literature firmly believes that older children and certainly no adults will make errors on Piaget's tests. However, Papalia (1972) demonstrated that older people are bad at the conservation task. It is possible that this might be because some of Papalia's participants were institutionalised older adults, so the results might be explicable by dementia or other illnesses. Again, it is possible that there is simply something quirky about the conservation experiment. However, later studies, using older adults who were community resident and non-dementing also found an age decline and on a wide range of Piagetian tasks.

For example, McDonald and Stuart-Hamilton (2002) conducted a replication of another of Piaget's studies, in which participants were placed at a table on which was a model of three mountains, each with a distinct feature (one had a snow cap, one had a house on it, etc.). The participants were shown a range of pictures showing views of the model from various positions around the table. Asked to select their own viewpoint, they could do this faultlessly. However, if now asked to select a picture representing what a doll positioned at another location around the table could 'see', participants made errors. Some of these were simple errors of spatial judgement (i.e. they chose a view that was close to that of the doll's, but nonetheless inaccurate). However, circa 15 per cent of older participants chose a view that was *their own*. This type of error – called an egocentric error – is illogical and is only otherwise seen when the task is given to younger children (typically aged 8 years or younger). There are similar surprising failings on other Piagetian tasks, such as moral reasoning (McDonald and Stuart-Hamilton, 1996), correctly drawing the water level in a tilting glass or bottle (Tran and Formann, 2008) and animism – the erroneous belief that some inanimate objects are alive (McDonald and Stuart-Hamilton, 2000; Parry and Stuart-Hamilton, 2009). Certainly, older people who fail Piagetian tasks are not incapable of performing them, since they can be easily retrained to do them correctly (Blackburn and Papalia, 1992).

Hooper, Fitzgerald and Papalia (1971) suggest that skills necessary to perform Piagetian tasks may be lost in the reverse of the order in which they were acquired during childhood, and may also be strongly linked with changes in fluid and crystallised intelligence. However, research by McDonald and Stuart-Hamilton (e.g. Stuart-Hamilton and McDonald, 1996, 1999, 2001) suggests a more complex tale. If older people's performance on a wide variety of Piagetian tasks is measured, then it is possible to create a 'Piaget score' (i.e. the total number of tests correctly performed). This is a better predictor of participants' ages than their intelligence-test scores (Stuart-Hamilton and McDonald, 1996). In turn, the best predictor of Piagetian score is a personality measure called *need for cognition* (Stuart-Hamilton and McDonald, 1999, 2001). This is a measure of the drive a person feels to pursue intellectually demanding tasks as part of their lifestyle, as opposed to their actual level of intelligence. Overall, this implies that the changes in Piagetian performance may reflect an older person's level of involvement with intellectual tasks and (for want of a better expression) an 'intellectual lifestyle'. As a person gets older, he or she may become less committed to certain intellectual pursuits, and his or her methods and styles of thinking shift. Such changes will correlate reasonably well with performance on intelligence test scores, but this is in part coincidental.

Summary

Intelligence change across the lifespan takes the form of the classic ageing curve – there is a rise in raw scores through early life, a plateau and then a drop. The age of onset of decline depends on many things – people show considerable individual differences in their pattern of change, and measures of age decline are distorted by the methods used to measure them: cross-sectional studies tend to exaggerate age changes whilst longitudinal studies tend to artificially shrink them. In addition, measures of age change tend to be distorted by incidental ageing effects such as slower movements and similar. The waters are further muddied when different types of intelligence are considered. Crystallised intelligence tends to remain intact throughout life, whilst fluid intelligence declines, but again, this is only a generalisation, and there are several caveats to this, not least that the way in which testing is conducted can strongly influence the size of the ageing effect that is found.

Studies of the cause of ageing change have tended to concentrate on the contrasting theories of general slowing and disuse. Both have their strengths and weaknesses and probably both explain some aspects of age-related change. Studies of ageing changes in other intellectual skills, notably Piagetian skills, indicate that ageing changes in mental processing might be even more complex than is traditionally assumed, and that older people might in some instances elect to adopt radically different thinking styles from those of younger adults.

Suggested further reading

Perhaps the best (and most readable) summary of the study of intelligence and how it is tested is provided by Deary (2001); although a short book, it covers a lot of ground and is very readable. More advanced texts covering a lot of the areas addressed in this chapter in much greater depth are Craik and Salthouse (2008) and Perfect and Maylor (2000). Readers should be cautioned that, although very erudite, these books require a high level of prior knowledge of advanced psychological and statistical techniques. The same caveat applies to Hertzog and Nesselroade's (2003) excellent critical review of methodological problems in testing older adults. Salthouse (2010) provides a concise overview of his model of ageing and intelligence.

CHAPTER 3

Memory

Introduction

Declining memory ability is probably the biggest single thing that most people associate with psychological ageing. People often assume that 'memory' is one skill, but in fact, it is composed of several different types of memory skill, each based in its own specialised part of the brain. In this chapter we shall look at some of the most intensively researched of these skills. As we shall see, age changes vary considerably between them.

Short-term memory (STM)

Short-term memory (STM) is generally defined as the ability to remember what has occurred in the last few seconds.[1] The most straightforward way of measuring STM is to read out a list of words[2] to a participant and get them to repeat them back immediately. Ageing has very little effect on this. If a large group of people is tested, a statistically significant decline is found, but it is rather small (Craik and Jennings, 1992; Craik *et al.*, 1995). However, if the task is made any harder than simply listening to and then parroting back items, the ageing decline is very much more pronounced (Bopp and Verhaeghen, 2005). For

---

1   Most researchers define it as the last 30 seconds.
2   Generally, either words are used, or numbers; if numbers are used, the test is often called a *digit span* measure.

example, in the *backward span* procedure, the participant is required to repeat the items back in reverse order of their presentation (e.g. the candidate hears *75123* and must reply *32157*). This is clearly harder than straightforward recall, since participants must keep in store the items in their correct order whilst simultaneously working out what they are in reverse. Bromley (1958), among others, has shown that older people are significantly worse at this task.

One suggested cause for this failure is that because the items in the forward and reverse lists are identical and only differ in their sequence, it is easy to confuse the two, and thus form a garbled amalgam. This implies a problem with frontal-lobe functioning (see Chapter 2; see also Thompson-Schill *et al.*, 2002). It is argued that the frontal lobes' failure to separate the forward and backwards lists is due to a failure to inhibit unwanted information,[3] and thus is often called the *inhibitory deficit hypothesis* (see Hasher, Zacks and May, 1999). This failure to inhibit applies to more than backward recall tasks. For example, memory experiments generally require the participants to do several trials in succession. It has been demonstrated that the more trials that are given, the more likely it is that people will erroneously 'remember' an item from an earlier list. For example, if on trial 8 of an experiment the participant is asked to remember the words *cat, dog, banana, orange, car* it is possible that they might erroneously recall *cab*, even though that word was from trial 2. Most people make this sort of error and it has been attributed to a failure of the frontal lobes to inhibit a response made earlier. In other words, people mix up what is new and old information. However, older people are especially prone to making this type of error (Bowles and Salthouse, 2003).

The effects of ageing on backward span illustrates a common theme in memory changes in old age. Namely, that a basic memory skill (such as straightforward tests of STM) are not affected much by ageing, as soon as the task is made harder by requiring more than just memorising, then older adults are disproportionately disadvantaged. This is again found in research on *working memory*. The term refers

---

3   Suppose a participant is given *2514* and is asked to repeat it backwards. Whilst they are trying to construct *4152* in their head, the original list *2514* in effect keeps 'butting in' until a garbled mess is produced. It is analogous to trying to hum a tune whilst someone is playing a completely different tune in the background.

to any task where someone must remember something whilst doing another task. An example often given is remembering a phone number you have been given whilst searching for a pen and paper to write it down and carrying on a conversation simultaneously. However, working memory is also used constantly whilst we are awake, often without us realising it, since we use working memory whenever what has just happened shapes what we are about to do. For example, in listening to what someone is saying, it enables us to remember what has just been said in order to make sense of the rest of what they say. All this is second nature to us, and so we rarely stop to think how vital an efficient working memory is to our everyday lives.

The widely accepted model of how working memory operates was devised by Baddeley and Hitch (1974). This argues that when something has to be remembered in STM, the information gets put into a mental store appropriate for the material to be memorised. Thus, anything consisting of words is put into a store called the *phonological loop*,[4] whilst anything consisting of visual material is stored in a store for visual information, etc. The stores such as the phonological loop have a limited capacity – in other words, there is a limit to how much they can store. Also, the stores are passive – in other words, they simply receive information rather than process it or seek it out. They are thus like an old-fashioned loop of recording tape, which can only record a brief message. Placing information onto the loop and retrieving it is the task of the *central executive*. This is a mental process that controls how working memory operates. If a person has to do another mental task whilst trying to remember something, it is the central executive's task to co-ordinate the psychological processes involved in doing this.

Baddeley (1986) cited the central executive as the prime cause of this age-related decline in STM. Given that the central executive is probably anatomically based in the frontal lobes (see Dahlin *et al.*, 2009) this makes intuitive sense. This concords with the argument raised above – namely, that the principal ageing deficit is not memory as such, but the tasks involved in organising the material that is to be remembered and in juggling different tasks when doing something more complex than simply remembering a list of items. For example, suppose a person is asked to remember a list of words, and whilst

---

4   Called the articulatory loop in some older texts. Note that 'words' in this instance includes numbers.

they are trying to do this they are given another mental task to do (what is known as a *distracting task*). It can be readily demonstrated that increasing the complexity of the distracting task disproportionately affects older people's recall (e.g. Mitchell *et al.*, 2000; Verhaeghen, 2011; Zeintl and Kliegel, 2010). Note that the distracting task does not have to be particularly intellectual. For example, Lindenberger, Marsiske and Baltes (2000) found that walking whilst memorising was sufficient to impair memory in older people, and the more complex the path to be walked, the disproportionately greater the decline in older adults' memories.

It is possible to improve memory by using various techniques. One of the simplest and most effective is *chunking*. If given a string of items to remember, a better strategy than trying to remember them as one long string is to think of them as a series of groups of three or four items. For example, instead of trying to remember *345172986142* as *345172986142*, a better strategy would be to think of it in chunks of three as *345 172 986 142*. Precisely this principle is used in the presentation of credit card and telephone numbers. Belmont, Freeseman and Mitchell (1988) demonstrated that older people are less likely than younger people to chunk long digit lists when trying to encode them. However, it is worth noting that some older participants *did* chunk, and their spans were as good as the best of the younger participants. Other researchers have also noted that older people do not arrange to-be-remembered (TBR) items, and that without prompting, they do not pay as close attention to them. In other words, they do not process the items 'deeply'[5] enough (e.g. Craik and Rabinowitz, 1984). Furthermore, older adults may at a broader level change their memory strategies. For example, Brébion, Smith and Ehrlich (1997) argue that when given a working-memory task in which a set of TBR items had to be remembered in tandem with performing a sentence comprehension task, the older participants tended to place greater emphasis on the comprehension task than the memory task.

---

5   This has a specialist meaning in Psychology. It can be used in the everyday sense of the word, but typically refers specifically to the quantity of information about an item that is mentally processed. Typically, the more an item has been mentally processed, the better remembered it is. There is a *vast* literature on this topic.

It can be concluded from this that older people's STM can be improved by making more effective use of strategies, and this is true (see Carretti, Borella and De Beni, 2007; Lemaire, 2010). However, the effect might not be very large, and other factors, such as an ageing nervous system are likely to cause an age decline regardless of strategy use (see Bailey, Dunlosky and Hertzog, 2009).

Long-term memory

Long-term memory (LTM) describes any memory longer than STM. This means that it describes memory for events of a few minutes to several decades ago. LTM used to be tested using fairly arid (and in the main unrealistic) tests under highly controlled conditions in the laboratory. Typically, participants were given lists of items to remember, and then their recall was tested minutes, hours, or even weeks later. Studies of this kind have almost invariably found that older people show bigger deficits than in STM tests (Albert, 1988). However, research over the past three decades has tended to look at how LTM is used in specific situations, and this is what we shall do here.

Remote memory

Remote memory is for non-autobiographical events that occurred within a person's lifetime. It is usually tested by giving participants a list of names and/or descriptions of events which have been 'in the news' over the past 50 or so years, and asking them to indicate which they can remember. One such example is the *Famous Names Test*, or FNT (Stevens, 1979), which comprises a list of names of people famous between the 1930s and 1970s. Stuart-Hamilton, Perfect and Rabbitt (1988) tested participants aged 50–80 years on the FNT, and found that for all ages, memory of recent names was better than for distant ones. This phenomenon has been observed by many other researchers (e.g. Craik, 1977; Perlmutter, 1978), and contradicts the once popular *Ribot's hypothesis* (Ribot, 1882), which argues that, in older people, memory for recent events should be worse than for remote ones.

However, a problem with remote memory tests is that it is difficult to know whether remote memory is being tested, or general knowledge. In the second part of the Stuart-Hamilton *et al.* (1988) study, a group of 20-year-olds, who could not possibly know the older names except as 'historical' figures, were given the FNT. However, they could still accurately recognise about 25 per cent from each decade group.[6] This means that a proportion of items on remote memory tests are probably recognised from general knowledge rather than as genuine 'only experienced at the time' remote memories. Furthermore, Stuart-Hamilton *et al.* found that the relative likelihood of a particular name on the FNT being recognised was similar for participants of different ages. In other words, if 'Miss X' were the tenth most recognised name amongst participants in their 70s, Miss X was likely to be at or around tenth position amongst those aged 60, 50 or 20. This suggests that supposedly 'remote' names may be rather more frequently aired in the media than researchers suspect, and the similar 'league tables' of popularity for different names implies that the impact of media coverage is remarkably consistent for different age groups.

This argument is supported by research by Basso, Schefft and Hamsher (2005), which found that in very old (aged 90+) participants, scores on the Presidents Test (a measure of knowledge of the temporal order in which the last eight US presidents had held office) are significantly worse. The same researchers also found that education level was positively correlated with remote memory. These results support the argument that remote memory tests might reflect exposure to the news media, since we would expect more highly educated people to read more and be more aware of recent history, and we might also hypothesise that very old people might find themselves less exposed to news media and similar through deteriorating senses.

Eyewitness testimony

As the name suggests, eyewitness testimony refers to the ability to remember information about an incident that has been seen once. In 'real life', eyewitness memory forms the basis of many legal cases, and experimental measures of eyewitness testimony have tended to present participants with an enacted incident (either 'in the flesh' or on video tape). Generally, older people are found to be as good as younger adults at remembering the main points of an incident, but show some worsening of recall of relatively minor points, such as details of the

---

6   The FNT contains a group of fictitious names to catch out anyone who dishonestly claims to recognise every name. However, the participants did not respond 'yes' to these, so the result was not simply the result of guessing.

clothing of the protagonists (e.g. Adams-Price, 1992). For example, if a simple 'score' of overall information recalled is made, then there is an appreciable age difference (e.g. Yarmey and Yarmey, 1997). This does not bode particularly well for the credibility of older adults as eyewitnesses.

Such a feeling is not enhanced by the findings of Coxon and Valentine (1997). They directly compared the responses of older and younger adults and children to a series of misleading and non-misleading questions about a crime video they had witnessed. It was found that both the older adults and children performed less well than the younger adults. A study by Karpel, Hoyer and Toglia (2001) found that older adults were more susceptible to misleading information surrounding a vignette depicting a theft. Not only did they subsequently report more pieces of misinformation as 'fact', but their level of certainty that the misinformation was real was significantly higher than in younger adults. Overall, therefore, the view is a pessimistic one (see LaVole, Mertz and Richmond, 2007) and is plausibly linked to a decline in frontal-lobe processing failing to suppress irrelevant information (Roediger and Geraci, 2007). Such considerations paint a grim picture of the status of an older person as a witness in a courtroom. Even if he or she is correct in the main points of their testimony (which arguably may be all that matters), a lawyer may quickly discredit this by playing on weaknesses over (what are after all irrelevant) recall of details (thereby reducing the older person's self-esteem as well). It is small surprise to find that older eyewitnesses' testimony is rated as being less credible (e.g. Kwong See, Hoffman and Wood, 2001). This is in spite of the fact that older people are generally perceived as being more honest (Kwong See *et al.*, 2001).

Text recall

Because recall of text is strongly linked with linguistic skills, this topic is dealt with in detail in Chapter 4. A summary of the findings is that, essentially, there are no or relatively few age differences in the recall of the main points of a story (the 'gist' of the text) but that memory for details may worsen, especially in older people who are also low scorers on intelligence tests. However, there are a number of occasions when this rule breaks down, and interested readers should consult the appropriate section in the next chapter.

Semantic memory

Semantic memory is memory for factual information, and is not concerned with, for example, memory of where and when something was learnt. *Very* loosely, it might be seen as being factual knowledge. In general, older adults are as good as, if not better than, younger adults at recalling facts and information held in semantic memory (e.g. Camp, 1988; Sharps, 1998). In part this is probably due to semantic memories being stored in a network that stretches across a relatively large part of the brain. This means that it is less sensitive to ageing loss than is a mental skill based in a relatively tightly conscribed part of the brain (Eichenbaum, 2003).

However, this does not mean that semantic memory is immune from ageing changes. A review by Luo and Craik (2008) notes that the preservation of semantic memory is strongest in frequently used areas of information; very specific information (e.g. people's names) is far less well preserved (see also Hough, 2006). Again, ability to retrieve items from memory might not be as fluent in later life. For example, Kozora and Cullum (1995) found that producing examples of particular semantic categories (e.g. tell me some types of trees) was less efficient in older adults.

Episodic memory

Episodic memory is defined by some researchers as memory of personal experiences from the relatively recent past. This is contrasted with autobiographical memory (see page 76). There is overwhelming evidence that there is a significant ageing decline in this skill (e.g. Naveh-Benjamin *et al.*, 2004; Plancher *et al.*, 2010). Commentators often contrast this with the relative preservation of semantic memory. Episodic memory is almost certain to show significant ageing effects because, by its very nature, it is more complex and prone to distortion than semantic memory. People are being asked to recall facts for once-only events (not like semantic memory where the same information might be encountered on numerous occasions), and must nail down what, where, when and often also by whom things were said or done (again, not something required of semantic memory). There is far more information that needs to be remembered, and therefore, far more that can go wrong. It is therefore not surprising that a key failing in the episodic memory abilities of older adults is what amounts to a failure to remember sufficient details surrounding the TBR items. Often this concerns the issue of *source memory* (essentially, remembering the context in which something was learnt). For example, McIntyre and Craik (1987) gave participants the task of remembering a new set of 'facts' (in reality false but plausible snippets of general knowledge). Over a week, the older adults showed little deficit in memory for the facts themselves, but were far worse than younger participants at remembering where they had first learnt the information (i.e. at the previous test session). Again, Simons *et al.* (2004) found that older adults were significantly worse at remembering specific source information (which of four people said a TBR item) and partial source information (the gender of the person who said a TBR item). The evidence collected by Simons *et al.* implies that memory for partial and specific information is equally affected.

It follows from the above that older people are probably more prone to false memories – and that generally appears to be the case, at least in laboratory studies (see Dehon and Brédart, 2004). This, *inter alia*, raises further concerns for the reliability of older adults' eyewitness memory. It is known, perhaps not surprisingly, that false-memory production is related to level of frontal-lobe functioning (Plancher *et al.*, 2010) and as in other instances reported in this chapter, older people are more likely to be (erroneously) confident that these false memories are in fact true (Shing *et al.*, 2009).

Implicit memory

Implicit memory is information that can be retrieved from memory that has not been explicitly stored. For example, if asked 'Did Margaret Thatcher have two legs?' we should be able to answer 'yes' almost immediately. However, it is wildly improbable that any of us explicitly remembered that Margaret Thatcher was a biped. However, because we could remember that Margaret Thatcher was human,[7] and we know that humans have two legs, we can work out the correct answer. Evidence on implicit memory points to there being no significant age difference, or, at worst, only a slight decline (e.g. Fay, Isingrini and Clarys, 2005; Mitchell and Schmitt, 2006).

---

7 Though admittedly some of her more extreme detractors might dispute this.

Autobiographical memory

Autobiographical memory can be loosely described as memory for events from one's own life. Some researchers argue this includes episodic memory (see page 74), whilst others argue that autobiographical memory solely refers to memories from a person's relatively distant past. There is an active debate about which definition is right in academic psychology, but for the purposes of this book the distinction is not an important one, and here we shall treat autobiographical memory as being memory for relatively distant events in a person's own life. Several major problems beset research in this field. The most often cited of these is the issue of reliability. For example, an older participant might reminisce about a picnic in 1936, held with her now-dead parents. How can one possibly verify the accuracy of this recollection? This is not to say that the participant is deliberately lying, but usually reminiscences have been recalled many times over a person's lifetime, and with each retelling, details often alter to improve the flow of the narrative (Bartlett, 1932). Thus, the recounting of a story five years after the event in question may have the same basic plot as a retelling 50 years on, but the details of the two narratives are likely to be different. This argument is supported by the findings of a longitudinal study by Field (1981). Comparing reminiscences of the same events 30 and 70 years, on, there was a reasonably high correlation[8] for points in the basic plot ($r = 0.88$), but only a 16 per cent concordance for recall of more peripheral details ($r = 0.43$). This finding is echoed in a study by Dijkstra and Misirlisoy (2009), who found that participants' accuracy in identifying altered transcripts of their own autobiographical memories a year after their telling was high for main details but low for peripheral information.

---

8   A statistical measure of how closely related two measurements are. There are two sorts of correlation – *positive correlation* occurs when one measure tends to rise if the other measure rises and tends to fall if the other falls (e.g. height and weight); *negative correlation* occurs when a rise in one measure tends to be met by a fall in the other (e.g. temperature and quantity of clothing worn). Correlations are measured using the *correlation coefficient*, or *r*. This can be between 0 (meaning absolutely no relationship) and 1 (meaning a totally matched relationship). A minus sign in front of the *r* value means a negative correlation. Typically, there is always *some* correlation between two variables simply by chance, and the statistical test used also calculates whether the result is statistically *significant* (i.e. in effect is not due to chance).

Another serious methodological flaw concerns how the memories are elicited. One general problem is that participants might censor their memories. It is a reasonable assumption that, human nature being what it is, people's most vivid memories include a largish proportion of sexual experiences. Curiously, these seem to be rarely mentioned by participants. Again, asking people to produce autobiographical memories by prompting them with cues[9] generally produces memories linked by being from roughly the same time period in a person's life. Asking people to produce an autobiographical memory and then recording any further memories that arise from the initial one produces memories linked conceptually rather than from the same period of a person's life (see Talarico and Mace, 2010). Also, the cueing method is sensitive to the choice of cues. For example, asking participants for their most *vivid* memories produces a glut of reminiscences from the early part of their lives. So does giving participants a cue word, and asking them to produce a reminiscence associated with it (e.g. *jam* – 'Oh yes, I remember helping my mother make jam when I was a child'), provided the participant has to put a date to each memory after producing it. However, if the participant is allowed to produce a whole list before any dating of memories is done, then the bias shifts in favour of a preponderance of memories from the recent past (Cohen, 1989). To further muddy the waters, words that are known to be better at producing clear mental images (e.g. *sandwich* as opposed to *procrastination*) tend to generate older memories (Rubin and Schulkind, 1997).

Thus, how the participant is asked determines the age of memories produced, and there is certainly no evidence to support the cliché that older people live in the past. Indeed, several studies have shown that younger and older adults produce equal numbers of reminiscences from childhood (e.g. Cohen and Faulkner, 1988). This is not necessarily due to participants wallowing in nostalgia. Rabbitt and Winthorpe (1988) found that, when memories are divided into 'pleasant' and 'unpleasant', reminiscences from early life fall predominantly into the latter category.

Related to the above, most studies of autobiographical memory have in effect examined *involuntary memory*. In other words, participants

---

9 For example, 'Tell me a memory associated with a picnic'. Alternatively, the participant might simply be given a single word (e.g. 'picnic').

are asked to produce memories that they would not have produced at that point in time. However, in real life, far more autobiographical memories are examples of *voluntary memory* – in other words, they are spontaneous recollections that appear unbidden or are prompted by an association with something encountered in the immediate present. Research on this potentially interesting topic is scarce, but the available evidence indicates that voluntary memories are less frequent in older people. The memories also tend to be more specific and positive in mood than involuntary memories (see Schlagman, Kvavilashvill and Schulz, 2007). Interestingly, voluntary memories are more likely to be cued by abstract thoughts than a specific sensory input such as a taste or smell (Mace, 2004). Although this does not discount Proust's famous account of the *madeleine* that kick starts *Remembrance of Things Past*, it indicates that this oft-cited memory cue is a less common source of reminiscence than might be supposed.

Notwithstanding the above considerations, the *reminiscence peak* (a.k.a. *reminiscence bump*) has been reported by many researchers. This is the phenomenon that when due allowance is made for testing methods, most autobiographical memories for relatively distant events (as opposed to the immediate past) are likely to come from the period when the individual was between 10 and 30 years old (e.g. Berntsen and Rubin, 2002). This is not surprising, since this is the time when most of the key life events (first forays into sex, employment, exams, marriage, parenthood, and so forth) usually occur.

In contrast, autobiographical memories from the very early years are scarce or non-existent (*childhood amnesia*). Freud and his followers believed that this was due to suppression of unpleasant memories and psychoanalytic conflicts, but it is now felt to be because young children lack the mental facilities to encode retrievable autobiographical memories.

There is growing evidence that brain activity during auto-biographical memory production involves the hippocampus (e.g. Viard *et al.*, 2007), an area known to be badly affected by ageing, and this might account for some of the perceived differences in vividness as well as differences in detail. Frontal-lobe functioning has also been associated (McKinnon *et al.*, 2008).

Many commentators believe that 'reminiscence therapy' for older people should be encouraged, since it enables them to come to terms with their lives (see Kermis, 1983; Pasupathi and Carstensen, 2003). There is also evidence that eliciting autobiographical memories can be an effective component in the treatment of older adults' depression for roughly the same reason (Serrano *et al.*, 2004). However, for many older people, reminiscence may simply be a response to boredom:

> Older people may experience an increasing contrast between an unmemorable present and an eventful past. Remote events may be more often researched and rehearsed in memory as the theatre of the mind becomes the only show in town. (Rabbitt and Winthorpe, 1988, p.302)

Prospective memory

Prospective memory is the ability to remember to do something in the future. It might be supposed that prospective memory is simply another form of LTM, since it involves retaining information over a long time period. However, the two skills are poorly correlated, indicating that they are separate entities (Jackson, Bogers and Kerstholdt, 1988).

In certain kinds of prospective memory tasks, there is either no age difference or even an ageing superiority. For example, a 'traditional' prospective memory task requires participants to remember to phone the experimenter at prearranged times. Moscovitch (1982) found that older participants remembered to phone more often and they were more punctual. However, this could in part be a cohort effect. Older people might lead more sedate lives and thus have less to distract them from making phone calls. Again, older people might have been brought up to place greater emphasis on punctuality and keeping appointments than younger people and thus were more motivated to make the calls. This latter supposition is supported by Poon and Schaffer's (1982, cited in West, 1988) finding that increasing the monetary reward for making a call improved the older people's performance, but not the younger people's. Again, Altgassen *et al.* (2010) found that when a prospective memory task had an attached social importance (as opposed to being simply part of a typical unrealistic laboratory experiment), older adults performed significantly better relative to younger adults. One method of minimising the cohort effect is to take participants in their 50s as the younger adult group. This age group will still intellectually perform more or less on a par with adults in their 20s (the age of a typical 'younger adult' group) but are more similar to older adults in their upbringing. Maylor (1990a) did this, and furthermore selected participants who had similar lifestyles. The participants had to phone once per day for five days, either at a specific time (the 'exact' condition) or between two specified times (the 'between' condition). Maylor found no significant difference between age groups in punctuality or in number of calls remembered. Studies other than Maylor's (i.e. where age differences have been found) have often used students as younger participants, who may be forced to take part in experiments as part of their degree programme (much psychological research takes place under the guise of practical classes). Given the typical undergraduate enthusiasm for practicals, the younger participants may be more apathetic than older participants, who are genuine volunteers and thus more motivated.

Maylor did find an age effect, however, in the efficiency with which participants used cues to remind themselves to phone. Those using *internal cues* (i.e. who reminded themselves to phone) who made errors were significantly older. Conversely, *external cue* users (who used a prompt such as a diary entry) who made errors were significantly younger. Thus, those participants who continue to rely solely on their memories worsen, whilst those who turn to external aids improve (probably because they become more practised).

Although 'traditional' prospective memory studies tend to favour older adults, under other circumstances, considerable age differences in prospective memory can be found. For example, one way of testing prospective memory is to ask participants at the start of a test session, where they will be doing several different tasks, to remember to do something at a particular point (e.g. 'when we finish looking at the pictures of famous people I want you to ask for your expenses claims form'). Generally, older participants are relatively poor at remembering to do this (Cockburn and Smith, 1988; West, 1988). Why older people should be better at some prospective memory tasks than others remains an open issue. Perhaps the most satisfying explanation is derived from Craik *et al.*'s (1995) observation that prospective memory tasks tend, perversely enough, to be most prone to age differences over relatively short time frames. Thus, if asked to do something as part of a fairly complex set of tasks, then this is more likely to be forgotten than, for example, remembering to do a single act in a week's time.

However, it is questionable whether the relatively long-term and naturalistic and relatively short-term and laboratory-based paradigms are assessing the same types of prospective memory. For example, suppose a person is asked to play a particularly taxing video game of the 'shoot 'em up' variety, and told that every time they shoot a red monster, they should shout out 'bananas'. If they forget to call out every time they kill a red monster, is this due to forgetting to do something in the future or a lapse in performing just another component of the ongoing task (akin to forgetting that, for example, shooting the yellow monsters gets twice as many points as shooting the blue monsters?). In comparison, forgetting to phone the experimenter at a particular time on a particular day is more likely to be a memory lapse rather than distraction by a large number of demands competing for the participant's attention at *precisely* the same moment in time. In other words, if older people are working at their own pace in their own world, and not trying to follow essentially unrealistic commands in an unrealistic situation over which they have little control, then their memories perform better.

The tip of the tongue state

Almost everyone knows the exasperation caused by a *tip of the tongue* (TOT) state. This occurs where we are aware of a lot of the features of a word, such as what it sounds like, etc., but we cannot retrieve the word itself. Brown and McNeill (1966) were the first to investigate the TOT phenomenon intensively, by giving participants definitions of obscure words, and asking them to provide the words. Often, participants either knew the word or simply had no idea, but on some occasions a TOT state was generated. Typically, participants could indeed provide details of the word (e.g. 57% of the time they could identify the first letter). The TOT state is nothing more than an annoyance when confined to defining rare words. However, if it creeps into everyday speech, then it is a potential disability. Burke, Worthley and Martin (1988) decided to study the TOT state in older people, in part because older volunteers in a study the experimenters were running had complained about it being a problem. Indeed, in general, older people can be bad at remembering words, and especially names[10] (Crook and West, 1990; James, 2006). It is unsurprising that names should give us especial problems because they are essentially arbitrary. The name 'James', for example, is a popular name for males in the UK, but it will tell you nothing whatsoever about what the person looks like, their age, or their psychological attributes.

Burke *et al.* (1988) asked their participants to keep diary records of all TOTs over a four-week period. They were asked to record all the details of the word they could remember whilst in the TOT state, and whether they ever discovered what the word they were searching for actually was (i.e. whether the TOT resolved itself). Burke *et al.* found that the older participants reported significantly more TOTs, although there was no age difference in the proportion of resolved TOTs (over 90% of the time both age groups eventually found the word they were looking for). However, whilst in the TOT state, the younger participants could report significantly more details of the word (a finding echoed by Maylor, 1990b). Subsequent research has indicated that younger people's TOTs contain more information and are closer to being recovered than are older people's. For example, White and Abrams (2002) found that if participants were given a phonological clue (e.g. the initial sound of the word the participants were searching for), then this would resolve the TOT state for younger but not older adults.

In a similar study to Burke *et al.*'s, Cohen and Faulkner (1989) had participants complete a two-week diary of TOTs for names. Surprisingly, the majority of these (68%) turned out to be for names of friends and acquaintances. Perhaps, as Cohen (1989, p.104) notes, 'there are more opportunities to forget names that are in frequent use'. It should also be noted that, in general, older adults are significantly and disproportionately worse than younger adults at remembering new names than new details about people, such as their occupation (James, 2004), probably due to a lowered efficiency of mental processing

---

10 For some reason, my own name seems particularly hard to remember. I have lost count of the number of times I have been called 'Stuart' as a first name, and I have seen just about every feasible misspelling of my surname, plus some unfeasible ones. My particular favourite is *Ivana Stewart-Hambleton*. This was, incidentally, in a textbook.

(simplistically, it is easier to remember a semantic category such as 'farmer' than the precise name 'Mr Farmer').

Neural changes and memory decline

Alas, the familiar complaint of many older people that their memories 'aren't what they used to be' seems in the main to be justified. Memory *does* decline in later life, and despite a few areas of relative preservation (e.g. 'basic' STM span and some aspects of prospective memory and metamemory), the outlook is downwards. To some extent this might be due to lowered self-image: older people believe they have poorer memories and so lack the confidence to perform well (see Earles *et al.*, 2004). However, there is too much evidence of a link between memory decline and physical ageing changes in the brain (e.g. Bäckman and Nyberg, 2010; Charlton *et al.*, 2008; Dahlin *et al.*, 2009; McArdle *et al.*, 2004) for this to be ignored.

The effects of neural change on memory are varied. It is known that memory loss is correlated with decline in brain volume[11] (Charlton *et al.*, 2010). This means that areas of the brain responsible for memory become less efficient, and the effects of frontal lobe decline have already been mentioned. However, there are other changes that also have an effect. For example, the *CRUNCH*[12] *model* (Reuter-Lorenz and Cappell, 2008) argues that as the ageing brain loses cells and interconnections between the surviving cells diminish, so more neurons have to be activated to handle a basic task, relative to younger adults. The upshot of this is that in younger adults, relatively small areas of the brain are activated when a memory task is being performed. But in older adults, these small areas no longer have enough neurons to do the task, so more areas of the brain have to be activated to cope with the demand. If brain scans of older and younger people doing memory tasks are compared, younger adults' brain activity tends to stay confined to specific areas of the brain as the tasks get more complex. In contrast, older adults' brains show increased activity across wider areas of the

---

11 In other words, how big the brain is. This in turn gives us a reasonable general measure of how many neurons have been lost.

12 Compensation-Related Utilization of Neural Circuits Hypothesis.

brain as task difficulty increases[13] (see Carp, Gmeindl and Reuter-Lorenz, 2010). Thus, memory changes in later life might be the result of the ageing brain compensating for loss as best it can by drawing as many resources as it can muster. This will work adequately (perhaps more than adequately) at lower task loads, but there will still not be enough forces when task demands increase.

Reuter-Lorenz and Park (2010) pursue this argument a step further by proposing an complementary *Scaffolding Theory of Aging and Cognition* (STAC). This argues that in order to offset the neural decline the brain recruits help from other sources – social engagement with others, compensation and similar. This theory thus brings together many of the models of ageing neural processes that have been considered in various forms within geropsychology (e.g. the general slowing hypothesis) and combines them with other models (e.g. compensation – see Reuter-Lorenz and Cappell, 2008) into an integrated theory that promises to describe much of cognitive ageing. However, the model is different in that it is flexible – no section of functioning is necessarily the most important, since the process works as an interactive whole, and indeed, the relative importance of different components might well vary considerably between individuals (see Kennedy, 2010). However, the theory at the time of writing is still in its relatively early days, and more research is still required.

It might be thought that neurological studies of ageing would only show irreversible decline, but this is not quite the case. For example, Lövdén *et al.* (2010) demonstrated that given extensive training in memory tasks (101 one-hour sessions over 180 days) resulted in growth in the corpus callosum[14] in young and old adults to the same extent. This is an example of experience-dependent plasticity (i.e. changes in brain structure in response to changing mental practice) and was once thought to only exist in younger people. However, it is now apparent that it survives into old age. Thus, the brain's neural structure is far from rigidly fixed in later life and mental exercise really can still have an effect on the brain's structure.

---

13 This is an example of *dedifferentiation*; this is the argument that in early development, areas of our brain take on specific functions (*differentiation*) but in old age, the functions of different areas become more diffuse (dedifferentiation).

14 A nerve pathway that links the two hemispheres of the brain.

A reality check

This chapter makes depressing reading if taken at face value. Memory defines us – besides mundane things like remembering shopping lists and appointments, it reminds us of who we are and locates us in time and space. These sound high flown, almost pretentious words, but all we have to do is think of books or movies based on a person having amnesia to appreciate just how disorienting a loss of memory would be. In addition, severe loss of memory is synonymous with dementia, and accordingly, memory loss has both a stigma and a fear attached to it. It is not surprising, therefore, that evidence of memory loss can be depressing.

However, we need to put things in perspective. Although we often use the term memory *loss*, it is far more accurate to use the term memory *decline*. We do not lose our memory ability, it simply gets a little bit worse. Of course this is deeply annoying, even upsetting at times. But we should be careful of over-dramatising this change. Put simply – our memories never have been perfect. They have always been easily distorted and prone to error. Age simply makes our fallibility a little more fallible. But it is NOT the same as the catastrophic loss seen in dementia. Most of us have encountered an older person who tells you how bad their memory is these days and gives a lengthy anecdote of how they forget things. But their memory must still be working well if they are able to remember in detail examples of how they forget things.

We live in a literate world. One of the great advantages of this is that we no longer rely on memory for storage of information, be it historical or more immediate (e.g. shopping lists). We should not be afraid of making use of this literacy, and indeed, given the fallibility of even the best memories, we would be foolish to do so. How many people would trust someone with a very good memory to get a weekly shopping list absolutely right? But this should not be an excuse for complacency. Maintaining good intellectual and memory functioning through mental exercise (augmented by regular physical exercise) is still a wise policy, as we have seen.

Summary

Most types of memory decline in later life. Generally speaking, the more complex the memory task, the worse an older person's memory gets. Often it is the tasks associated with basic memorisation that do the most damage. For example, remembering a list of numbers might not be particularly problematic for an older person; but remember a list whilst doing a mental arithmetic problem causes a disproportionate loss in ability. In a similar vein, older people are often perfectly capable of remembering the essential information, but the peripheral details are far less well remembered. It is therefore questionable where the effects of a decline in memory stop and a decline in general cognitive skills take over. However, this does not alter the fact that whatever the root cause, there is a real decline in memory skills. However, not all types of memory decline to the same extent, and it is important to remember that a lot of the loss can be offset by use of diaries or notepads.

Suggested further reading

Baddeley (1983) provides an immensely readable introduction to the general psychology of memory, and the book is warmly recommended. Baddeley, Eysenck and Anderson (2009) is a more advanced text, but still reasonably accessible to a non-specialist. A useful briefer survey of ageing and memory is provided by Old and Naveh-Benjamin (2008). There is an excellent introduction to the topic of brain ageing and the CRUNCH model by Reuter-Lorenz and Lustig (2005).

CHAPTER 4

Language

Introduction

The majority of research on ageing and language has used cross-sectional studies. Where longitudinal research has been conducted on linguistic changes, then, as with measurements of cognitive performance (see Chapter 2), it has generally found smaller-scale changes than have cross-sectional studies (e.g. Connor *et al.*, 2004). Thus, some of the studies reported in this chapter might be exaggerating the true size of ageing decline. It should also be emphasised that, as with intelligence and memory, the changes we will examine are *relative* and not, repeat *not*, absolute. Discussion of a decline in speech comprehension and similar can lead to the misguided but understandable impression that researchers have conclusively proved that older people are incapable of understanding a single thing beyond the most elemental and simple of concepts. This is not the case. Although under certain laboratory conditions, older people will perform less well, such situations are often far from realistic and simply demonstrate what happens *in extremis*. Such scenarios are sometimes necessary to discover how a particular process operates, but they might have little bearing on everyday experience. In a similar way, sometimes an engine's performance is only truly tested by pushing it to its limits, but this has little bearing on the performance of the same engine in a family car consigned to the school run and weekend shopping. In most situations corresponding to normal everyday life, older people's comprehension and use of language in all its manifestations operate within acceptable bounds (see Whitbourne and Whitbourne, 2011).

The role of reading in older people's lifestyles

Reading can be used for various media. We tend to think of it in terms of books, magazines and newspapers, but it can also include mundane everyday items such as posters and timetables, as well as relatively recent innovations such as text on a computer screen or ebook. With regard to book reading, the percentage of people who read a book for pleasure declines slightly from a peak in middle age, but is still higher than many younger age groups (e.g. National Endowment for the Arts, 2007). Regarding other types of print reading, particularly newspapers, in the USA at least, a higher percentage of older adults read these than many younger adult age groups (National Endowment for the Arts, 2007). Furthermore, these figures have remained relatively stable for older adults, whilst the figures for younger adults have shown a decline (National Endowment for the Arts, 2007). It should also be noted that the internet and other digital media are increasing as a source of reading material for older adults. For example, in the USA, although they are the smallest by percentage consumers of digital media, almost a quarter of older adults claim to have accessed digital media in the past day as a source of news (Pew Research Center, 2010). It should also be noted that although there are similarities, the precise pattern of reading activity between cultures varies somewhat (e.g. Chen, 2008).

Reading in later life appears to be beneficial. For example, Verghese *et al.* (2003) found that reading was a leisure activity (along with playing board games or musical instruments and dancing) that was correlated with a lower risk of developing dementia. Lachman *et al.* (2010) found that reading, as part of a package of cognitive activities (the others were writing, word games, and lecture attending) appeared to offset some indices of cognitive decline. Again, Dellenbach and Zimprich (2008) demonstrated that reading was a key predictor of level of *typical intellectual engagement* (TIE), a measure of willingness to engage in cognitively demanding activities (a concept akin to the need for cognition measure cited in Chapter 2). These examples might be seen as further proof of the disuse theory (see Chapter 2) since reading is mental exercise and thus presumably keeps the mind and brain active.

Reading can play a greater role than simply being a type of mental exercise, since it is a principal means of deriving information. For example, research evidence almost overwhelmingly supports the argument that *health literacy* (the ability to access and constructively use healthcare information) is beneficial both in reducing mortality and increasing quality of life (see Perlow, 2010). However, this is not a simplistic scenario in which if people read more about their health they will act on the advice and get better (see Sudore *et al.*, 2006). Generally, when reading is found to be a predictor, it is often one of several factors cited as having a significant influence on health behaviour (e.g. Scazufca, Almeida and Menezes, 2010). For example, Kim and Yu (2010) demonstrated that if a person has low self-efficacy (i.e. they feel they cannot change their own lives for the better), then reading about health matters will have negligible impact.

However, even if at times reading activity might be only one of several factors, it is still an important one. A case in point is the finding by Beckman, Parker and Thorslund (2005) on older people's ability to dose themselves correctly with medicine. Nearly 10 per cent of their participants (aged 77+ and demographically representative) *could not even read the instructions on a sample medicine container.* That is worrying enough – but an even higher proportion could not comprehend the instructions they had read. Factor in physical issues, such as difficulties undoing the safety cap on a pill bottle and similar, and two thirds of the participants tested had at least one problem that limited their competence to dose themselves correctly with medicines. Banning (2007) reviews the implications of poor patient comprehension in older adults in the UK population and points to some serious practical shortcomings that can result, not only in health dangers to the older people themselves, but also the gross waste of resources that could be easily prevented by increasing the ease of comprehension and similar.

Physical constraints

As was noted in Chapter 1, the eyesight of most older people worsens, and visual acuity ('focusing power') is reduced. Even in older adults with relatively normal sight, diminishing text size within a range easily visible by younger adults will cause a decline in older people's reading skills (Hasegawa *et al.*, 2006). One study (Bell, 1980) estimates that about 23 per cent of community resident older people are incapable of reading normal print. A solution to this problem is to print books in a larger typeface or to increase the font size on an ebook. There is some evidence that this might slow down reading rate (Lovie and Whittaker, 1998), but physically altering text does not seem to differentially affect older relative to younger readers (Cerella and Fozard, 1984).

Considerations about print size may eventually become outmoded because of the rise in availability of talking books or the talking text option found in some ebooks. For example, Bouchard Ryan *et al.* (2003) observed that older adults with visual problems were more likely to change from reading newspapers and magazines (which typically have small print and poor contrast) to listening to talking books. The authors also noted that circa a quarter of their sample used computer technology to enlarge print. However, although talking books offer a solution to people with sight difficulties, they are not, as is commonly supposed, a direct substitute for reading. Two reasons can be cited. First, the narrator will almost certainly place emphases upon what is being read out that may not match what the listener would emphasise were he or she reading for themselves. Second, in reading it is easy to move back over a passage of print just read, or to skim read through a section of prose. This is either very difficult or impossible to do when using a talking book.

It should be noted that many older people are unaware that they have problems with their vision. Holland and Rabbitt (1989) noted that all participants from the age of 50 onwards gave near-identical subjective ratings of their vision, though in reality there was a marked deterioration in the older participants. This is important, because sensory loss can directly affect the efficiency with which information is processed. For example, Rabbitt (1989) noted that older people with mild hearing loss (35–50 dB) had great difficulty remembering lists of spoken words, even though they were earlier able to repeat them all perfectly as they were spoken to them. It appears that hearing-impaired older people can perceive words, but it takes greater effort to do this, leaving fewer mental resources to encode and remember them. That there is nothing especially wrong with their memories can be shown by the fact that if the participants were shown *printed* lists of words, then there was no difference between their and normal hearing controls' performance (i.e. the effect was confined to when hearing was part of the processing chain). Again, Cervera *et al.* (2009) demonstrated that age differences in speech recognition and memory tasks were eliminated when hearing ability was partialled out of the equation.

The voice also undergoes changes, becoming weaker and higher pitched. This loss of vocal efficiency shows itself in a slowing of articulation rate for normal impromptu speech, reading a passage of prose and reaction times to pronouncing words (e.g. Laver and Burke, 1993; Oyer and Deal, 1989). Handwriting undergoes changes (see Miller, 1987), largely tied to physical deterioration. Dixon, Kurzman and Friesen (1993) found that overall, writing speed decreases with age across a wide variety of writing tasks. However, to some extent this is shaped by the level of familiarity of the tasks: the more familiar the task, the less the age difference.

General cognitive constraints

Given the findings reported elsewhere in this book, it might be intuitively supposed that anything that increases processing load or otherwise makes a linguistic task 'harder' will be disproportionately disadvantageous for older adults. However, the results are surprisingly mixed. For example, Smiler, Gagne and Stine-Morrow (2004) found that reading speed was unaffected by having to perform another task simultaneously. Similarly, Stuart-Hamilton and Rabbitt (1997b) found that manipulating aspects of text (e.g. syntactic complexity and/or amount of the text that could be seen at any one time) did not affect the reading speed of older adults relative to younger adult controls.

With regard to eye movements, Kemper, Crow and Kemtes (2004) found relatively few age differences except that older adults tended to look back over ambiguous text (e.g. to use one of the authors' examples, *The experienced soldiers warned about the dangers conducted the midnight raid*) more than did younger adults. This implies that older adults can process less information in a single 'bite' and thus need to re-check complex text more often than younger adults. Analogous findings were reported by Rayner *et al.* (2006). They examined eye movements in reading text that was manipulated in various ways, including predictability and frequency[1] of words used. The researchers found that older readers tended to 'skip' their eyes over words[2] far more than younger readers did. Rayner *et al.* concluded that older adults have slower processing speeds than younger adults and compensate for this by taking more chances and skipping over words whose identity is highly predictable, thereby increasing the speed at which they can get through a passage of text. This explains why the researchers found that their older participants were significantly more affected by predictability and frequency of the text.

Supporting evidence for Rayner *et al.*'s conclusions comes from Christianson *et al.* (2006), who gave participants an assortment of *garden path sentences*. These are sentences that appear to be saying one thing but at a certain point it becomes obvious that another meaning is intended (e.g. *While David drank the wine was poured*). When given comprehension questions later, participants sometimes gave answers that were only correct if just the first bit of the sentence is taken into account (e.g. answering 'yes' to the question *Did David drink the wine?*). Christianson *et al.* found that older adults gave more of these 'good enough' answers (which are of course errors), and they argue that this is because in later life, people become more dependent upon heuristics to compensate for declines in basic skills. It is worth making a caveat here that many garden path sentences can be made easier to understand when spoken, and prosody (i.e. how something is said) is taken into account. Hoyte, Brownell and Wingfield (2009) gave participants sentences whose interpretation was ambiguous and whose intended meaning could only be determined by the prosodic pattern (e.g. *The doctor said the nurse is thirsty*). Aspects of the prosody were systematically varied (namely, pitch, amplitude and timing), but for old and young adults alike, timing variation had the most significant effects.

---

1   That is, how frequently the words occur in everyday language (e.g. *the* is a high-frequency word, whilst *defenestration* is not).

2   Incredible as this seems the first time one hears about it, studies of eye movements in reading show that we either do not look at or barely notice 'filler words' – that is, words like *the*, *and*, etc. that are required to be there for grammatical purposes, but are so predictable that they barely merit our attention. Subjectively, we think we read each word 'equally' but this is far from the case, and indeed some filler words can be replaced by a nonsense letter string (e.g. *kfa* for *the*) and we will not notice it. This might produce the occasional error, but it is arguably worth it for the speeding up of reading.

Kemper, Herman and Lian (2003) gave participants the task of giving spoken responses to questions whilst engaged in another activity (walking and finger tapping). The researchers found that older participants produced less fluent and syntactically less complex speech than younger participants, thus supporting the argument that older adults have a lowered working-memory span[3] (see Chapter 3). Interestingly, the researchers also found that younger adults adopted a different strategy from older participants; namely, they used grammatically simpler and shorter sentences, whereas the older adults slowed their speech rate. Kemper *et al.* (2010) found analogous results when they examined language production by adults as they conducted a simultaneous task. Unsurprisingly, as the task was made more demanding, linguistic skills deteriorated. Kemper *et al.* found that participants with higher levels of vocabulary and working-memory capacity showed less deterioration in linguistic skills, and this effect was more pronounced for older than for younger adult participants. Conversely, faster processing speeds were associated with a lesser linguistic decline in younger more than in older adults.

Other effects are more complex and not uniform across all types of linguistic activity. For example, Gilchrist, Cowan and Naveh-Benjamin (2008) measured recall of spoken sentences with various structures. The researchers found that although older participants recalled fewer words than younger participants, there was no age difference in the percentage of complete clauses accessed. Gilchrist *et al.* concluded that older adults simply recall fewer chunks (see Chapter 3) in verbal recall tasks.

Thus, although there are instances where linguistic skills are affected by general cognitive decline and a lowering of cognitive capacity, the effects are not always clear cut, with some skills apparently largely immune to these effects. This is something of a recurrent theme in ageing and language, with some instances of decline that fit with the general findings of intellectual and memory changes and others where there is a surprisingly well-preserved skill that goes against intuitive expectations.

---

3   In other words, there isn't enough 'mental processing space' to give full attention to all the tasks required, so something has to give – in this instance, speech becomes simpler and so uses up less of the processing space.

Word recognition

There are a variety of ways to test the ability to read single words, but two of the commonest are the *lexical-decision* and the *naming-latency* tasks. The former requires participants simply to decide whether a group of letters forms a word (note that the participants do not have to identify what the word 'says'). A naming-latency task measures how quickly a participant can read a word aloud. Generally, older people are no worse at these tasks than younger adults when the task is presented in its conventional form (e.g. Bowles and Poon, 1985). Duñabeitia *et al.* (2009) gave participants a lexical-decision task. In the condition of interest here, participants were shown compound words (i.e. words made up of two or more individual words such as *bookshop*) preceded by a priming word,[4] which was either the first word within the compound word, the second word, or an unrelated word (e.g. if the word is *bookshop*, the primes would be *book*, *shop* and e.g. *house* respectively). Duñabeitia *et al.* found that there was no difference in priming effects for younger and older adult participants, implying that *morphological processing* (the processing of word structure) remains intact in later life.

However, if the tasks are made harder or more complex, then often an age decrement appears. For example, Ratcliff *et al.* (2004) found that in two lexical-decision tasks, older adults were slower but more accurate than younger participants. Bowles and Poon (1981) found further evidence of age-related decline when they gave participants a modified lexical-decision task. Participants had to judge pairs of letter groupings, both of which had to form real words for a 'yes' response to be given. Again, Madden (1992) found age differences were greater when the visual appearance of the words was manipulated. Generally, as lexical-decision task difficulty increases, then so does the size of the age difference (Myerson *et al.*, 1997).

Word recognition can be speeded up if, just before seeing the word, a semantically related word is shown to the participant (e.g. *butter* will be recognised faster if the participant has just seen *bread* rather than *soap*). This is known as *semantic facilitation.* Generally

---

4   Priming is a commonly used technique in lexical-decision tasks. If the prime leads to a faster response (a *priming effect*), this is taken as evidence that the same mental processes used to process the prime also are used to process the next word as well.

speaking, older people are slower than younger people at performing semantic facilitation tasks. Proportionately speaking, older adults gain a bigger advantage from semantic facilitation, compared with recognising words presented in isolation (Laver and Burke, 1993; Myerson *et al.*, 1992). One explanation for this draws on the argument that 'a slow horse will save more time than a fast horse when the distance is reduced by a constant amount' (Laver and Burke, 1993, p.35). If one horse runs at 40 kph and another at 20 kph, then cutting the race distance from 40 to 20 kilometres will save 30 minutes for the faster horse and an hour for the slower one. In a similar manner, if older people are reacting less quickly, then facilitation (which in effect decreases the computational 'distance') will be of greater benefit to older participants (see also Bennett and McEvoy, 1999).

Spelling

Knowledge of spelling rules is a crystallised skill, and as such should be relatively immune from ageing effects. However, there is evidence that this is not always the case. Certainly it is generally true that when participants are simply asked to judge if a word is correctly spelt, there is relatively little effect of ageing (see Shafto, 2010). However, there are (as is almost inevitably the case in psychogerontology) exceptions to this rule. For example, MacKay, Abrams and Pedroza (1999) observed that older participants were as adept as younger participants at detecting misspellings in a list of words. However, there was an age difference involved in being able subsequently to retrieve the correctly and incorrectly spelt words from memory. Abrams, Farrell and Margolin (2010) found that if *solely* older adults were considered, who were then grouped into age decades (60s, 70s and 80s), the two oldest groups were both slower and less accurate at detecting misspellings when reading sentences in which words were presented one at a time.

When *production* of words is considered, generally an ageing decline is observed. For example, MacKay and Abrams (1998) found that misspellings increased in later life, as did Stuart-Hamilton and Rabbitt (1997a). These age-related deficits are not directly attributable to general slowing, crystallised intelligence or education level. Stuart-Hamilton and Rabbitt found fluid intelligence to be a good predictor of spelling skills, whilst MacKay and co-researchers link the decline to a more specific linguistic coding deficit (see MacKay *et al.*, 1999).

Tip of the tongue states

These have already been mentioned in Chapter 3, which addressed memory. Tip of the tongue states (TOTs) describe the familiar experience of remembering a number of features of a word (what it sounds like, etc.) without being able to bring the word to mind. The study of TOTs is often treated as a memory issue, but of course it is also of considerable interest in psycholinguistics, since it can inform us of the processes by which words are produced. Generally speaking, psycholinguists are interested in TOTs for what they can tell us about retrieval from memory, whilst cognitive psychologists are generally more interested in the 'phenomenological experience' of having a TOT state (Schwartz and Frazier, 2005). However, this is a generalisation and there are plenty of exceptions. See Chapter 3 for further discussion of TOTs.

Pronunciation

Knowledge of pronunciation of words might also be expected to be preserved in later life, because it is ostensibly a crystallised skill, and indeed this would appear to be generally the case. Typically, pronunciation is tested by presenting participants with a list of irregularly spelt words (e.g. *yacht, dessert*), and asking them to say them out loud. Because the words do not obey conventional spelling rules, their pronunciation cannot be calculated from first principles. For example, pronouncing *dessert* by conventional spelling rules would yield the spoken presentation of *desert* [in the sense of a large area of sand] (and vice versa). Those readers who have already read Chapter 2 will appreciate that pronunciation abilities are therefore seen as part and parcel of crystallised intelligence (loosely speaking, general knowledge), which is largely ageing-proof. It follows from this that pronunciation ability should remain stable in later life.

Nelson and O'Connell (1978) examined the pronunciation abilities of 120 adults aged 20–70 years, and found no significant correlation between test score and chronological age (Nelson and McKenna, 1973). This word list was developed into the *National Adult*

Reading Test, or NART. A subsequent study by Crawford *et al.* (1988) found a slight negative correlation between age and NART score, but this disappeared when either length of education or social class was controlled for. Hence, concluded the authors, 'age has little or no effect on NART performance' (p.182). Because of such arguments, the NART has become widely used as a quick assessor of crystallised intelligence (see Deary, Johnson and Starr, 2010), particularly where older participants with dementia or some other kinds of brain damage have retained the ability to read whilst being incapable of some other intellectual tasks (e.g. Starr and Lonie, 2007). The NART is not necessarily a totally accurate guide, however. When words from the NART are placed in the context of a sentence, then performance generally improves (Conway and O'Carroll, 1997, who developed this format into a new test – the *Cambridge Contextual Reading Test* (CCRT) – see Beardsall, 1998).

In other instances, the NART may overestimate intelligence levels (Mockler, Riordan and Sharma, 1996), whilst researchers using an American version of the NART (called, not surprisingly, the *American NART* or AMNART or ANART) found somewhat different patterns of results within groups of White-American and African-American older people who were either non-demented or suffering from dementia (Boekamp, Strauss and Adams, 1995). There are also question marks about the general advisability of using reading tests across groups of older people in multiethnic and multilingual groups (see Cosentino, Manly and Mungas, 2007). It is difficult to get a clear overall picture from these and similar studies simply because different samples of people have been used (e.g. some have dementia, some have not; amongst studies of dementia, different grading criteria have been used, and so forth). The general conclusion of many researchers is that the NART is a fair *general* predictor of intellectual status, even if the shortened (and quicker) format arguably lacks accuracy (Bucks *et al.*, 1996) and the full test is not absolutely precise (see Law and O'Carroll, 1998).

Semantic processing
In Chapter 2, it was demonstrated that knowledge of word meaning is the key component of many measures of crystallised intelligence, and

it is known that, although age does not affect crystallised intelligence (and thus knowledge of word meanings) as much as, for example, tasks heavily based on fluid intelligence, nonetheless there is a decline in later life. Principally, older adults are slower to produce responses, and definitions offered are likely to be less precise than younger people's. For example, McGinnis and Zelinski (2000) gave participants the task of providing definitions of unfamiliar words that could be gleaned from the context in which they were presented. The researchers found that older adults picked up fewer of the available pieces of information available in the text, and produced more vague generalised definitions. In a second experiment, McGinnis and Zelinski provided four definitions for each unfamiliar word and asked participants to choose the correct definition. One definition was rigorously correct; one was more generalised (thus, not quite 'wrong' but certainly vague); one was a generalised interpretation of the story; and one was irrelevant. Younger adults relatively favoured the exact definitions, whilst the oldest old participants (those aged 75 years and over) were more likely to select the generalised definitions.

In a follow-up study, the authors gave participants the task of reading a passage of prose that contained an unfamiliar word. Whilst reading, the participants were asked to 'think aloud' about what they were reading, and afterwards were asked to rate a set of definitions derived from the passage for accuracy (McGinnis and Zelinski, 2003). The researchers found that the older participants produced more generalised comments about the passages whilst thinking aloud, and rated generalised and irrelevant definitions more highly. Overall, McGinnis and Zelinski concluded that older adults have appreciable problems processing the relatively complex information required to extract meaning from context. More specifically, they fail to think at a sufficiently abstract level and thus fail to draw adequate inferences. This echoes the findings of Albert *et al.* (1987), who found that older adults have especial problems providing definitions of sayings and proverbs. It might also be noted that older adults take significantly longer than younger adults to distinguish between metaphors and literally untrue statements (Morrone *et al.*, 2010). This failure too can be seen as a reduced ability to see beyond the literal to the underlying symbolic structure. At a neurological level, this has been attributed to a decline in frontal-lobe functioning (Uekermann, Thoma and Daum, 2008).

It should be noted, however, that semantic processing almost invariably is predicated on the use of other skills, and thus age differences may be the result of a wide variety of potential factors. It is rather like judging the worth of different brands of flour in cake recipes. Whilst a reasonable estimate of differences may be gauged, the influence of the other ingredients will always be there and will vary from recipe to recipe. Similarly, whilst semantic skills can be measured, participants have by definition to use other skills (e.g. phonological processing) to perform a semantic task. Thus, the field is wide open for other variables to have an effect. For example, Taylor and Burke (2002) presented participants with pictures of objects. The participants had to name these objects, whilst distracting words were read out. In some instances, the name of the object was a homophone (i.e. had more than one meaning – the authors cite the example of *ball*). If the participant was looking at a picture of an item and a word semantically related to its other meaning was spoken (e.g. the participant sees a picture of a ball and hears the word 'dance' spoken), then this aided the response times of younger participants, but not older participants. Other distracters generally did not differentially affect the responses of the age groups. Taylor and Burke use this finding to develop an interesting and rather complex model in which ageing has an asymmetric effect on phonological and semantic mechanisms.

Relatively basic semantic processes appear to be age-resistant. For example, Lahar, Tun and Wingfield (2004) demonstrated that filling in a missing word in a sentence where the answer can be gauged from the context appears to be relatively unaffected by ageing. Again, presented with the relatively uncomplicated task of providing a definition of a new word just encountered in a passage of prose, older adults produced more complete definitions (Long and Shaw, 2000). It is only with more complex semantic skills that the evidence is more circumspect.

Syntactic processing

Relatively little research has been conducted on semantic or syntactic processing independent of the concurrent considerations of text recall. However, one notable exception is a series of excellent papers and articles by Susan Kemper on changes in syntactic processing in older people. Kemper (1986) requested younger and older adults to imitate sentences by creating new ones with the same syntactic structure. She found that the older participants could only reliably imitate short sentences: long sentences, particularly those containing embedded clauses, were the hardest to imitate. Baum (1993) likewise found that increasing the syntactic complexity of sentences resulted in age-group differences in a sentence-repetition task; this also occurred when the sentences were used in a lexical-decision task. Obler *et al.* (1991) found similar effects of syntax on sentence comprehension. This syntactic decline is also reflected in spontaneous everyday language. Kynette and Kemper (1986) noted that the diversity of syntactic structures declines with age, whilst there is an increase in errors such as the omission of articles and the use of incorrect tenses. In a similar vein, Kemper (1992) found that older and younger adults had the same number of sentence fragments in their spontaneous speech. However, the younger adults' fragments tended to be of 'better quality', being false starts to statements, whereas older adults tended to produce these incomplete statements as a 'filler' during a pause.

Kemper and Rush (1988) reported other examples of this decline. For example, the average number of syntactic clauses per sentence fell from 2.8 for those aged 50–59 to 1.7 for those aged 80–89. The researchers also assessed the *Yngve depth* of the syntax. This is a fairly complex technique that gives a syntactic complexity 'score' to a phrase or sentence (the higher the score, the more sophisticated the construction). Yngve scores declined with age, but more intriguingly, they correlated well ($r = 0.76$) with digit span. Thus, the better the memory, the better the syntax. There is an attractively simple explanation for this finding. Syntactically complex sentences are almost invariably longer than simple ones and to construct or comprehend them, greater demands are placed on memory. Or, put simply, more words have to be remembered at one time. This general principle is illustrated in a study by Stine-Morrow *et al.* (2010), who demonstrated that older readers tend to slow down their reading more when they reach the end of a phrase, in effect to allow their syntactic processing extra time to 'catch up'.

The simplification and shortening of phrases can be seen in more realistic studies of everyday language. For example, Gould and Dixon (1993) asked younger and older married couples to describe a vacation they had taken together, and analysed their descriptions for linguistic content. The general finding was that the younger couple produces a greater amount of detail. The researchers attributed the older couples' 'failure' to do this to a decline in working memory. However, they also acknowledge it is possible that the age-related change is due to a shift in attitude – 'the younger couples...may have given less consideration to being entertaining than did the older couples' (Gould and Dixon, 1993, p.15). Adams (1991) noted that compared with a group of younger controls, older adults' written summaries of stories tended to interpret the text at a more abstract level, and placed emphasis on a précis of the story's structure. This qualitative difference may arise because of a loss of processing capacity. For example, if the older participants cannot remember as much about the story, then talking about it in abstract terms might be a wise option. Kemper and Anagnopoulos (1993) likewise argue that older people may use various strategies to make up for deficiencies or discrepancies in their syntactic processing skills.

Kemper (1987) examined six diaries kept by people for most of their adult lifespans. Drawn from museum archives, the diaries commenced between 1856 and 1876, and finished between 1943 and 1957. Kemper found that the language used became simpler over the writers' lifespans. Sentence length decreased, as did complexity of syntax. Again, an ingenious study of the letters of King James VI/I[5] by Williams *et al.* (2003) demonstrates an age-related decline in writing complexity that can also be correlated with well-documented bouts of illness. In a slightly more prosaic format (no pun intended) Kemper, Thompson and Marquis (2001) conducted a longitudinal study of the writing of older volunteers. Annual samples of language were taken and cognitive tests were also administered. The researchers demonstrated an age-related decline (particularly after the mid-70s) in grammatical complexity and propositional content, and this was linked to cognitive changes. Kemper and Sumner (2001) demonstrated that grammatical complexity was linked to working memory, and sentence length to verbal intelligence.

---

5 He was King James VI of Scotland and then became King James I of England.

Story comprehension

The basic 'story comprehension' paradigm is simple – a participant listens to or reads a short passage of text (usually 300–400 words long) and then in one form or another either repeats back as much as possible, or is given a multiple-choice recognition test. Most studies have shown that older people remember less (e.g. Light and Anderson, 1985 and Petros *et al.*, 1983 in cross-sectional studies; Zelinski and Burnight, 1997 and Zelinski and Stewart, 1998 in longitudinal studies) and may generalise more (e.g. Zelinski and Hyde, 1996). However, whilst this is a general finding, it is not a universal truth, and varying the types of experimental participants and/or test materials can have a crucial effect.

Studies using 'old' participants who are in their 60s have often found no difference with young adults (e.g. Mandel and Johnson, 1984). Age differences are only reliably found when the 'old' participants are in their mid-70s or older (Meyer, 1987). Also, participants with a high verbal ability generally show no age difference (e.g. Taub, 1979). The findings on prior experience are more complex. Soederberg Miller (2003) gave participants various texts to read, some of which related to cookery. The readers varied in cookery expertise, and the greater their knowledge (not surprisingly) the greater their encoding and memory of cookery-related items. However, the age of the participants had no effect on this phenomenon. In contrast, Soederberg Miller (2009) performed an experiment in which participants of various ages differed in their level of knowledge about cookery. She measured 'reading efficiency', defined as time spent reading divided by quantity of information recalled from each passage read. When reading prose passages about cookery, younger adults' reading efficiency was unaffected by their prior knowledge of cookery. However, for older adults, efficiency rose the greater their prior knowledge. An analogous result was found when participants were classified by working memory ability. Those with a high level of working-memory were unaffected by cookery knowledge, whereas those with a low level of working memory performed better if they had a high prior knowledge of cookery.

This provides evidence for a compensatory strategy, often termed within reading research an *allocation policy*, which, it is argued, can be very consistent across time and tasks (Stine-Morrow, Soederberg Miller and Hertzog, 2006). In effect, older adults cut their suit according to their cloth. Stine-Morrow *et al.* (2008) demonstrated that if, for example, participants had lower working memory span, then greater resources were allocated to word processing (i.e. simply working out what the individual words mean). In contrast, those with higher verbal abilities diverted more resources into processing the meaning of the text. A further example of allocation policy can be seen in the findings of Crowley, Mayer and Stuart-Hamilton (2009). They tested children and younger and older adults on a series of measures of general reading (as measured by word recognition), spelling, phonological processing skills (e.g. identifying the reason why two words sound similar because of a shared phoneme) and measures of fluid and crystallised intelligence. The researchers found that in children and younger adults, reading and spelling were best predicted by phonological test performance. However, older adults' reading and spelling abilities were best predicted by fluid intelligence and chronological age. These findings suggest that as we age, there can be considerable shifts in our reliance on specific sub-skills involved in the reading and spelling processes.

The choice of intended listener can also make a difference. Adams *et al.* (2002) gave older and younger women the task of remembering a story that they were told had to be told to either an adult or a child. Although both younger and older adults simplified the story and did more elaborations of key points when retelling the story to a child, older adults did this to a greater extent. When an adult was the listener, the retelling was more 'sophisticated' and younger adults produced a significantly higher proportion of propositions from the original story. This does not necessarily indicate a superiority of older adults in the child-as-listener condition (arguably it is easier and the additional elaboration may represent a different level of pragmatic awareness rather than a cognitive superiority). However, as Adams *et al.* point out, it does mean that social context may be a confounding variable of some importance in this area of research, and researchers should be careful over choice of the 'listener' when participants are recalling stories and other information.

Generally, and as with much else in psychogerontology, complexity increases the age difference. For example, Byrd (1985) found older people were impaired on straightforward recall of a passage of text, but were disproportionately disadvantaged when asked to *summarise* it. In other words, when the passage had to be simultaneously remembered and processed, older people were at a severe disadvantage. Again, Hamm and Hasher (1992) found that older people had greater difficulty in drawing inferences from ambiguous stories in which the text began by implying one thing before finally resolving itself in a different direction from the one initially anticipated. They attributed the age-related decline to a lessening ability to process information in working memory (i.e. to keep the initial story 'in mind' whilst resolving the contradiction introduced at the end of the story).

It is tempting to ascribe the above changes to a decline in the memory skills of older people. Certainly, under some circumstances the age difference in memory does seem to play a significant role, but not in all. For example, De Beni, Borella and Carretti (2007) tested young (18–30), young-old (60–75) and old-old (75+) participants on a series of measures, including metacomprehension (understanding of how comprehension processes work) and working memory. All participants showed an equivalent level of comprehension for text when it was in a narrative format (e.g. 'first x happened, then y'). However, when expository text (i.e. text intended to explain and present a series of facts and arguments, not necessarily in chronological or other sequence) was used, there was a significant age difference. Furthermore, this age difference was attributable to levels of metacomprehension and working memory, not chronological age.

An oft-reported finding is that older participants remember as many main points of a story as younger adults, but that they are significantly worse at remembering details (Cohen, 1989). For example, Jeong and Kim (2009) found that recall of content of text was significantly better in younger adults. However, there was no age difference in ability to *interpret* the text. McGinnis (2009) compared young and young-old and old-old participants. She found that although the old-old group performed significantly the worst on comprehension measures, they also scored the highest marks on measures of generalised and elaborative inference. Therefore, 'comprehension', as traditionally measured by psychologists, might only be tapping one type of skill and not all of the factors that would be understood by a layperson to constitute 'comprehension'.

Furthermore, many of the changes in comprehension that are often attributed to old age might start earlier in adult life. In a study by Ferstl (2006), young, middle-aged and older adult participants showed no age difference on the ability to judge the implied meaning of sentences, but the ability to recognise words that had appeared in test materials declined steadily with age. Of key interest here is that Ferstl demonstrated that decline was notable in *middle-aged* participants. Studies of age changes have typically compared 'young' adults in their 20s with people in their 60s or older, with middle-aged people largely ignored. Therefore, a research literature has developed where it is almost tacitly assumed that decline begins in old age. However, Ferstl's study demonstrates that change might occur far earlier in some skills than is often realised.

It is perhaps worth noting that in many studies of comprehension, the young adult participants are students – a cohort that perhaps more than any other has been drilled to note everything and not just the superficial details. Finding that younger adults have better memory for story details is not surprising, since older people probably have less processing capacity to note and encode details having memorised the main points (Cohen, 1988; Holland and Rabbitt, 1990). But could there also be a cohort effect? If we ask someone what a book or a movie is about, we just want the bare outline, not the details. Many people might learn to give 'just the facts' and ignore the details as an irrelevance. It is often only students who have a mindset of noting as much as possible.

The possibility of a cohort effect raises its head again in considering a specific aspect of this issue – namely, humour comprehension (in other words, understanding jokes). Mak and Carpenter (2007) found that older adults appeared to have a lower comprehension of humour (verbal and non-verbal). The researchers found that this correlated with a decline in cognitive skills. Similar findings were reported by Uekermann, Channon and Daum (2006), who found older adults were significantly worse at selecting the punchline to a joke in a multiple-choice task.

As has been often noted, nothing kills a joke more effectively than trying to explain it. The simple fact is that either you comprehend a joke or you do not. A large part of humour relies upon the joke teller and the recipient having a shared culture and often a shared set of common responses to the same events. Take the following cartoon the author once saw in a student magazine, which shows a young man in the 1920s driving along in an open-top sports car. Out of his head there is a thought bubble, which reads – *I know, I'll get Isadora a scarf for her birthday*. Now if you get the reference to Isadora Duncan, then you will understand the joke (which, it should be said, is in appallingly bad taste, as anyone who has just looked up 'Isadora Duncan' on Google will have found out). But unless you have the requisite knowledge shared with the joke teller and can make the logical connection to an oblique reference, then the joke will make no sense.[6] Humour comprehension is thus about having the cognitive skills to make the connections, but also about having the shared experiences and assumptions of the joke teller. Older people, from a different cohort, will therefore possibly not have sufficient shared culture to appreciate the same humour as younger adults. The study of age differences in humour comprehension is potentially a rich field of research and it is regrettable that relatively little has been done in this area. As Mak and Carpenter acknowledge, the full picture is as yet far from clear.

The above findings on comprehension have to be weighed against the argument that the experiments reported above lack *ecological validity* (in other words, they are not very realistic). The standard story-recall test – of reading a passage of 300–400 words then attempting to regurgitate it whole – is hardly an everyday activity. Given that a moderately sized novel is circa 60,000 words, even the longest texts currently being used in standard experiments fall well short of a realistically long piece of prose. The reason for this observation is that, as librarians know to their cost, older adults are often appallingly bad not only at remembering the plots of books, but also *which* books they have read before. Clive James, the writer and television presenter, once worked as a librarian and describes the phenomenon thus:

> I ran out of answers for the little old ladies who wanted to know if they had already read the books they were thinking about taking out. The smart ones used personalised coding systems... There were hundreds of them at it all the time. If you picked up a book by Dorothy L. Sayers or Margery Allingham and flicked through it, you would see a kaleidoscope of dots, crosses, blobs, circles, swastikas, etc. (James, 1983, p.243)

---

6   Take another example: Comic Sans walks into a bar and the bartender says, *Sorry, but we don't serve your type here.*

The phenomenon seems to be widespread. The author has spoken to a number of librarians who practically gave a paraphrase of Mr James's observations. However, this shining failure of recall for lengthy passages of prose seems to have escaped researchers' attention.

Summary

The study of language changes in older people is currently fragmented. Some areas have been covered in depth, whilst others have barely been touched upon. Because of this, interpretations must be guarded.

It should first be noted that declines in sight and hearing will affect linguistic skills. More generally, a decline in physical health may generally lessen access to the 'outside world', and with it conversational opportunities, library visits, and so forth. Thus there may be an appreciable alteration in the practice of reading and other linguistic skills for many older people. This may in part account for the more general changes in language. However, the usual suspects of general slowing and intelligence must also be cited (though, surprisingly, crystallised intelligence may not play a particularly major role).

Concentrating on specific skills such as word recognition, syntactic processing and story recall, it can be seen that there are age-related declines. However, the magnitude of any age differences is probably inflated by experimental artefacts such as the types of test materials used, cohort effects, and so forth. Perhaps the biggest criticism is that many reading tests are unrealistic – people do not normally spend their time learning very short stories verbatim, pronouncing obscure words or deciding whether a string of letters on a computer screen forms a word or not. Thus, a loud note of caution needs to be sounded over these results, since the measures used probably do not directly match real-life experiences.

Suggested further reading

There are surprisingly few textbooks that deal specifically with language and ageing that are specifically targeted at the general reader. Light and Burke's (1988) edited collection of papers on ageing linguistic skills is probably still the most comprehensive review of this type currently available. A more recent book by De Bot and Makoni (2005), though more directed towards multilingual issues, may also be of interest. Although outside the remit of this book, there is a useful sociolinguistic study of older people's language by Coupland, Coupland and Giles (1991), which some readers may find of interest. For those interested in reading more about psycholinguistics, Aitchison (2007) is recommended. For a recent review of the practical options available to older adults with vision problems, see Dunning (2009).

CHAPTER 5

Ageing, Personality and Lifestyle

Introduction

So far, most of the topics addressed in this book have principally concerned the internal mental world of the older person. How people think, how people memorise, and so forth, all largely address how the brain and mind process information. In this chapter, we will consider psychological factors that are largely concerned with how older people interact with the world around them, through their personality and lifestyles. We will also consider related issues, such as how older people view themselves, lifestyle choices, and the attitudes of others towards older people and ageing.

Trait models of personality

Personality traits are sets of related behaviours that everyone possesses, but the strength with which traits manifest themselves varies from person to person. This concept becomes easier to understand if we consider an example. A commonly measured trait is *extraversion-introversion*, often shortened to the single letter *E*. This describes the degree to which a person is outgoing and assertive. A person with a high E score is thus very outward-going and is likely to be what is often called the life and soul of the party. Somebody with a low E score, on the other hand, will be very shy and retiring. Most people tend to be towards the middle of the E scale – in other words, neither very outward going nor very quiet and withdrawn. However, *everybody* can be measured on this same single scale – we all possess the same trait; all that differs is the strength with which this trait is held.

An early study of personality traits in later life was conducted by Hans Eysenck (Eysenck, 1987; Eysenck and Eysenck, 1985). Eysenck argued that personality could be adequately summed up using just three traits: the aforementioned extraversion-introversion,[1] plus *psychoticism* (P) and *neuroticism* (N). These measure the degree to which a person is emotionally 'cold' and antisocial, and the extent to which a person is anxious and emotionally unstable, respectively.[2] Eysenck argued that E, P and N alter as people get older, and gender also has an important influence. P declines with age, but the rate of decline is much greater for men than women. At 16 years, male P scores are almost double those of females, but by the age of 70, this difference is practically non-existent. More curious is the change in E. Both men and women become more introverted as they get older. Males in their late teens are more extraverted than females, but thereafter, their extraversion declines at a much greater rate, so that by their 60s, males are more *introverted* than females (the crossover point, where the two sexes are equally introverted, occurs in the 40s). The changes in N are less spectacular. There is a decline in neuroticism for both sexes, but at all ages, female scores remain higher than male scores.

Eysenck argued that personality changes across the lifespan are primarily the result of physiological changes altering levels of excitation within the nervous system. This argument is disputed by many psychologists and a plausible case can be made for changes in lifestyle being the prime cause of shifts in E, P and N.[3] For example, older people may become more introverted, not because of changing

---

1   Note this is the correct spelling – 'extroversion' is not used in Psychology.

2   High scores on the P and N scales do not necessarily mean that a person is mentally disturbed, but rather that under stress, they are likely to display psychotic or neurotic characteristics.

3   In fairness to Eysenck, recent genetic studies indicate that neuroticism and extraversion are linked to genetic causes that could interact in complex physiological ways – see Terracciano *et al.* (2010).

levels of neural excitation, but because, as they age, society becomes less geared to their needs.

Other researchers have tended to use a broader range of personality traits than the three used by Eysenck. A very popular choice is the *Big Five* model (a.k.a. five-factor personality model) by Costa and McCrae (see Costa and McCrae, 1980, 1982). This is predicated, as its name implies, on the assumption that personality is best described using five basic personality traits – conscientiousness (how reliable a person is), agreeableness (how compliant with others' wishes), openness (how willing to cope with the unfamiliar), extraversion and neuroticism.[4] The results of studies using the Big Five and other personality trait measures point to a rather less cut-and-dried picture than the one Eysenck presented, possibly because different tests were used, but perhaps also because different measurement methods were used. In particular, several studies based on longitudinal data are now available. For example, in a longitudinal study of Dutch people, Steunenberg *et al.* (2005) found a mild decrease in N between the mid-50s and 70 and then a slight rise. Field and Millsap (1991) found that extraversion declined slightly in a longitudinal study of older adults. Again, Mroczek and Spiro (2003) conducted a longitudinal study on a group of 1600 men (initially aged 43–91) over a 12-year period. They found considerable variability in E and N scores over this time. They also found that significant life events (e.g. death of spouse) were related to these changes.

Roberts, Walton and Viechtbauer (2006) conducted a meta-analysis[5] of 92 longitudinal studies of personality and found that overall there was evidence for cumulative change in many traits. The picture they present is complex, because not all the studies they analysed used exactly the same tests. However, overall, there appeared to be relative stability in some personality attributes such as sociability, whilst traits such as conscientiousness and agreeableness increase in later life. However, openness to experience (essentially, level of mental flexibility) declines in old age (thus perhaps providing an explanation

---

4   Sometimes referred to as *emotional stability*, since emotional stability and neuroticism form opposite ends of the same continuum, akin to extraversion and introversion.

5   Basically, an overview of studies, often using complex statistical techniques to compare the findings and produce an aggregate result across studies.

for the stereotype of hidebound older adults[6]). Allemand, Zimprich and Hendriks (2008), using a cross-sectional study, similarly found that agreeableness and conscientiousness increased in later life.

Overall, these findings seem to point to some traits remaining relatively stable, some (e.g. neuroticism) showing a slight rise, others showing a bigger rise (e.g. agreeableness and conscientiousness). However, it is difficult to know how much weight to put on many of the findings on personality traits because of variability: in other words, scores on many measures of traits fluctuate across the lifespan (e.g. Lucas and Donellan, 2009; Ojha and Pramanick, 2010). Just to muddy the waters a bit further, it should also be noted that through all these fluctuations, the positioning of an *individual* relative to people of their own age remains remarkably constant. It was noted in Chapter 2 that although raw scores on intelligence tests fluctuate, the IQ of the individual participant remains relatively stable. The same applies to an individual's personality test scores – although their raw scores on tests fluctuate, relative to their age group, they remain on roughly the same percentile relative to the rest of their age group (see Roberts and DelVecchio, 2000). A further point is that there is evidence that personality traits have shifted towards being more flexible and accommodating across birth cohorts in the 20th century (see Schaie and Willis, 1991; Mroczek and Spiro, 2003). This might in part also explain the stereotype that older adults become more conservative and hidebound. It is not ageing *per se* that makes someone hidebound – rather, older groups belong to less tolerant cohorts. But more importantly for the argument being presented here, if there are cohort effects, then comparisons of scores between age groups are not necessarily comparing just on age – there could be a significant cohort effect colouring the analyses.

Although studies of general personality change across the lifespan yield somewhat conflicting and confusing results, other aspects of research on personality in later life have produced more substantial findings. A key example is the study of the effects of neuroticism. It is intuitively plausible that a person who worries a lot and has brooding preoccupations is unlikely to enjoy a healthy lifestyle.

---

6   Though note the changes are *relative* and not absolute. Thus, a decline in openness means a person is slightly less flexible, not that they suddenly become a complete curmudgeon, clinging with limpet-like tenacity to old ideas and practices.

The worrying in itself might raise blood pressure, whilst attempts to alleviate the worry (e.g. drink, drugs, over-eating) will further worsen the neurotic person's health. Furthermore, once a person becomes ill, then excessively worrying about the illness will only make matters worse. This is not only intuitively plausible, as a plethora of studies have supported these suppositions. For example:

- Wilson *et al.*'s (2004) longitudinal study found a strong correlation between neuroticism and mortality with those with the top 10 per cent of N scores having double the risk of dying compared with the scorers with the lowest 10 per cent of N scores.

- Lauver and Johnson (1997) demonstrated that higher levels of neuroticism were disadvantageous in coping with chronic pain in later life.

- Spiro *et al.*'s (1995) longitudinal study found neuroticism to be correlated with high blood pressure.

- People with high N scores are significantly more likely to have memory failures on days with high stress levels (Neupert, Mroczek and Spiro, 2008).

It is thus readily apparent that a high level of neuroticism is disadvantageous in later life for a whole host of reasons. However, it would be unwise to assume that neuroticism is the *sole* personality trait that is at fault. Several studies report that although N scores have a major influence, either an appreciable amount of variance is unaccounted for[7] (e.g. 60 per cent in the study by Mroczek, Spiro and Turiano, 2009) or other factors are of near-equal importance (e.g. physical health in the study by Steunenberg *et al.*, 2007).

Research on extraversion has yielded findings of various levels of predictability. The discovery that extraversion is related to likelihood of doing voluntary work in later life (Okun, Pugliese and

---

7   That is, N accounts for some of the differences between people in their health, but not all of the difference is explained, meaning that other factors must also be at work.

Rook, 2007) is perhaps not all that unpredictable.[8] Again, a higher level of extraversion appears to be advantageous in recovering from a stroke (Elmstahl, Sommer and Hagberg, 1996) and more generally in maintaining a high level of morale (Adkins, Martin and Poon, 1996) and having a more positive outlook on future health (Chapman *et al.*, 2006). These are perhaps not too surprising, since we often perceive the outgoing personality as being more robust and thus healthy. However, researchers often report that extraversion has no correlation with other factors of interest, even when it might be intuitively expected. For example, Iwasa *et al.* (2009) found that E scores did not significantly predict older people's participation in health check-ups. In other instances, although E scores at other ages are significantly related to the measure in question, by later life they are not. For example, Gomez *et al.* (2009) found that although extraversion scores were significantly correlated with subjective well-being (SWB) in young adults, they were not a significant predictor of SWB in older people. Finally, in some rare instances, extraversion has been reported as being actually disadvantageous. For example, one study found a negative relationship between E scores and driving performance in older people (Adrian *et al.*, 2011).

Openness to experience is correlated with a range of measures, including risk of developing Alzheimer's disease (Duberstein *et al.*, 2011) and ability at creativity tests (Shimonaka and Nakazato, 2007). The link with greater creativity and imagination possibly accounts for the association some researchers have found between openness and successful or at least more contented ageing (see Gregory, Nettlebeck and Wilson, 2010). However, like extraversion, there are also measures where openness has no significant predictive role (e.g. medication adherence – see Jerant *et al.*, 2011).

A lowered level of agreeableness (including, one assumes, a willingness to endure unpopularity when necessary) has been shown, along with higher level of extraversion, to increase older people's use of hospital emergency departments for treatment (Chapman *et al.*, 2009). Conversely, a high level of agreeableness has been associated with more effective regulation of responses to saddening events and images (Pearman, Andreoletti and Isaacowitz, 2010).

---

8   In fairness to Okun *et al.*, a key theme of the paper is the pattern of the relationship and the effects of social capital.

Research on conscientiousness shows similarly piecemeal results, with relationships found between disparate measures, such as lower overall effect of multiple simultaneously occurring illnesses and conditions (Chapman, Lyness and Duberstein, 2007) and increased life expectancy (Terracciano *et al.*, 2008).

It can thus be concluded that although the manner in which traits change over the lifespan is open to question, traits nonetheless can be significantly related to key indices of health and activity. The role of neuroticism is probably the most unremittingly negative. However, we must be careful not to overplay this argument. Although measures such as neuroticism do indeed appear to have an effect, it is rarely an effect that accounts for all the observed variability.

Psychoanalytic and type models of personality

Some of the earliest attempts to codify the ageing personality came from *psychoanalysis*. It is difficult to give a concise definition of this term. In its usual sense, it means any treatment regime based upon an integrated theory of the subconscious and its effects on behaviour. However, the term sometimes applies (particularly with later practitioners) to broader-based models that whilst having roots in psychoanalysis, also integrate findings from the behavioural sciences. Often psychoanalytic theories are named after their author (e.g. 'Freudian' after Sigmund Freud, 'Jungian' after Carl Jung). Strictly speaking, psychoanalysis is not part of mainstream psychology and many psychologists have questioned its efficacy (e.g. Eysenck, 1952). However, from a historical viewpoint at the very least, a brief examination is necessary. The founding father of psychoanalysis, Sigmund Freud, was sceptical about the value of therapy being administered to older patients, because they had relatively little remaining life in which to enjoy the benefits of treatment (generally, the treatment of older people has been a minority subject within the psychoanalytic literature, though this position has changed in recent years – see Settlage, 1996). It is worth noting that, although Freud did little formal work on ageing, in his private life and correspondence he appears to have had a very melancholy and illogical attitude towards the subject (Woodward, 1991).

Erikson (see Erikson, 1982) felt that personality developed throughout the lifespan – unlike many other psychoanalysts, who felt that it was essentially determined by childhood habits. He argued that at different ages different conflicts had to be resolved. For example, in infancy, individuals must resolve the conflicting impulses to trust or to mistrust by developing a sense of trust. There are eight of these conflicts to resolve, of which only the final one occurs in later life. The goal of this stage is *ego integration* – the acceptance that earlier goals have been satisfied or resolved, and there are no 'loose ends'. A person who feels that not everything has been achieved can feel a sense of despair because, with death approaching, it is too late to make amends. Thus, the person comes to fear death, and he or she ends life feeling anxious and depressed.

The *Rochester Adult Longitudinal Study* (RALS) has examined several cohorts of students from Rochester University in the USA, using Eriksonian measures. The study has found that adults change in a consistent fashion on these measures in the directions predicted by the theory (see Krauss Whitbourne and Whitbourne, 2011). However, Rochester University alumni are not necessarily demographically representative, and thus these findings might not apply to the population as a whole.

Peck (1968) expanded on Erikson's theory, and argued that in later life, three conflicts need to be resolved. The first of these is *ego differentiation versus work-role preoccupation*. Many working people (particularly men) establish their status and self-concept through their work. Thus, a professional person may develop a high self-esteem simply because they have an occupation that society regards favourably. However, when a person retires, this status disappears with the job. Thus, retirees must find something in themselves that makes them unique or worthy of an esteem previously conferred on them by a job title. The second conflict is *body transcendence versus body preoccupation*. For most individuals, ageing brings a decline in health and general physical status. If an older person overemphasises bodily well-being in extracting enjoyment from life, then disappointment will almost inevitably result. Successful ageing involves an ability to overcome physical discomfort, or at least finding enjoyable activities where bodily status is unimportant. The third of Peck's conflicts is *ego transcendence versus ego preoccupation*. This essentially means that a person comes to terms with the fact that he or she will inevitably die. This is obviously an unpleasant thought, but Peck argues that, by attempting to provide for those left after a person has died, and continually striving to improve the surroundings and well-being of loved ones, an overweening concern for the self and the self's fate can be overcome.

Levinson's view of ageing is akin to Erikson's and Peck's but concentrates rather more on the role of the older person in family and society (e.g. Levinson, 1980). Changing physical and occupational status means that in the early to mid-60s (the *late adult transition*), people must come to terms with the fact that they are no longer the prime movers in either work or in family. To remain content, older people must therefore learn to shed leadership and take a 'back seat' (other researchers have reported similar conflicts, e.g. Settersen and Haegestad, 1996). This does not mean that all cares and duties can be avoided, since aside from assuming the role of wise counsellor to family and younger friends, older people must come to terms with their past (in a manner similar to that described by Erikson). Levinson refers to this process as the 'view from the bridge'.

Research has tended to support psychoanalytic descriptions, at least in broad terms. We have already seen the RALS study in support of the Eriksonian model. Reichard, Livson and Peterson (1962) interviewed 87 American men aged 55–84, half of them in retirement, and half in full- or part-time employment (note that for some jobs in the USA there is no compulsory retirement age). Many points raised by Reichard *et al.* support the psychoanalytic theories. For example, participants approaching retirement seemed to be particularly 'on edge' and self-deprecatory, indicating that the period in question was perceived as being one of change and of anxiety. Overall, five main *personality types* were identified. In the first section of this chapter, we saw that trait models of personality assume that people share personality attributes in common – what makes us different from each other is the relative strength with which we have these attributes or traits. Personality type models take a different viewpoint. They assume that we are best described by grouping us into distinct categories.

The five types identified by Reichard were as follows. *Constructiveness* is akin to the optimal resolution envisaged by Erikson's and Peck's theories – people possessing this trait had come to terms with their lives, and were relatively free from worries, while striving to interact with others. The *dependent* or 'rocking chair' type created some contentment, but individuals were dissatisfied with products of their own efforts, and relied on others to help or serve them, regarding later life as a time of leisure. The *defensiveness* or 'armoured approach' type is essentially neurotic. Participants possessing it carried on working or were engaged in a high level of activity as if to 'prove' that they were healthy and did not need other people's help. The fourth type – *hostility* – involves blaming others for personal misfortune. Participants unrealistically attributed failures throughout their lives to factors other than themselves. In part this sprang from a failure to plan adequately. The final type identified by Reichard *et al.* was *self-hatred*. The self-hating individuals were akin to the hostile type possessors, except that they turned their hatred and resentment inwards. Reichard *et al.* found that people possessing the first three types were well adjusted towards later life, whilst those possessing one of the latter two were less successful. However, given that the researchers' personality descriptions contain implicit value judgements of quality of lifestyle, this is not surprising.

Reichard *et al.* also observed that people's personalities had developed long before the onset of later life. In other words, the types are not the result of 'being old' *per se*. It follows from this that, in order to enjoy later life, one must prepare for it. This argument is somewhat supported by the findings of a longitudinal study reported by Haan (1972). Participants were studied from their teens to the onset of middle age. Various personality types were identified, but these can be principally divided into: the stable and secure; those akin to Reichard *et al.*'s defensive personalities; and the insecure who blamed others for their misfortunes and who often had disorganised lifestyles. These types are remarkably similar to those found in studies of older people, and it is reasonable to conclude that those found in later life are probably those which have been there since early adulthood (Kermis, 1986).

It is interesting to note that some personality types may be better adapted to early rather than late adulthood and vice versa. *Type A personalities* are very hard-edged, competitive types who find it difficult to relax – in Eighties parlance, they are ideal 'yuppie' material. *Type B personalities* are the opposite – easy-going, carefree, and so forth. It might be expected that Type As will be best suited to early adulthood when there are perhaps the greatest chances to exhibit competitiveness in career chasing, sport, and so on. Later life should not suit Type As because of its emphasis on a sedentary lifestyle. For Type Bs, the reverse should hold true. Strube *et al.* (1985) measured the psychological well-being of a group of people aged 18–89, and found that, in general, Type A and B personalities fulfilled this prediction, although the results were mediated by factors such as the social environments of individuals. Again, Shimonaka, Nakazato and Homma (1996) found Type B personalities to be more prevalent amongst centenarians.

A notable feature of type models is that they show relatively little change across the lifespan, or show a predictable pattern of change from one outlook to another. Why should type models find relatively little change when traits alter considerably? The reason is largely an artefact of the measurements used. People can vary in the strength with which they show a particular set of behaviours and still remain within the same broad category of personality. On the other hand, traits are a scale and thus *any* change is registered. However, this does not mean that there is absolutely *no* change in types over the lifespan. In a review of the literature, Aiken (1989) noted that while some of the more stable personality types may not alter greatly over the lifespan, the less stable types may be more labile in response to age changes. A more recent longitudinal study by Cramer (2003) echoes this.

The personality type literature indicates there is more than one way to age successfully, but all essentially involve accepting limitations and renouncing responsibilities without suffering a feeling of loss. A slightly less successful strategy is to maintain a fear of the ravages of ageing, and to fight them by keeping as active as possible. However, as this involves a failure to come to terms with ageing, it is ultimately less satisfying. The worst option is to have no strategy at all and to blame all the wrong factors for one's present state. However, the argument presented is a generalisation and a potentially misleading one. Successful ageing involves accepting limitations and abnegating responsibility, but this might be because of societal pressure to hand over the reins of power. Accepting this change willingly might be akin to surrendering gracefully to a stronger opponent on the principle that if one is going to lose, one may as well do so with the minimum of hurt. In other words, the 'successfully' aged older person has not gained a philosophical insight as much as grasped a point of pragmatics. Another important consideration is socio-economic class. The 'unsuccessful' aged person might rant and rail about external forces precisely because their social position has yielded them fewer privileges and 'lucky breaks' (often researchers note that such individuals are downwardly socially mobile). In contrast, someone who has had an emotionally and materially successful life will be more likely to have a relaxed view of things. Accordingly, the older personality might be as much a product of social and economic circumstances as of any internally motivating factors. This consideration does not refute the theories described, but one should be careful not to consider personality as a purely internally driven entity.

However, this is perhaps too bleak a conclusion to draw. There is a grave danger that we can see personality as something that, because it is shaped by earlier life, is irredeemably fixed. But it is not. The longitudinal studies presented in this section show that personality types are categorically *not* set in stone, and though it is difficult to move from one type to another, it is not impossible. Arguing that because of previous experiences a poor conclusion is inevitable might describe what typically happens, but it should never be an excuse to avoid attempting to change if the person wants to. There is a rather trite cliché that when you drive a car, which turnings you take are dependent on your steering now, not where you have chosen to drive in the past. However, assuming a positive outlook and setting one's resolve is far from stupid – *provided a person changes their behaviour to match their changing attitudes.* Consider the following:

- Whitbourne (2010) demonstrated that adults lagging behind in Eriksonian developmental stages can and do catch up and even overtake others in later life. The current situation thus does not totally dictate the future self.

- McMamish-Svensson *et al.* (1999) demonstrated that subjective health is a significantly better predictor of life expectancy than formal medical diagnosis. This does not mean that one can wishfully think oneself a longer life, but a robust attitude will certainly not be harmful.

- As was demonstrated in Chapter 2, taking up even moderate exercise can and does significantly improve cognitive skills. Altering lifestyle and behaviour does make a difference.

- Measures of personality are variable and not totally accurate predictors. Performance on formal psychological tests are not in and of themselves utterly accurate prophets of future performance and behaviour.

Thus, personality measures are only a guide – they are not a life sentence.

Dependency

Not all studies of how people interact with the world around them are concerned with personality. A significant body of research concerns facets of social behaviour and how old age affects these. A key instance of this is *dependency*. This is essentially the degree to which a person is capable of performing routine daily activities without the necessary assistance of others. Put another way, the more a person relies on others to do things for them, the more dependent they are.

One of the common features of old age is a loss of the means to be totally independent. Physical ailments can impede an older person's mobility to the point where they can no longer easily walk and require a wheelchair to move more than a few steps. Worsening vision can cause a person to stop driving. The onset of marked cognitive decline can lead a person to stop cooking (e.g. for fear of them forgetting to turn off the heat under a pan, leading to a fire). There are many reasons why an older person might have to abnegate a routine activity that they once took for granted. However, these routine activities still need to be performed: housebound older people still need to visit places (even if it is just to go to their doctor or dentist), older people barred from cooking still need to eat, etc. And in order to perform these activities, older people become dependent on the help of others.

The issue of dependency is loaded with value judgements. If an adult is dependent on others for basic daily tasks (e.g. meal preparation, transport to other places) then in many societies (particularly Western ones), this is seen as demeaning (see Cordingly and Webb, 1997). Individualism and 'standing on one's own feet' are measures of societal approval. Thus, an older person in need of assistance might be seen as having a lowered status. There is, however, another side to this issue. There are many welfare organisations (e.g. local and national government agencies, charities) whose specific purpose is to offer assistance to older people in need, such as tending to people living in the community or in residential homes, sheltered accommodation and similar. If older people do not use these services, this can be seen not in terms of older people trying to preserve their independence, but as a 'failure' of older people to make use of all that the organisations are generously offering. For example, Baltes and Wahl (1996) found that older people's requests for help tend to be met, whilst independent behaviour is ignored.

Baltes (1996) examined the issue of dependency in detail and argued that it can be both good and bad, depending upon the type of dependency and the circumstances in which it is acquired. Bad dependency might result from bad motives. Thus, an institutional environment in which older residents are denied any autonomy is a clear example of this. However, bad dependency can also be produced from good intentions. For example, a social worker might provide an older person with the specific help they need, but then swamp them with lots of other forms of assistance (even though the older person neither asked for them nor needs them), because they are seen as a generous aid package. Of course at one level they are, but this largesse is also forcing an older person to become dependent on a system to a much greater extent than they need. However, not all dependency is bad. Baltes notes that increased dependency can be good, if, for example, it liberates an older person from trivial cares or tasks that are too problematic. It should also be noted that bad dependency can be reversed or at least lessened through intervention. Thus, dependency is in itself neither good nor bad – it is how and why it is used that matters. Fiori, Consedine and Magai (2008) found a complex interrelationship between what might be termed good and bad dependency and other factors. For example, they found that what they termed 'healthy dependency' was related to higher levels of self-reported health. A 'dysfunctional dependency' was, on the other hand, related to an increased probability of being on medication for hypertension, and 'over-dependency' to a higher level of depression.

Attitudes to ageing

Attitudes to ageing shape the way in which we treat and regard older adults. It is therefore not encouraging to find that overall, they are regarded less favourably than younger adults (e.g. DePaola *et al.*, 2003). This is undesirable on many levels. First, such attitudes are damaging to older people themselves. We have already seen that failing to take a positive self-image can have serious repercussions for health and longevity in later life. It is well established that older people have an aversion to being called 'old', with only a fifth of people in their 60s and a half of those in their 70s being content with this label (Ward, 1984). The author of the study that produced this finding noted that, ironically, older people are often hoist by their own petard, since when they were younger they formed the illogical stereotypes of ageing which now haunt them. Stereotyping seems to affect older people's confidence; and generally, the more older people believe in stereotypes, the lower their self-esteem (Ward, 1977). This argument was reinforced in a study by Ryff (1991). She asked younger, middle-aged and older adults to rate their past, present and future selves and well-being. She found that the younger and middle-aged adults tended to see themselves on a path of self-improvement – they were better than their past selves, and in the future would get even better. The older participants, on the other hand, saw the best behind them and a decline in front of them.

Such generally negative attitudes occur even when considering nursing and medical staff, who have a professional duty of care towards older adults, but still are often found to have ageist attitudes on a par with the general population (Duerson *et al.*, 1992). This can lead to the phenomenon that even when presenting with identical symptoms, older and younger patients were diagnosed and treated completely differently (Duerson *et al.*, 1992). Again, Helmes and Gee (2003) found that when presented with a (fictional) description of a patient presenting with symptoms of depression, both psychologists and counsellors were significantly less optimistic about the prognosis for the patient if they were described as 'elderly'. Peake and Thompson (2003) followed the progress of circa 1600 patients diagnosed with lung cancer. They found that treatment was directed more intensively towards the younger patients, even when other health factors were equal. For example, one commonly used surgical treatment was given to 37 per cent of younger patients versus only 15 per cent of patients aged over 75 years. Six months after diagnosis, the mortality rate for patients aged under 65 was 42 per cent versus 57 per cent in those aged over 75, a difference that arguably cannot be accounted for simply by differences in other health indices. Negative attitudes about older patients amongst clinicians are nothing new. We saw earlier in this chapter that Freud was unwilling to consider psychotherapy for older clients, and in a similar vein, psychiatrists have sometimes regarded treatment of older adults as unwarranted because they have too little remaining life to benefit from therapy (James and Haley, 1995). In addition, the negativity surrounding geriatric care can deter practitioners from specialising in the area (see Goncalves *et al.*, 2011). This is at a time when specialists in ageing are needed as never before (see Lun, 2011).

In part, this inequality of attitude might reflect an ignorance of the full facts about ageing and the attitudes of practitioners. For example, Knapp, Beaver and Reed (2002) found that church ministers and students for the ministry were surprisingly unaware of very basic facts about ageing and later life. Nurses are similarly often lacking in knowledge about ageing and the specific needs of older people (see Alsenany, 2009; Wells *et al.*, 2004), although specialists in nursing older adults will probably outscore other student groups (Flood and Clark, 2009). However, some research suggests that negative attitudes can be changed. For example, Guo, Erber and Szuchman (1999) demonstrated that exposing participants to positive reports about ageing can improve subsequent judgements of older people's skills. Likewise, Schwartz and Simmons (2001) reported that positive experiences of older adults (rather than simple frequency of meetings) was a significant determinant of younger adults' positive opinions of older people. Similar findings were reported by Ferrario *et al.* (2008) when participants in a training course were given greater exposure to the concept of successful/healthy ageing as part of their training.

However, how deeply these attitudes are profoundly changed by such manipulations, and the degree to which they express true opinions is open to question. The measure of attitudes used in the above studies addresses *explicit attitudes* – in other words, the expressed attitude of a person who has had time to prepare their answer. However, even under very rigid conditions of anonymity, such attitudes are prone to self-presentational bias (Goffman, 1959). There are thus sound grounds for questioning whether explicit attitudes are expressions of what a person 'really' thinks. Instead, they are arguably a measure of how far a person is prepared to express their true opinions. This implies that there could be more than a hint of impression management in the responses of participants to many attitudes to ageing studies, and there is some evidence for this.

For example, Harris and Dollinger (2001) found that students taking a course on the psychology of ageing improved their knowledge of ageing but their own anxieties about growing old had not significantly altered. In short, training had improved *knowledge* of ageing, but had not really affected underlying emotions or opinions on the subject. Stuart-Hamilton and Mahoney (2003) conducted a study in which younger adult participants (employees of a local government district in the UK) were given a half-day training session intended to increase awareness of ageing and older adults. Prior to the session, participants were given two questionnaires – one measured attitudes to ageing (The Fraboni Scale of Ageism – Fraboni, Saltstone and Hughes, 1990) and the other knowledge of ageing. Two months after the training session, participants were given the same tests again. Not surprisingly, it was found that knowledge of ageing improved following training. However, attitudes to ageing and older adults remained unaffected, except for an increased awareness not to use ageist language. This is a potentially worrying finding. Many studies of anti-ageism training use a measure of knowledge of ageing as a gauge of whether training has been successful (see Stuart-Hamilton and Mahoney, 2003). However, just as with the Harris and Dollinger study, *knowledge* can change without significant changes in the underlying *attitudes* (in the same way that an army general in battle can learn a great deal about the state of the opposing forces without changing his or her dislike for them). Indeed, Stuart-Hamilton and Mahoney found that knowledge and attitude scores did not correlate significantly, a finding echoed by Cottle and Glover (2007). The degree to which attitudes can truly change is therefore still open to question, and it may therefore be assumed that anti-ageing stereotypes are still strong in many instances, despite whatever the measures of explicit attitudes claim to show.

Note that the findings discussed so far are from studies where participants have at least some conscious control over what they are saying. What then might attitudes to ageing be like if we could identify what people think *before* they have had time to impose conscious control and in effect, impose a layer of impression management onto their opinions? This leads to the study of *implicit attitudes*. These have been defined by Greenwald and Banaji (1995, p.8) as 'introspectively unidentified (or inaccurately identified) traces of past experience that mediate favourable or unfavourable feeling, thought or action toward social objects'. They are in effect the very first reaction a person has before they have had time to think about whether their thought is socially acceptable or accords with their other beliefs. It is tempting to see implicit attitudes as a measure of what the person 'really' thinks, but although this is plausible, it cannot definitely be proved. For example, it is also possible that a person might have a 'knee-jerk reaction' to a phenomenon, but because this does not accord with genuinely held values, it is amended.

There are various ways of measuring implicit attitudes, but the most widely used is probably the *implicit attitudes test*, or IAT (Greenwald and Banaji, 1995). The IAT is based on the well-established premise that the more strongly two items are associated together, the faster a person responds to them. For example, people will associate the words *bread* and *butter* with each other faster than, for example, *bread* and *razor*. If people are implicitly ageist, then it follows that they should associate unpleasant words faster with older people and pleasant words faster with younger people. These are what are termed the 'congruent conditions'. Conversely, ageist people should be relatively slower at associating pleasant words with older people and unpleasant words with younger people. These are called the 'incongruent conditions'. However, if people are *not* ageist, then they should associate the words in the congruent and incongruent conditions at equal speed. Over several blocks of trials, participants are shown pairings in different combinations. Before each block begins, participants are told to press one response button if one type of pairing appears, and another button if another pairing appears. The full procedure is laborious to describe, but in short, when the test is over, it is possible to measure the difference in mean response times to congruent and incongruent pairings – the larger the difference, the stronger the implicit attitude.

Although the IAT has been widely used to examine implicit attitudes to a range of things (see Baron and Banaji, 2006), studies of attitudes to ageing and old people are at the time of writing relatively rare. Jelenec and Steffens (2002) demonstrated pronounced ageist attitudes using the IAT, a finding more recently replicated by Turner and

Crisp (2010). These researchers found that implicit attitude scores were less prejudicial the greater the contact the participants had with older people. This should bode well for many nursing and medical situations, since it implies that people who work regularly with older adults will have more positive implicit attitudes. However, it is important to bear in mind that all the researchers found was a *relative* lessening of prejudice, not necessarily an absence of it. Older people were still seen negatively even by those with the greatest contact with them. A study by Nash, Stuart-Hamilton and Mayer (2009) demonstrated a further worrying trend. Nursing students with regular exposure to older patients had negative implicit attitudes, but their *explicit* attitudes were positive. In short, the students appear to pay lip service to explicit support for older adults whilst their implicit attitudes are ageist. These students were followed over a year, during which time this situation did not significantly change in this regard. Furthermore, performance on the implicit and explicit measures did not correlate significantly. Studies of implicit attitudes towards ageing and older adults are still in their relative infancy, but the existing findings indicate that many measures of explicit attitudes might be the expressions of very shallow beliefs.

Cross-cultural differences

So far, a high proportion of the research discussed has been conducted in industrialised nations with Western cultures. This is not wilful bias, but a simple reflection of the fact that this is where a lot of the research has been conducted. Generally, this is of little concern: age changes in working memory are likely to be reasonably similar from Austria to Zambia, and the same applies to nearly all cognitive ageing. There are exceptions (e.g. some relatively minor differences in the way stories are recalled – see Hosokawa and Hosokawa, 2006), but in the main this argument probably holds. However, in studies of how older people present themselves to the outside world, clearly culture could potentially have an impact. If a country is generally accepting and supportive of old age, then a person might have different attitudes and behaviours compared with a person living in a more ageist environment.

In practically any discussion of attitudes to ageing in the popular media, a sharp contrast is drawn between attitudes in the East and

West. A visual cliché of documentary makers is to contrast shots of an impoverished pensioner in a British planning-blight apartment block with serene Asian octogenarians doing communal Tai Chi exercises. Certainly, there are East–West differences to be found. For example, older people in Hong Kong have a higher proportion of immediate family members and lower proportion of acquaintances in their social circle with increasing age. The reverse applies to older people in Germany (Fung *et al.*, 2008). Generally in the Far East, later life *is* revered to a greater extent than in the West. However, this is a generalised statement. First, it is generally *active* old age that is prized, where the older adult can still make a contribution (see Okamoto and Tanaka, 2004). A later life of infirmity and reliance is regarded less positively. Again, as globalisation continues its seemingly inexorable progress, there are signs of some change towards Western values in Eastern countries – in other words, views about ageing are becoming more negative (see Ingersoll-Dayton and Saengtienchai, 1999).

Eastern cultures are sometimes treated by Western observers as homogeneous, but in reality, not all Eastern cultures have the same strengths of attitude. For example, Levy (1999) reports that Japanese people tend to have less negative attitudes towards older people than do Chinese. Also, note that even at best the view of ageing is still often negative in absolute terms – it was merely the *strength* of the view's expression that differs between cultures. Western cultures are similarly varied. For example, Clarke and Smith (2011) demonstrated that American older adults have a significantly higher sense of personal control than British older adults. Again, differences in the representation of ageing have been found between Italian and Brazilian participants (Wachelke and Contarello, 2010).

A key measure of well-being in many older people is *quality of life* (QOL). This is essentially a gauge of how contented a person is with their lifestyle and day-to-day experiences. However, different cultures have different expectations of what constitutes the good life, so what a typical person in one culture considers to be a barely adequate and thus unsatisfying existence might be seen by a person in another culture as living in the lap of luxury. This means that comparisons of quality of life in different cultures can be fraught with difficulty if due allowance is not made for cultural differences (Bowling and Stenner, 2011).

Tangential to this, in general, non-industrialised and developing societies have a higher regard for later life, according it a special status. This may be because later life is relatively rare in such groups, and in peoples lacking a written language system, older people may be especially valued for their memories of the past. However, as with many Eastern countries, the very elderly and physically and mentally infirm are often regarded far less favourably (see Perlmutter and Hall, 1992). It is also important to recognise that within developing countries, just as with the East, attitudes to ageing are not in stasis. For example, Aboderin (2004) has identified significant shifts in attitudes to ageing amongst urban Ghanaians, with an increasing expectation that older adults show self-reliance rather than (as was traditional) relying on younger members of the family to provide a high level of support. Aboderin attributes this sea change in attitudes to the increasingly materialist culture of Ghana.

Ethnic minority groups within industrialised countries tend to have a higher regard for, and more inclusive treatment of, older adults. This may in part be attributed to a higher proportion of multigenerational households, and closer-knit communities. Even where the traditional family unit is becoming less common, a support system may still remain in place that leaves older adults satisfied with the level of support from younger family members and their social network (e.g. Cornman *et al.*, 2004).

However, it is dangerous to overgeneralise such arguments and assume that cultural differences are uniquely the product of particular cultures and are fundamentally different to the core. Almost inevitably there are confounding factors, such as the fact that ethnic minorities tend to have a lower socio-economic standing and thus may be forced to be more inter-reliant through economic necessity, and these are difficult to tease apart from other factors. For example, Fung, Lai and Ng (2001) demonstrated that the life expectancy of an ethnic group can significantly shape matters. In comparing social preferences of older Taiwanese people against those of typically shorter-lived mainland Chinese people, statistically controlling for differences in life expectancy also removed cultural differences. In addition, studies across different ethnic/cultural groups have found common themes and expectations, such as recognising the importance of mutual assistance and reciprocity between generations, even if the relative emphasis placed on individual factors within the system varies between groups (e.g. Becker *et al.*, 2003). Furthermore, level of education is a consistent predictor of health and health change across Eastern and Western cultures (Farias *et al.*, 2011).

Notwithstanding these comments, older people within an ethnic minority face what has been termed *double jeopardy* – the problem that not only will they be treated prejudicially because they are older, but also because of their ethnic identity. It is certainly true that in many countries, older people from ethnic minorities under-use health and social care programmes.

However, findings that older people from minority groups have poorer health cannot be taken at face value, since minority groups often have lower socio-economic status, and this, as we have seen, can be a powerful confounding variable. Many early researchers were thus sceptical about how genuine a problem was there, and gave the concept of double jeopardy equivocal support (see Perlmutter and Hall, 1992). However, more recent studies, which have adjusted data for socio-economic variables, have found that older people from ethnic minorities are physically unhealthy significantly more often than majority culture older people; and furthermore, this difference is significantly larger in older than in younger adults from the same cultures (Carreon and Noymer, 2011). The research literature is packed with further examples. For example, Nielsen *et al.* (2011) demonstrated that dementia is under-diagnosed in older adults from ethic minorities, but conversely, it is *over*-diagnosed in people aged under 60. White-Means (2000) found that older African-Americans are less likely to use various medical services, and this explanation holds even after financial differences have been accounted for. Hardy *et al.* (2011) found differences between ethnic groups in use of hospice care.

Thus, although the findings on cultural differences in later life are at times mixed, one thing that is very clear is that ethnic minorities often face appreciable health problems. The argument that in part this is due to the confounding effects of socio-economic class is important for researchers; but in moral terms, it does not excuse failure to rectify this problem. However, it is important to note that although ethnic minorities as a group might experience problems, this cannot be automatically said of every individual member of any cultural group, and there is a wide variability between individual experiences in many studies (see Whitfield and Baker-Thomas, 1999). Thus, discussions of ethnic minority problems are descriptive, not prescriptive.

Retirement

Although some people think about retirement in terms of a set 'retirement age', this is often inaccurate. As noted in Chapter 1, the idea of a formal pensionable age is largely a phenomenon of the 20th century, and even then, it was not obeyed rigorously or indeed at the same age in all countries. For example, the formal retirement age for many public sector workers such as school teachers varies from the late 50s to the 60s, depending upon the country in question. In addition, not everyone waits for the formal retirement age to retire. Companies wishing to shed surplus workers often find it financially easiest to offer early retirement packages to the oldest workers.[9] In addition, the advent of more humane employment laws means that early paid retirement through chronic ill health is on the rise. Conversely, other people choose to work past retirement age (if their country's laws permit it) and in the case of self-employed people, there is almost always no legally defined age at which a person must retire. This means that retirement, although probabilistically an experience of old age, is not automatically so, and the precise age of retirement, and the reasons for it, can vary widely (see McDonald, 2011). It is therefore not totally surprising that a study by Settersen (1998) found that for many people age was now an irrelevant criterion on which to judge retirement. It should also be noted in passing that over the past 40 years, the proportion of men still working from aged 55 to 65 has significantly declined, whilst the comparable figures for women have risen (McDonald, 2011).

From psychological studies of retirement, two recurring questions have emerged. First, what determines the nature of retirement? (In other words, how happy people will be once retired, and what will they do?) Second, how do people plan for retirement?

With regard to the first of these questions, the answer has often focused on the degree to which a person feels they have controlled their

---

9   If common office folklore is to be believed, early retirement is also a useful way of getting rid of the most inefficient/most work-shy individuals, a consideration that does not seem to have been examined by many researchers.

retirement for themselves. In general, if a person feels they were forced to retire and/or they had no say in the arrangements leading up to retirement, then they have a lower sense of well-being and mental and physical health (e.g. de Vaus *et al.*, 2007; Gallo *et al.*, 2000). However, other factors also play a part. For example, Price and Balaswamy (2009) found that financial status was a significant predictor. In a study of British civil servants[10] opting for early retirement, Mein *et al.* (2000) found that the principal reasons were high income (i.e. could afford to retire early on a good pension), ill health or dislike of the job. Older workers who had material difficulties (e.g. debts) usually felt compelled to carry on working. Again, van Solinge and Henkens (2007) found that whilst degree of choice over when to retire was a key consideration, so were other measures such as the social environment the retirees lived in. Body satisfaction and perceived health have also been found to be key predictors of retirement satisfaction (van den Berg, Elders and Burdorf, 2010). Findings on whether it is better to go from working one day to being fully retired the next, or to retire by gradually working less and less each week, is somewhat equivocal (see de Vaus *et al.* 2007).

The effects of retirement on health are often hard to gauge. Since retirees are also generally in old age, this means that many of the health changes that occur post-retirement are probably age- rather than retirement-related. Fonseca (2007), studying Portuguese retirees, argued that many people find retirement itself relaxing and pleasurable (absence from stress and 'being your own boss' were often cited). Many of the negative factors surrounding retirement are, Fonseca argued, the product of ageing, rather than retirement *per se*. Hult *et al.* (2010) studied a group of retired Swedish construction workers, comparing how early they had taken retirement. The researchers found that there was no link between mortality and age at retirement. Although some early retirees died earlier than the norm, the researchers concluded that this was due to the underlying physical health of the worker, rather than retirement. Thus, the clichéd story that retirement kills people is a myth. Undoubtedly there are unfortunate people who die soon after retirement,[11] but this is very much the exception rather than the rule.

---

10 In essence, government officials.
11 The dedicatee of this book being a sad case in point, alas.

To turn to the second question raised above (*How do people plan for retirement?*), the answer is again a multifaceted one. It is clear that retirement is seen as a deeply desirable thing by most people. European readers of this will have witnessed the furore in many countries that greeted proposals to increase the pensionable age. The right to retire and enjoy the fruits of one's labours is seen as an inalienable right, even though, as we have seen, state pensions are a relatively new invention. Be that as it may, surveys of attitudes to working past retirement age are typically met with extreme opposition in many workers (e.g. Davies and Cartwright, 2011). In part this may be because people often have a rose-tinted view of what retirement years will be like. A key interest is often the prospect of taking up a new activity, such as a hobby, that will be for their own pleasure rather than satisfying others. Stephan, Fouquereau and Fernandez (2008a, 2008b) found that this was the typical reason for engaging in post-retirement activities within a university-run organisation. However, this is only one type of activity and does not necessarily universally apply to all. For example, Hopkins, Roster and Wood (2006) categorised (American) retirees according to the attitude they took to retirement. They found that expenditure was increased on more outward-looking activities if the individuals concerned regarded retirement either as a 'new start' or a 'disruption'. On the other hand, if retirees saw retirement as the 'continuation of life' or 'onset of old age' then expenditure tended to increase on inward-looking activities.

Other popular dreams of retirement are the prospect of long life and a pleasant place to live. These seem utterly reasonable wishes, but people often fail to examine the issues in sufficient depth. Ayalon and King-Kallimanis (2010) posed the following question to their (American) participants: whether they would prefer fewer years of remaining life in perfect health or more years of life in imperfect health. Those participants already in imperfect health tended to prefer fewer years of perfect health; white participants preferred fewer years of perfect health, whilst black participants preferred more years of imperfect health; people with lower levels of education preferred more years of imperfect health.

The conundrum presented by Ayalon and King-Mallimanis is one to which arguably there is no correct answer. However, in other instances, planning for the future does involve decisions that are more clearly right or wrong. For example, advanced financial planning is clearly important. Barely a week seems to go by (in the UK at least) without a new study in the popular media showing that an alarming proportion of the population do not save adequately for retirement.[12] A study of Dutch participants by van Rooij, Lusardi and Alessie (2011) demonstrated that the greater the financial literacy of the participant, the more likely they were to have planned for retirement. This is perhaps not very surprising, since an awareness of retirement planning is part and parcel of financial literacy. However, a key issue raised by this and similar studies is the necessity for financial education to begin early, since planning for retirement takes decades of saving. Another key issue is provision of key amenities. Retirement advisers often talk despairingly of the 'roses round the cottage door' phenomenon – in other words, retirees who entertain an over-romanticised dream of living in a quiet country cottage miles from anywhere. Such places might be bearable when young and with reliable transport, but are much less convenient when older, in need of frequent visits to the doctor/hospital, but without a car, and sporadic (at best) public transport. The great 19th-century writer, the Reverend Sydney Smith, once complained that stuck in a country parish in Yorkshire, he was 12 miles from the nearest lemon. This is often taken as being a whimsical joke, but like much of Smith's wit there is a serious point to it. Rural locations are often the very worst places to live without adequate access to modern amenities. And yet, retirees often head with seemingly lemming-like determination to what is pretty rather than practical. This is neatly summed up in a study by Oishi *et al.* (2009), who studied retirement location choices of retirees and non-retirees in Korea and the USA. Non-retirees assumed that places with nice weather and plenty of cultural amenities were the best choice.[13] However, retirees who had gone for the practical (easy access to medical services and routine daily amenities) were significantly happier than other retirees.

---

12 Obviously purely coincidentally, many of these studies seem to be sponsored by banks or building societies.

13 However, the assumption that urban equals better provision than rural does not always hold true (e.g. Peterson and Litaker (2010) demonstrated that healthcare provision was equally unmet in urban and rural settings in poverty-affected regions).

In summary – retirement is not necessarily a time of problems, perpetual ill health and misery. However, it does need to be carefully planned for, and that planning (particularly the financial) needs to start in early adulthood.

Psychosocial factors and health

Psychosocial factors, such as personality and social environment, are all related to health, and health is linked to feelings of well-being. Indeed, we have already seen how personality traits are related to health in an earlier section of this chapter. However, as has also already been seen, there is rarely a simple one-to-one link between things in real life, and many aspects of health are influenced by multiple factors.

Governments across the world are keen that people pursue a 'healthy' lifestyle, and thus live a longer healthier life without being a burden to the health services and thus the taxpayer. The links between smoking, diet, exercise and health/life expectancy are too well known to need reiterating here, and it may be assumed that a healthy lifestyle is a good thing. How, though, can older adults be persuaded to adopt it if they have not already? Certainly some of the signs are not propitious. For example, several studies have noted that older adults have poorer eating habits (e.g. Souter and Keller, 2002), though there are exceptions (e.g. older Greek people – see Kossioni and Bellou, 2011). Other factors may have roots much further in a person's past. People rarely take up 'bad habits' in later life (e.g. older smokers have usually been abusing their bodies for several decades); accordingly, attempts to make older people change their ways may in some instances be fighting decades of maladaptive behaviour (see Keranen *et al.*, 2009).

Self-motivation is a key factor in initiating and maintaining an exercise regime (e.g. Thogersen-Ntoumani and Ntoumanis, 2006). Therefore, any factor that lowers motivation is a marked impediment to taking up exercise. For example, older adults might be more reluctant to take up exercise because they fear the risks outweigh the benefits, such as having a heart attack through over-exertion (Wilcox *et al.*, 2003). This is not helped by the finding that older adults have fewer people to encourage (or nag) them about their health-related behaviour (Tucker, Klein and Elliott, 2004). However, once past these barriers, numerous studies, across many diverse cultures, have found that health improves following the adoption of a more healthy lifestyle (e.g. Bookwala, Harralson and Parmelee, 2003; Park *et al.*, 2011).

The adoption of a healthy lifestyle can thus lead to better health. This is not surprising. However, what of correlations found between general healthiness of lifestyle and health? What causes what? We have already seen from studies of personality traits that personality traits in early life predict health in later life. In a seven-year longitudinal study, Ostir, Ottenbacher and Markides (2004) found that positive affect (i.e. mood or emotion) was associated with a significantly lowered risk of frailty amongst older Mexican-Americans. Exposure even to subliminal presentations of negative stereotypical statements about older adults and ageing can raise blood pressure and other physiological measures of stress in older participants (Levy *et al.*, 2000). Therefore, over the long term, exposure to persistent negative comments about ageing and older people may have a deleterious effect on health (thus refuting the adage about sticks and stones). Conversely, there is evidence that physical health affects psychological functioning. For example, Druley *et al.* (2003) found that the more severe the response to the physical pain of osteoarthritis in older married women, the greater the negative impact on both their and their husbands' behaviour.

However, it would be naive to assume that such an issue as this can be explained simply in terms of 'A causes B' or 'B causes A' arguments. A far more probable explanation is that the effects are multidirectional, and that in effect 'vicious circles' of maladaptive functioning can be created (e.g. physical decline causes a rise in stress and depression, which makes the physical decline worse, which in turn... etc.). A case in point is falls in older adults. A fall is unpleasant at any age, but it brings with it increased health risks in later life. This is principally because more brittle bones mean that breaks of the hip and leg bones are a distinct possibility, and if not these, then other unpleasant injuries are likely; one study found that an older person has a one in three chance of suffering a functional decline following a fall (Stel *et al.*, 2004). Older people who have fallen over once are understandably unwilling to repeat the experience, but the added caution this feeling engenders may make matters worse. A longitudinal study by Delbaere *et al.* (2004) found that older adults who had fallen were more frightened of falling again and had lower levels of daily activity. But this greater fear and lower activity were the best predictors of having a fall in the subsequent year. (On a more positive note, methods for reducing fear of falling are available – see Li *et al.*, 2005.) Findings such as this must be treated with some degree of caution as it is possible that an underlying physical cause may be causing people to fall, and it is not difficult to find evidence of physical causes of falls (see Vassallo *et al.*, 2003). However, on *a priori* grounds, the vicious circle argument must hold true for at least some instances of fall behaviour. Nor can it be denied that a fear of falling can have negative consequences not only for quality of life but also for general health if mobility is unduly restricted (Li *et al.*, 2003).

A related topic is that of *hostility* and ageing. Hostility in this instance has largely the same meaning as in everyday language, and indicates a consistently negative attitude towards others. Some studies have reported higher levels of hostility amongst younger adults and older elderly people, with a drop in hostility between these two ages (see Barefoot *et al.*, 1993). This may in part be adaptive, because a healthy cynicism is arguably a useful tool for both younger adults first finding their way in the world, and older people in increased dependence on health and social welfare services. However, as many commentators have argued, it can also be disadvantageous, because high hostility levels are associated with an increased risk of heart disease (see Schott *et al.* 2009) and other illnesses (see Ranchor *et al.*, 1997).

However, it is also possible to overestimate the relationship between physical health and psychosocial factors. For example, a good predictor of physical health in later life is physical health in earlier life. Almost 40 years ago, Maas and Kuypers (1974) observed that many illnesses of later life are preceded by related physical complaints earlier in life. In turn this may be related to socio-economic status (SES) – low childhood SES is significantly related to lower health status in later life. In part this is because of the long-term effects of childhood illness, but also because of lower income and living standards in adult life (Luo and Waite, 2005). Again, Krause, Shaw and Cairney (2004) found that suffering trauma in early adulthood is strongly correlated with worse health in later life. This means at the very least that if there is a change in personality in response to illness, it may not just be the illness in later life that is causing this – it could be an effect accumulated across the lifespan.

It should also be noted that throughout this section, much of the discussion has centred on quantitative methods of research that emphasise reducing complex data to an underlying numerical pattern. However, although it can appear a trite cliché, we should remember that it is the health and suffering of *individuals* that is ultimately the focus of these studies. Black and Rubinstein (2004) examined older adults' experience of illness, and noted that many of their findings can only be regarded at an individual level, and defy simple reductionist techniques. Therefore, global statements about this topic potentially overlook important details.

Marriage

Generally, older married couples are found to be as happy as, or even more content than, younger married adults (Cunningham and Brookbank, 1988) and report a reduction in negative interactions with increasing age (see Akiyama *et al.*, 2003). This may in part be due to reduced work and parenting responsibilities[14] (Orbuch *et al.*, 1996). Other research suggests a rather less cosy picture. For example, Chipperfield and Havens (2001) observed older adults over a seven-year period and observed changes in life satisfaction for those whose marital status remained unchanged over the period versus those for whom there had been a marital change (principally, loss or divorce of a partner). The basic finding of the study was that men benefited more from marriage than women. Thus, if there was no change in marital status, women's life satisfaction tended to diminish, while men's remained relatively stable. Loss of a partner affected both genders badly, but men more than women. If a couple married, then the man's satisfaction tended to rise, whilst the woman's was unaffected. Reasons for the relative levels of satisfaction may be dependent on a number of factors. For example, the degree to which each partner relies on the other for support.

---

14 It might be supposed that adults in their 50s and 60s would be more willing to consider marriage/remarriage because of the potential material gains and lack of parental responsibilities, but this group is significantly less willing to marry/remarry than younger adults, even allowing for factors such as religiosity, child dependents, etc. (Mahay and Lewin, 2007).

Gurung, Taylor and Seeman (2003) found that older husbands relied principally on their wives for emotional support, whilst wives were more likely to use friends and close family members. As older friends die and families move further apart, it is easy to see how women could lose many of their sources of support. De Jong Gierveld *et al.* (2009) note that in circa 20 per cent of marriages of older couples, at least one of the partners has significant symptoms of loneliness. Emotional loneliness is relatively stronger in women in second marriages, whilst social loneliness is relatively more frequent in men with disabled wives. Perhaps unsurprisingly, having a smaller circle of friends, a marriage marked by general poor communication and/or arguments also increased the sense of loneliness. The study by de Jong Gierveld *et al.* indicates that changes in marriages can occur in response to changed circumstances and attributes of the spouse. Similar findings have been reported by other researchers. For example, Hoppmann, Gerstorf and Hibbert (2011) found that a functional decline in one spouse can be met by an increased level of depression in the other.

Discussion so far has concentrated on married couples. It might be tempting, given today's social mores, to assume that the findings will be true for cohabiting couples as well. Research on older cohabitees is still in its relative infancy (see Brown and Kawamura, 2010). Some research indicates that there is little difference between married and cohabiting couples (e.g. Brown and Kawamura, 2010). However, other research suggests that marriage is often more advantageous. For example, Brown, Roebuck Bulanda and Lee (2005) found that the male partners in cohabiting couples had significantly higher levels of depression than husbands in married couples, even after controlling for socio-economic factors, health and levels of social support.[15]

---

15 Comparing Canadian marrieds vs. singles, married men were found to be less likely to be depressed than unmarried men, whilst the proportion of depressed women was similar in married and unmarried women (St John and Montgomery, 2009).

Sexuality and ageing[16]

It is a commonplace observation that the media portray sex as being for the young and slim, and ageist humour dictates that older people wanting a sex life are either 'dirty old men' or ugly and desperate (see Nay, McAuliffe and Bauer, 2007; Scherrer, 2009). Even those older people whom the media have labelled 'sexy' are chosen because, generally, they do not 'look their age' (see Walz, 2002). Accordingly, older people do not receive support from everyday sources that wanting a sex life in later adulthood is normal and healthy. It is therefore unsurprising to find that people's professed interest in sex decreases after the age of 50 (Arias-Castillo *et al.*, 2009), and in part this is attributed to negative societal views (though illnesses and medical treatments affecting sex drive are also major contributors). There is also a gender difference. Waite *et al.* (2009) studied a sample of people aged 57–85 and found that men at all ages were more likely to have a partner (unsurprising, given the longer life expectancies of women – see Chapter 1) and were also more likely to be sexually active and have more permissive sexual views. There is potentially a cohort effect involved, since the groups questioned were amongst the last where women were less likely to be outwardly sexual in their behaviour.

Perversely enough, the lowering of sexual activity and expectations of the same might not be altogether bad. Some loss of sexual opportunity is almost inevitable in later life due to death of partners, loss of physical functioning, etc. A stereotype that informs older adults that less (or even no) opportunity for sex in later life is to be expected may therefore act as a comfort. Examinations of older adults' reactions to a loss of sexual functioning and/or partner show that the negative effects may be lessened or negated by the expectation that this is part of 'normal ageing' (Gott and Hinchliff, 2003). This does not mean that older adults should be discouraged from an enjoyable sex life (far from it), but arguing too vociferously that sex is an automatic right might be misinterpreted by those who lack the opportunity (or physical means) that they have 'failed'.

---

16 This section deals with ageing rather than middle age, but the related issue of the menopause is clearly of importance (see e.g. Dennerstein, Alexander and Kotz, 2003; Palacios, Tobar and Menendez, 2002). It also is, *purely* for the sake of space, devoted to majority heterosexual practices. For an excellent survey of gay behaviour and ageing, see Heaphy, Yip and Thompson (2004).

There are a variety of problems associated with studying sexuality in the later years. The first concerns the general reticence most people feel about discussing their sex lives. Castelo-Branco *et al.* (2010) found that women aged between 45 and 64 were far more frank about their sexual activities in anonymous questionnaires than in interviews. For example, the questionnaire group was twice as likely to admit to having what the authors termed 'occasional or unconventional partners'. This reticence might easily be magnified further by a cohort effect – older people were brought up in less permissive times, and are not accustomed (and indeed might lack the vocabulary) to talk about sexual issues. Surveying the history of studies of sexual activity in later life, Gibson (1992) observed that the more recent the study, the more often older people admit to having sexual relations. Therefore, older groups might provide less information, not because they have sex less often, but because they are less willing to talk about it.

Another problem often cited by researchers concerns what constitutes 'sex'. If penetrative intercourse is taken as the only measure of sex, then older people might show a greater decline in activity than if a wider range of activities is considered. But older adults in many cultures might in reality still engage in sexual activity of other kinds such as caressing, kissing and hugging and in effect 'renegotiate' what 'sex' means to them. However, this is not true for all cultures. For example, older Chinese people tend to restrict the definition of sex very rigidly to penetrative heterosexual intercourse (Yan *et al.*, 2011). It is worth noting, however, that sexually active older people generally report great satisfaction in whatever activity they indulge in (see Gott, 2004).

A further problem facing older adults is one of opportunity. Since women on average live longer than men, it follows that there are a lot more older women than men. Thus, older women's opportunities for heterosexual contact are diminished, and activity might cease not because of lack of capability or willing, but because of lack of a suitable partner. For those older people who attempt to find sexual contact through higher-risk behaviours, such as using prostitutes, there is an increased risk of contracting sexually transmitted diseases, including AIDS (Gott, 2004). For example, a study of circa 800 Swiss people aged over 45 found that they had behaviours presenting an increased risk of contracting AIDS compared with younger adults

(Abel and Werner, 2003). A more recent study by Kott (2011) found that 34 per cent of older (aged 50+) HIV positive adults had recently had unprotected sex. This was significantly correlated with drug use and loneliness. An additional factor is that the 'baby boomers' generation, which was arguably the first to embrace substance abuse on a widespread scale has shown less reluctance to drop their habits as they have grown older, relative to previous generations of substance abusers (Topolski *et al.*, 2002). Continued intravenous drug use of course drastically raises the risk of HIV/AIDS, but in addition, the lifestyle associated with substance abuse is also probabilistically linked to a higher level of risky sexual practices, such as those identified by Kott (2011). Another key risk factor is level of self-esteem – the lower this is, the higher the probability of engaging in (or being persuaded/coerced into) risky sexual behaviours, such as unprotected sex (Jacobs and Kane, 2011). Older adults are no less vulnerable than any other age group when it comes to infection by AIDS – as proof of this, in the USA, circa 15 per cent of all HIV/AIDS cases are in people aged over 50 (Emlet, 2004). Similarly, 14 per cent of male deaths from HIV in the UK are in men aged over 65 (Office for National Statistics, 2011).

A final problem to be mentioned here is the relative under-treatment by health professionals, who may undervalue or ignore older people's sexuality (see Elias and Ryan, 2011) and may be unaware of the prevalence of HIV/AIDS in older adults (Emlet, 2004). Generally, a high proportion of cases of sexual dysfunction in older adults remains untreated (see Godschalk, Sison and Mulligan, 1997). In many instances, there is a clear and pressing need for healthcare professionals to become far better versed in issues surrounding sexuality and sexual behaviours in later life (see Sharpe, 2004).

In addition to limitations of physical health, the level of sexual activity is dependent upon the level of activity in early adulthood (e.g. Martin, 1981). This implies that, once again, the state of one's later life is determined by one's earlier behaviour. However, it is worth remembering that sexual drives differ markedly between individuals (e.g. Masters and Johnson, 1966). In later life, a key determinant of sexual activity is the level of importance of sex to the individual (DeLamater and Sill, 2005). Although this may to some extent be a circular argument (e.g. if a person cannot have sex then arguably it may become less important, especially with a stereotype that loss of libido is 'normal' in later life) it cannot *all* be circular. Put simply, it is wrong to assume that there is a 'correct' level of sexual activity, or indeed, that sexual activity is necessary at all, for successful ageing to occur.

Disengagement and activity theories

It has been tacitly acknowledged in various parts of the research literature that part of ageing is a preparation for death. Nowhere is this made more explicit than in the *disengagement theory* by Cumming and Henry (1961), based on a large study of residents in Kansas City. This argued that as people get older, their contact with the world lessens. At a social level, the loss of spouses and friends, and other social estrangements such as retirement, cause older people to disengage from contact with others. This was seen by Cumming and Henry as a rational process, initiated by older people and aided and abetted by societal conventions. It is as if older people are preparing to die by shedding their links with the physical world. The theory can be criticised (and indeed was) for presenting the behaviour of passively waiting for the Grim Reaper as a good role model for older people. This is perhaps being a little harsh on Cumming and Henry, who were talking about relative rather than total disengagement. In addition, as Coleman and O'Hanlon (2004) observe, the prevailing societal attitude (in the USA at least) was that old age 'should' ideally be like middle age – therefore, old age was seen as an unhealthy decline from the norm. Rather than denigrating later life, Cumming and Henry were in fact making a vigorous stand celebrating the separate identity of later life and in effect empowering people in senescent decline as undergoing a natural rather than aberrant experience.

In any case, later evidence indicated that disengagement was largely confined to individuals who were always reclusive (e.g. Maddox, 1970a, 1970b) or in some cases to people who had loneliness thrust upon them by force of circumstances. In other instances it was linked to level of economic hardship. For example, Magai *et al.* (2001) found that the greater the hardship, the greater the isolation, and this in turn was probabilistically related to racial grouping (African-Americans were on average poorer and more isolated than European-Americans). It has also been argued that people who disengage from society have probably been doing so for most of their lives – in other words, it is not purely a response to ageing, and this is supported by a longitudinal study by Barnes *et al.* (2004), which found that such behaviour was present before participants entered old age. Stalker (2011) similarly found that level of engagement in activities is dependent on a large number of factors including not only age but also, for example, ethnicity and socio-economic status.

Researchers and commentators responding to Cumming and Henry's work argued that the best policy for older people is to keep as active as possible. Their argument is roughly as follows. Older people usually want to keep active, and life satisfaction is found to be greatest in those with an active involvement. In addition, greater social involvement (or at least, a more supportive social network) appears to lessen the impact of negative social exchanges (Rook, 2003) and be associated with a lower level of cognitive decline (Holtzman *et al.*, 2004). It is important to stress that 'activity' in this context does not have to be physically demanding – the term refers to any sort of behaviour with a social component. Thus, in assisted-living facilities, the simple act of getting together with other people at mealtimes and enjoying friendly relations with staff and residents constitute 'activity' and can be demonstrated to promote well-being (Park, 2009). Indeed, some researchers have argued that the activity itself is of little consequence – what matters is the social interaction that comes with the activity. For example, Litwin and Shiovitz-Ezra (2006) demonstrated that after accounting for quality of social interaction during an activity, the length the activity went on for had no significant effect on well-being.

Thus, greater social involvement is associated with beneficial things, and it is not surprising that a theoretical stance that older people should be encouraged to be socially active developed. However, in its extreme form this *activity theory* is as unattractive as the argument it tried to replace. The image of hordes of social workers forcing older people to mix with others 'for their own good', with compulsory whist drives and so forth, is not a pleasant one. Nor is it necessarily effective. Social activity is often confounded with level of health (i.e. an older person has to be relatively healthy in order to engage in social activities, so the finding that older adults who engage in social activities are also the healthiest may not be surprising). Lennartsson and Silverstein (2001) found that when health was statistically controlled for, the most beneficial activities with regard to older people's further life expectancy were solitary activities.

The modern consensus is that disengagement and activity theories describe the optimal strategies for some but not all older individuals, and which is better depends on a variety of factors, such as financial circumstances (e.g. can one afford an active lifestyle?), health (e.g. does one still have the vigour for some hobbies?) and personality types (e.g. introverts may hate a socially active lifestyle). To some extent, level of activity in later life is explained by behaviour in earlier life. For example, in a longitudinal study, Holahan and Chapman (2002) found that level of purposiveness at age 40 predicted the goals being actively sought from activities at age 80. However, it should also be noted that disengagement can also be indicative of encroaching illness and is correlated with mortality level (e.g. Bennett, 2002). Hence, although caution should be exercised in labelling particular behaviours as undesirable, withdrawal may in some instances be an early warning of serious health problems.

The role of the family

In Western nations at least, most older people, given the choice, would like to live independently, but to have family close by. The family can have distinct advantages. For example, the effects of hardship can be at least partly offset by family factors (e.g. Ferraro and Su, 1999). However, does the family have to actually be *physically* close? In the past, families had to be close together because the children of the aged parents had to be nearby to provide financial and practical assistance. However, in a modern world, with far better communications and transport, this is not as necessary. Financial assistance can be sent electronically, payment for cleaning services and similar can also be done at a distance, etc. For example, in Thailand, many older people living in rural areas have witnessed all or some of their children leaving the village to earn more money in the cities. Traditionally, the elders relied on younger family members to support them, but now that the children can send financial assistance from the city back to the village with ease, at least financial care is possible even if they are physically absent. Abas *et al.* (2009) found that migration of children from urban areas was not, on the surface, associated with depression in the older parents left behind. More remarkably, after confounding variables had been controlled for, older adults with migrated children were actually *less* depressed than other older villagers.

The danger with studying the effects of family on older adults is that most readers come armed with a set of assumptions. High amongst these is the *golden age myth* – the idea that in the past, extended families were the norm, with multigenerational families living in joy amidst the squalor, as described in some of the more glutinously sentimental passages in Dickens. In reality, the fate of many older people who were too poor to care for themselves was the workhouse, and the extended family (where three generations live under the same roof) was the exception rather than the rule in pre-20th century Europe (e.g. Laslett, 1976). In short, there has never been a golden age (see Thane, 2000). However, regardless of reality, there is often a temptation amongst non-experts to assume that there is a traditional duty to care for elderly parents by housing them in the family home, and anything short of that is a 'failure'. Another common assumption is that some cultures take much greater care of older adults than others. We have already seen in the section on cultural differences above that this is not entirely accurate. Willis (2008) found that with the exception of black Caribbean families (who provided less), all cultural and ethnic minority UK groups were as likely as white British people to support older members of their own families. Nor, in spite of the saccharin images of doting grandparents so beloved of the popular media and numerous pieces of fiction, can it be assumed that the state of the rest of the family is necessarily all that older people live for. For example, Sener *et al.* (2008) found that for older women, health and education made the highest contribution to life satisfaction; whilst for older men, it was solely health. For both sexes, the influence of family relationships was relatively minor. Likewise, older adults' views on the ability of their adult children to provide for them are often ambivalent (Radermacher *et al.*, 2010).

The above caveats indicate that the role of the family in older people's lives is not as cut and dried as might have been initially supposed. However, that does not mean it is unimportant. Family members recognise the importance of harmonious relationships. In a masterly review of the literature up to that time, Bengston and Treas (1980) observed that while family members were the usual and preferred source of comfort and help in a crisis, older people were more depressed the greater their expectations of assistance from their relatives. In other words, expect too much, and disappointment will almost inevitably follow, indicating that people clearly have expectations that family relationships 'should' work.

In addition, perceptions of family harmony seem to be greater the smaller the family – a study by Fingerman and Birditt (2003) found that people who cited a smaller number of family members tended to rate these relatives as being 'closer' and the incidence of problematic relationships to be lower. Interestingly, older adults were less likely to report problematic relationships than were younger members of the same family. It is possible to offer a cynical interpretation of these results – namely, that the smaller the family, the more obliged members feel to get along; and simultaneously, the older one gets, the more oblivious one becomes to problems within the family. However, this is perhaps an unduly bleak view. It should also be noted that in the case of childless older adults, where there may be no younger generation to interact with, greater psychological stress is not inevitable, but may depend on specific circumstances (e.g. men without a living partner had higher levels of loneliness and often depression, but men with a living partner did not – see Zhang and Hayward, 2001).

Religion and ageing[17]

The role of religion in a time of crisis is something known to many people, and its beneficial nature is well documented. For example, it is known that strength of religious faith is negatively correlated with depression (see Lee, 2007) and faith is of value in lessening the negative effects of caregiving for an elderly sick relative with, for example, dementia. Similarly, religious attendance is inversely correlated with anxiety (Ellison, Burdette and Hill, 2009). More generally, religiosity is strongly correlated with well-being even after controlling for gender, birth cohort and socio-economic group (Wink and Dillon, 2003). Religiosity may also be associated with better physical health,

---

17 To the best of the author's knowledge, the majority of research on religious practice and ageing has looked at the Christian faith as practised in industrialised nations, and particularly in the USA. No offence is intended to other belief systems by the concentration of discussion on Christianity in this section.

possibly through the intermediary step of increasing optimism and thereby presumably lowering stress (Krause, 2002).

Researchers and non-researchers often make a distinction between religion and spirituality. In very general terms, 'religion' applies to religious belief that is expressed by regular religious practice, such as visits to a place of worship. 'Spirituality' is a more nebulous concept. It can indicate level of sensitivity to spiritual/religious issues and imply an awareness of a deity that embraces all religious practices. However, it can also be used to describe any vaguely religious or mystical feelings, without any adherence to established religious practice. It would appear that many older people think of religion as being formal practice and spirituality as a rather wider concept (Schlehofer, Omoto and Adelman, 2008). For religion to be beneficial in earthly terms, regular formal practice and observance appears to be required. Sullivan (2010) found that amongst various Christian worshippers in the USA, regular church attendance was associated with lower mortality levels, even after confounding factors have been accounted for. People with strong religious beliefs might argue that this proves the power of faith. However, it is possible that particular psychological processes that make a person particularly faithful to religious practice might also have other life-prolonging properties. Currently, this question is unanswered. However, it must not be assumed that spirituality (as opposed to religion) is without value in terms of physical health and well-being. For example, Kirby, Coleman and Daley (2004) found that level of spirituality helped lessen the effects of illness and physical frailty on the well-being of very old adults.

Integrating religious belief into cognitive-behaviour therapy can bring significant improvement in depression and anxiety in older patients (Paukert *et al.*, 2009). At the end of life, religion is often supposed to provide comfort, but relatively few empirical studies have been conducted (for obvious ethical reasons). One of the few studies to examine the issue found that dying people who had religious belief were comforted by, *inter alia*, the promise of an afterlife and the concept of death being part of a larger cosmic order (see Pevey, Jones and Yarber, 2009). A longitudinal study by Idler, Kasl and Hays (2001) found that level of religious feeling remained stable or even increased in the last year of life, even though attendance at religious services declined (perhaps because of physical limitations). Ultimately, what is important is that either the application of religious belief to everyday life or (more probably) a correlate of this brings with it greater life satisfaction to some people.

Summary

The findings of research on personality and lifestyle are varied. There is not a personality type unique to later life, nor do personality traits necessarily follow a predictable pattern. On the other hand, some types of personality enable people to cope with later life better than others. However, all these arguments must be weighed against the considerable criticisms of personality testing and research methodologies. Again, it should be noted that many personality taxonomies incorporate implicit value judgements. For example, a successfully ageing person is held to have a placid and almost stoic attitude towards life. However, this conforms to the stereotype that older adults should be quiet wisdom-dispensing archetypal grandparent figures. Or in other words, people who make little fuss and make themselves available to others. The relationship between lifestyle and well-being is similarly more complicated than it may first appear, however. Socio-economic class, ethnicity, widowhood, familial relations, finances, and many other factors interact to provide a complex web of events and pressures whose effects are far from fully mapped.

However, the final words in this chapter must go to another reality check. Much of what is discussed in this chapter is *relative*. Anybody's life can be seen to be miserable if you set high enough standards. Someone reading this book might think themselves impoverished and leading a dull life compared with the stereotypical rich banker or hedge fund manager. But equally, a typical reader, living in a typical modest three-bedroomed house on a typical modern housing estate is living at a level of material comfort beyond the dreams of avarice for a high proportion of the world's population and beyond credence to their forebears in the 19th century. Of course, material possessions are far from everything, as we have seen. And there is abundant evidence that many older adults have a strong sense of well-being in spite of material or emotional problems – what is sometimes referred to as the *paradox of well-being* (Mroczek and Kolarz, 1998). Even when people are faced with issues that money cannot solve, such as many relationship and health problems, these issues are rarely omnipresent. The existence of problems in later life does not mean that they dominate to the exclusion of everything else. Or if someone is that burdened with problems, they are almost certainly very neurotic, and for such individuals, even if a solution to a problem is found, another problem will be immediately found to take its place (Hoyer and Roodin, 2003).

Suggested further reading

An excellent overview of many of the issues covered in this chapter (particularly psychoanalytic theories) is provided by Coleman and O'Hanlon (2004). An overview of personality research in general is provided by Caspi, Roberts and Shiner (2005). A more detailed discussion of the level of dependency exhibited by older people is an excellent book by the late Margaret Baltes (Baltes, 1996). Gibson (1992, 1997) provides an intelligent overview of sexual and emotional changes. Krauss Whitbourne and Whitbourne (2011) provide a readable survey of many of the topics covered in this chapter, and their book as a whole is an intelligent and thoughtful survey of the psychology of ageing and midlife adulthood. McDonald (2011) provides an excellent overview of issues surrounding retirement from a broader academic perspective.

CHAPTER 6

Mental Health in Later Life

Introduction

Older people are less likely to suffer from mental health problems than any other age group (Smyer and Qualls, 1999). All conditions, other than dementia, are at a lower level. This does not of course mean that mental health issues in later life can be dismissed. They are a serious problem at any age, but in older people may be compounded by generally poorer health and lowered intellectual skills. The number of chronic conditions an average person suffers from increases over the lifespan, and the problem is greater the lower the socio-economic group being considered (House *et al.*, 1992). In the present chapter, an overview will be presented of some of the key types of illness and disability.

Mild cognitive impairment/mild neurocognitive disorder

With no pun intended, this condition is what many commentators justifiably describe as a 'grey area'. It undoubtedly exists, but defining it in precise terms is difficult. In Chapters 2 and 3 of this book, we saw that older people often have significantly worse memories and other cognitive skills than younger adults. For most older people, this has little real impact on everyday life. Being a little slower to learn how to use a new mobile phone or retrieve the name of a person is irksome, but that is all. However, for some older people, the problem is worse than this without being totally handicapping. These individuals do not have dementia, but their worsening memories and/or cognitive skills are sufficient for them to have noticed a decline in everyday life. However, the decline is not so large that normal functioning is stopped – memory loss is far from total, and cognitive changes are not destroyed but are *very* noticeably slower and less efficient. Such loss has often been termed *mild cognitive impairment* (MCI) in older textbooks. There is no precise definition for this, and to further confuse matters, many other similar terms have been used.[1] More recently, the American Psychiatric Association (2013) has proposed another term – *mild neurocognitive disorder* (mild NCD).

Regardless of the niceties of definitions, MCI/mild NCD is of great interest to clinicians.[2] Although at times irksome, mild NCD by definition does not drastically affect a person's daily life. And happily, for many people, that is how things stay. They develop mild NCD and remain slightly forgetful and occasionally confused, but their cognitive abilities are still sufficiently intact that they can enjoy the rest of their days. However, for some individuals, the mild symptoms of mild NCD worsen until dementia develops (see Chertkow *et al.*, 2009). The likelihood of developing dementia from mild NCD is uncertain as different researchers have often used different measurement systems, but Woods (2011) cites a conversion rate of between 10 and 20 per cent. Other researchers have been more pessimistic. For example, Plassman *et al.* (2011) found that new cases of mild NCD outnumber dementia cases by about 2:1.[3] However, over a near six-year period in Plassman *et al.*'s longitudinal study, approximately two thirds of the people with mild NCD went on to show symptoms of dementia. Therefore, it has been argued that identifying cases of mild NCD is a key concern, since with early intervention, the progression of the condition to full-blown dementia might be slowed down.

---

1   Woods (2011, p.19) cites the following: *benign senescent forgetfulness*; *mild dementia*; *very mild cognitive decline*; *questionable dementia*; *limited cognitive disturbance*; *minimal dementia*; *age-associated memory impairment*; and *age-associated cognitive decline*.

2   For the sake of convenience, from now on, only the term *mild NCD* will be used, even if the original study used another term.

3   At 60.4 cases per 1000 patient-years versus 33.3/1000 for dementia. *Patient years* are the number of patients in the group being studied multiplied by the number of years the patients are observed for (e.g. 20 patients observed for 10 years equals 200 patient years).

It is important to note that not everyone with mild NCD will develop dementia. However, given the present state of knowledge, it is impossible to tell who has got dementia in its *prodromal* (early stage) phase, and who is not going to deteriorate further. What is needed is a *smoking gun symptom*. This is a symptom that unambiguously indicates one illness and one illness only. In this instance, if a symptom could be found in people with mild NCD that is only present in people who will then develop dementia, this would be fantastically useful as a diagnostic tool. However, so far such a symptom has not been found, although Ritchie and Tuokko (2010) noted that a pronounced failure of memory retrieval was a good (but not perfect) predictor of developing dementia.

Dementia

Dementia may be defined as widespread deterioration of intellectual functioning[4] resulting from atrophy of the central nervous system. Most authorities argue that the decline in intellectual functioning must include a decline in memory plus at least one other cognitive skill (Woods, 2011). However, not all authorities agree. The American Psychiatric Association (APA) periodically produces a highly influential taxonomy of mental illnesses, called the *Diagnostic and Statistical Manual of Mental Disorders*. At the time of writing, the most recent edition is the fifth, known by the abbreviation DSM-5 (American Psychiatric Association, 2013). In previous editions of the DSM, the APA has argued that memory loss must be present for a diagnosis of dementia to be made. However, in the DSM-5, it is argued that memory loss does not have to be present, and that severe declines in other aspects of intellectual functioning are sufficient. Furthermore, the APA has argued that the term 'dementia' should be replaced with *major neurocognitive disorder* (major NCD). This, it is argued, has fewer negative connotations than the word 'dementia'. It is fair to say that at the time of writing, these arguments have not won the universal approval of the psychiatric or psychological professions. However, once one gets past this particular argument, much of what is contained

---

4 'Intellectual' in this case means any sort of higher mental functioning, and thus, besides memory and intelligence, includes, for example, linguistic skills and highly accomplished movement skills, such as writing.

in the DSM-5 with regard to dementia concurs with mainstream opinion, and in what follows, it can be assumed that what is written concurs with the majority view, unless otherwise indicated.

To distinguish dementia from mild NCD and related conditions, there is typically a requirement that the deterioration is sufficient to interfere with daily activities. To distinguish it from conditions that cause temporary mental deterioration, there is a further requirement. Namely, that the deterioration occurs in the absence of intoxication or other factors that could cause a temporary confused state. There are three common misconceptions about dementia:

- It is a disease that only old people get.

- It causes memory loss.

- It is synonymous with Alzheimer's disease (AD).

All three of these assumptions are only partially correct. First, it is not solely a disease of old age. Cases of *early-onset dementia* (EOD), where the first symptoms present themselves before the age of 60, are well documented in the research literature (e.g. Garre-Olmo *et al.*, 2010). However, cases of dementia in younger adults are very rare. For example, Garre-Olmo *et al.* (2010) found that in the age group 30–49 years, the incidence of EOD was circa five cases per 100,000 person-years. In the UK, it is estimated that only about 2 per cent of all dementia cases are EOD (Alzheimer's Society, 2007). As age increases, the probability of developing dementia increases. The rate of expansion appears to be a doubling of cases roughly every five years (Corrada *et al.*, 2010), and this is consistent across the world (Ziegler-Graham *et al.*, 2008). Thus, dementia is not totally a condition that occurs in old age – it is simply far more *probable* that if a person develops dementia it will be in late rather than early adulthood. Second, although dementia causes memory loss, it is not *solely* a matter of memory loss. We shall examine this more below. Third, dementia is not synonymous with Alzheimer's disease. Most commentators argue that Alzheimer's is the commonest form of dementia, but it is not the sole type of dementia. At least 50 types of dementia have been identified (Haase, 1977), although admittedly a lot of these are extremely rare.

Dementia is a significant problem both in health and economic terms. *Dementia UK* (Alzheimer's Society, 2007), a report produced by the London School of Economics and the Institute of Psychiatry for the charity the Alzheimer's Society, calculated that at the time of publication, there were circa 680,000 people with dementia[5] in the UK alone – or, 1.1 per cent of the population. By 2051, this number could have conceivably swelled to 1,735,087. This increase of 155 per cent is not because there is an 'epidemic' of dementia as such, but simply because more people are living into old age. The cost to the UK alone of extra care, etc., needed for people with dementia is over £17 billion p.a. – and this figure is going to carry on rising (see Alzheimer's Society, 2007). However, it is important to note that not everybody will have dementia to the same level of severity. Approximately half of all cases of dementia are in the early and relatively mild stage; about a third have a moderate level, and the remainder have severe dementia. It should also be noted that severe dementia becomes commoner the older the patient being considered, rising from circa 6 per cent in people aged 65–69 to circa 23 per cent for those aged 95 and older (Alzheimer's Society, 2007). Reading between the lines, it is clear that, cold comfort as this is, a considerable proportion of older people die before they enter the moderate or severe stages of the illness.

Functional impairment

An early step in diagnosing dementia is to discover the extent of the disability suffered by the patient when they first seek help. As already noted, dementia is often heralded by relatively minor changes in cognitive function that in themselves do not impinge upon daily functioning to any appreciable extent. Because dementia often develops gradually, the stage in the illness when the patient first presents for medical help can vary greatly. Perhaps not surprisingly, younger adults are likely to go to a medical practitioner much sooner (McMurtray, Clark *et al.*, 2006), because memory loss and other signs of intellectual decline are considered atypical in their age group. In older adults, the symptoms might have reached a more pronounced stage, simply because the early symptoms of decline, which are treated with alarm by younger adults are dismissed as being no more than 'typical' age-related loss (see Roe *et al.*, 2008).

---

5   *Dementia UK* estimated that roughly two thirds of people with late-onset dementia lived at home, and a third in care homes. The likelihood of living in a care home rose with age of patient and severity of illness.

Once the patient's problem has been noticed, there are a number of basic measures of intellectual functioning to provide a rough guide to the degree of impairment. A widely used British test of this type is the *Blessed Dementia Scale* (Blessed, Tomlinson and Roth, 1968). In the USA, the equivalents are the *Mental Status Questionnaire* MSQ (Kahn *et al.*, 1960) and the *Mini-Mental State Examination* (MMSE). These ask the patient such memory questions as 'Who is the current Prime Minister/President?', 'What is the day today?' and 'What is your name?'. In short, these are questions that no non-demented person should get wrong. The more questions the patient answers incorrectly, the greater the degree of their impairment and the more pronounced their illness is held to be. In addition, a questionnaire on the patient's behaviour may be given to a caregiver to determine the extent to which the patient is still functionally independent, by asking questions such as the degree of help he or she requires in getting dressed. This has the dual advantage of not only giving a further gauge of the patient's degree of impairment but also judging the level of nursing care the patient requires. Scales such as the Blessed and the MSQ can also be used as the illness progresses to check on the general status and needs of the patient.

A more detailed method of describing the level of functioning of the demented patient is provided by Reisberg *et al.*'s (1989) *Functional Assessment Stages*, or FAST. The method was originally devised to describe the functional status of Alzheimer's disease patients, but is applicable to other dementias as well. Patients are placed into one of seven categories, with Stages 6 and 7 divided into sub-stages. Stage 1 describes normal functioning. In Stage 2, there are subjective feelings of loss of intellectual power, although these are not perceived as serious by other people. In Stage 3, intellectual impairment (particularly in memory) is evident in complex tasks that previously posed no problems, and in Stage 4 this has extended to relatively complex everyday tasks that, although demanding, are usually managed by most people (e.g. 'ability to handle finances'). Stage 5 is defined as 'deficient performance in choosing the proper clothing to wear', and in Stage 6 the patient is no longer able to dress him- or herself or properly attend to personal hygiene (the stage is divided into five hierarchical sub-stages, ranging from problems with dressing through to faecal incontinence). Stage 7 describes the loss of motor and speech skills (with six sub-stages, beginning with the loss of speech through to 'loss of ability to hold up head'). The authors also place estimates of the length of time a patient is likely to remain in a particular stage if he or she does not die during it (Stage 3 = 7 years; 4 = 2 years; 5 = 18 months; 6 = 2 years 5 months; 7 = 6 years+). A slightly simpler assessment is provided by the *Clinical Dementia Rating* (CDR), which is a checklist of level of functioning on a variety of tasks (e.g. memory, orientation, behaviour in the home). Based on the scores, the patient is graded as having no dementia, or 'questionable', 'mild', 'moderate' or 'severe' forms of the illness (Berg, 1988).

It is also worth noting that incidences of *agitation* increase in demented individuals (c. 60% of all demented patients exhibit it – see Eisdorfer, Cohen and Paveza, 1992). The term is generally taken to describe a group of symptoms, including aggression (physical and verbal), lack of co-operation, shouting, grabbing, restless behaviour, etc. Cohen-Mansfield (2007) found that in most cases, agitation increases from waking through to circa 4.00 p.m. and then decreases. However, about a quarter of those observed in Cohen-Mansfield's study showed increased agitation later in the day. Several methods of reducing the level of agitated behaviour have been suggested. For example:

- training caregivers to respond in an appropriate way (see Roth *et al.*, 2002), including offering positive verbal responses

- involving institutionalized dementing patients in an indoor gardening project (Lee and Kim, 2008)

- bright light therapy (Burns *et al.*, 2009)

- increased physical activity (Scherder *et al.*, 2010)

- listening to favourite music and hand massage (Hicks-Moore and Robinson, 2008).

However, no single method appears to be totally effective and some patients appear to be resistant to behavioural intervention, in which case drug therapy might be the only plausible solution (Brown, 2010; Salzman *et al.*, 2008).

The different types of dementia[6] all have the general characteristics described above. However, within this general decline, each has a unique pattern of dysfunction. We shall now consider the principal forms the illness takes.

Alzheimer's disease (AD)[7]

Alzheimer's disease (AD) is named after Alois Alzheimer, a clinician who was the first to identify the symptoms in a study of a 51-year-old woman in 1907. Early symptoms include:

- Severe memory failure well beyond the scope of everyday experience. This may include forgetting very simple lists or instructions, or getting lost in familiar surroundings, such as a local shopping centre or streets around the home. Standardised memory tests will typically show a gross failure to remember new information for more than a few minutes or even seconds, and short-term memory (STM) measures for digit span and similar may also show a decline (see Terry *et al.*, 2011).

- *Apraxia* (inability to perform skilled movements) (see Capone *et al.*, 2003).

- *Visual agnosia* (inability to recognise by sight) (see Giannakopoulos *et al.*, 1999).

- Impoverished verbal skills. Patients may have difficulty in producing the appropriate words (see Clark *et al.*, 2009), and may fail to comprehend abstract phrases, such as proverbs (see Rapp and Wild, 2011).

Patients' responses to their symptoms vary. Some are depressed, others apathetic and unconcerned; others are aware of a problem, but either discount it or underestimate its severity. Others develop a paranoia

---

6   Sometimes called dementias of different aetiologies or etiologies.

7   Also known by several other names, including *senile dementia of the Alzheimer type* (SDAT) and *dementia of the Alzheimer type* (DAT). For the sake of convenience, Alzheimer's disease or AD is principally used in this book. Some older textbooks restrict the use of 'Alzheimer's disease' to cases arising before the age of 60 and use the term *senile dementia* to describe those occurring after this age. However, this use has in recent years been largely outmoded.

that people are deliberately hiding things or stealing from them (see Murayama *et al.*, 2009).

As the illness progresses, so the severity of symptoms increases, though there is considerable variability in the rate and order in which the symptoms appear (see Stopford *et al.*, 2008):

- Memory for new items is now severely curtailed, often even for items in STM.

- Memory for remote events, learnt before the onset of the illness, also worsens.

- Recognition declines, even to the point of being incapable of recognising friends and family (which obviously causes great distress).

- Language worsens considerably, and *aphasia* (language failure) becomes a key feature of the latter stages of AD. Speech can be reduced to a few words and a series of garbled speech-like sounds, or can consist of recognisable words produced in a nonsensical order (see Whitworth and Larson, 1988).

- Sometimes the ability to read aloud is remarkably well preserved, with proper observation of punctuation and intonation (see Raymer and Berndt, 1996). However, patients have typically very poor recall of what they have read.

- The external appearance of patients reflects their inward decline. Without the aid of dedicated helpers, patients' grooming and general demeanour inevitably worsen.

- Movement begins to appear crabbed and awkward. A shuffling gait, characteristic of *Parkinsonism*[8] becomes commonplace.

---

8   Set of symptoms, including a shuffling gait and trembling hands, *bradykinesia* (very slow movement) and *hypokinesia* (difficulty imitating a movement). This set of symptoms is found in patients with various kinds of dementia and other brain injuries, and can be a side-effect of some drug treatments. It is also found in *Parkinson's disease* (caused by damage to an area of the brain called the *substantia nigra*, responsible, amongst other things, for producing the neurotransmitter dopamine).

In the terminal stages of the illness, the patient usually falls into an uncommunicative state and incontinence becomes habitual. For further discussion of the mid- and late stages, see Burns (2006).

Death typically occurs about five years or more after the appearance of the first 'major' symptoms (though note there are huge variations between studies, depending on what is counted as a 'major symptom', etc.). Certainly, length of survival after being admitted to institutional care has increased since the 1960s (Wood, Whitfield and Christie, 1995), probably reflecting improvements in general medical care. Death is most commonly ascribed to respiratory failure, presumably exacerbated by the relative immobility of patients in the later stages of the disease (see Burns, 1995).

Patients who develop AD before the age of 60 generally have a higher mortality risk (Koedam *et al.*, 2008) and are considerably more likely to have close family members who also have the disease (McMurtray, Ringman *et al.*, 2006). However, early- and late-onset AD are still considered to be fundamentally the same disease (see Miyoshi, 2009, for an overview).

At a cellular level, the brains of people with AD typically have two key characteristics. The first is a large number of *senile plaques*. Plaques are tiny lumps of a protein called *beta amyloid*, and they are found lying in between neurons. Almost all older people have some senile plaques, but in people with AD, they are found in much greater numbers. The second is *neurofibrillary tangles*. Nerve cells in part keep their structure thanks to a protein called *tau*. In AD, tau becomes distorted, leading to the nerve fibres becoming distorted and forming tangles. The tangles mean that communication between the affected neurons is lost (for some excellent illustrations of tangles and plaques, see Hyman *et al.*, 1993). Researchers are unclear as yet about whether plaques and tangles are the root cause of the symptoms found in AD or whether they are by-products of a deeper process. However, it is known that plaques and tangles correlate with some psychological symptoms. For example, the number of plaques and tangles correlates significantly with cognitive performance (Braskie *et al.*, 2010).

There is typically heavy brain cell loss in AD, and this tends to be concentrated in specific areas of the brain. The wrinkled 'top' layer of the brain, known as the *cortex*, is especially badly affected, particularly the frontal regions. As was noted in Chapter 2, decline in the frontal lobes is believed to be responsible for a significant proportion of normal ageing decline. The frontal lobes are very badly affected in many AD patients. However, this is not the only area of the brain to show a higher than normal level of cell loss. Also badly affected are several parts of the brain that lie underneath the cortex, principally the amygdala, the hippocampus and the brain stem (Braskie *et al.*, 2010). Damage to the hippocampus is particularly interesting to psychologists, because it is known that it is heavily involved in the formation of new memories.

Nerve cells use chemicals to transmit signals to each other. These chemicals are called *neurotransmitters*. Several different neurotransmitters are used in the brain, but a large number of brain cells use the neurotransmitter *acetylcholine*, and these cells are known collectively as the *cholinergic system*. It is known that in non-dementing people, suppressing the working of the cholinergic system impairs memory. The argument follows that perhaps part of the memory problem that AD patients face is because their cholinergic system is not functioning properly. This is known as the *cholinergic hypothesis*. Certainly, there is ample evidence that cognitive decline in AD is correlated with poorer cholinergic system functioning (e.g. Bohnen *et al.*, 2005). This leads to the argument that if neural damage cannot be repaired, perhaps pharmacologically stimulating what is left of the cholinergic system will be beneficial. Some of the so-called 'anti-dementing' drugs work in this manner, and although they do not cure or even stop the course of the disease, they can reduce symptoms and retard the disease's development (Sabbagh and Cummings, 2011).

Thus, in AD patients, as cell death increases, intellectual performance decreases. This has been an established general truth since the earliest studies in this field (e.g. Tomlinson, Blessed and Roth, 1968). However, as with much else in ageing research, we must sound a note of caution. Although plaques, tangles and similar indices correlate with psychological symptoms in AD, plaques *et al.* can be found in older adults with *no* signs of dementia (Erten-Lyons *et al.*, 2009). So therefore, the link between cellular abnormalities and behavioural manifestations cannot be a simplistic one of 'greater cellular damage = more symptoms', otherwise, many more people would have the disease.

Furthermore, other factors can disrupt the rate at which the disease manifests itself and develops. For example, an oft-cited case is the effect of education. Older adults with more education are likely to present for treatment at an earlier age than older adults with less education. Furthermore, those with less education are likely to have more pronounced symptoms when they first present for treatment (Roe *et al.*, 2008). The explanation for this is straightforward. People with a higher level of education are also likely to be more intelligent and be engaged in more 'intellectual' activities. Thus, the effects of dementia are likely to be recognised as being atypical much sooner.[9] Older adults with less education might lack the knowledge to distinguish between normal ageing and early dementia and thus be unconcerned about the symptoms until they become far more pronounced. However, an even stronger claim for the beneficial effects of education can be made than this. Namely, at death, older people can be found who have the neurological symptoms of AD but in their lifetime had no cognitive deficits (Roe *et al.*, 2007); Roe *et al.* attribute this to cognitive reserve – in other words, the higher the education, the greater the surplus processing power. This in turn means that far more decay is required before this extra reserve is used up and psychological effects become noticeable. It is also possible that more educated individuals have more heuristics to help them deal with cognitive tasks, thereby further lessening the difficulty of tasks and keeping the effects of dementia at bay longer. In other words, more education allows a person to mask the problem (see Gilleard, 1997). However, note that any advantageous effects from education are absent by the time the late stages of AD are reached (Koepsell *et al.*, 2008). Koepsell *et al.* suggest that in the early stages of the illness, greater test-taking skills or cognitive reserve might account for differences, but by the final stages of the illness, such skills have long since decayed.

Beyond the effects of cellular loss and the protective effect of education, there is the question of the origins of AD. There is occasional mention in the media of a 'dementia gene' but this is potentially misleading. What is known with certainty is that possession of some genes greatly increases the risk of developing AD. For example, the

9　This also explains the finding that subjective memory complaints are significantly more likely to be the harbinger of AD the higher the education level of the person concerned (van Oijen *et al.*, 2007).

Apoliproprotein E (apoE) gene has attracted considerable attention. More specifically, a variant of apoE known as apoE e4[10] appears to confer a significantly greater risk of developing late-onset AD, and even in non-dementing people is associated with a significant worsening of memory in later life (see Hofer *et al.*, 2002; van der Vlies *et al.*, 2007). However, note that apoE does not account for the majority of late-onset AD cases. Several other genetic links to early-onset AD have been found (see Bekris *et al.*, 2011; O'Brien and Wong, 2011).

Finding genes that are strongly associated with AD implies that the disease has a genetic cause. However, this is simply not true. Identical twins have identical genes. It follows from this that if one identical twin develops AD then, if genes are the cause, the other twin is also bound to get AD. However, in reality it is far from certain that the second twin will *ever* develop it (Alzheimer's Society, 2007; Scheinin *et al.*, 2011). Furthermore, if they do develop it, the age of onset can vary hugely (e.g. by 4–18 years in the study of such twins by Brickell *et al.*, 2007). Therefore, AD is not a purely genetic condition. The most likely current explanation is that something in the environment is the cause. Genes still have a role to play, since it is assumed that our genetic makeup makes us less or more susceptible to this environmental cause. Some people are born with genes that make it relatively easy for them to 'catch' AD, whilst others are less susceptible.

A number of candidates for this lurking menace have been suggested. Dodge *et al.* (2011) found that vascular disease can increase the risk of developing AD by circa 10 per cent, and there is at least tentative evidence that a decline in death rates from stroke and heart disease in the USA is being met by a decline in dementia and mild NCD (Rocca *et al.*, 2011). In recent years, aluminium has been suggested as a likely cause of AD. This is because brain cells in AD patients have been found to contain tiny grains of the metal, and it has been known for over a hundred years that aluminium poisoning produces symptoms very akin to AD (Tomijenovic, 2011). Some worried people stopped using aluminium cooking utensils and similar; probably a futile gesture, since aluminium is a very common element, present in a great many 'natural' things and foodstuffs. Why AD patients are especially vulnerable to aluminium is still something

---

10 Or epsilon 4.

of a mystery. It is possible that the aluminium uptake is a symptom rather than a cause of the decline. For example, dying cells within an AD patient's brain may just happen to absorb aluminium, rather than the aluminium causing the cells to die. This is illustrated by the finding that attempting to restrict aluminium uptake into the brains of AD patients does not affect the progression of the illness (Shore and Wyatt, 1983). However, more recent studies suggest that aluminium has a role in the formation of neurofibrillary tangles (Walton, 2010). Another proposal is that the illness is caused by a slow-acting virus. It is known that some dementing illnesses such as *kuru* (which affects a few native tribes in Papua New Guinea) can be caught by handling diseased nervous tissue. However, generally the evidence on causes of AD is inconclusive (Mahley and Huang, 2009; Mondragon-Rodriguez *et al.*, 2010) and the search continues.

Vascular dementia

Vascular dementia (VaD) is an umbrella term referring to dementia caused by damage to the blood vessels within the brain. This may be due to a blood vessel becoming blocked by the formation of a clot (*thrombosis*), a detached clot lodging in an artery (causing an *embolism*) or a rupture in the wall of a blood vessel (a *haemorrhage*) causing damage to the surrounding tissue. The damage in turn causes the surrounding brain tissue to die, the dead tissue being called an *infarct*. Dementia can result from a single infarct (*single infarct dementia*), but more commonly it results from multiple infarcts, each in itself too tiny for the patient usually to notice its effects (*multi-infarct dementia* or MID). The majority of cases of vascular dementia are MID.[11] In total, VaD is probably the second commonest type of dementia after AD. Note that it is relatively rare in its 'pure' form, where only symptoms of VaD and no other type of dementia are present (accounting for circa 10 per cent of all cases of dementia). However, VaD also occurs reasonably frequently in conjunction with symptoms of AD, where it is termed a *mixed dementia*. Distinguishing between AD, VaD and mixed dementia can be difficult and there is no smoking gun symptom that can be used. Several methods are in use, including using the number

---

11 Note that older texts tend to refer to *all* cases of vascular dementia as MID or arteriosclerotic dementia.

of neurofibrillary tangles to categorise the type of dementia (Gold *et al.*, 2007).

In most cases, the infarcts in VaD can be anywhere in the brain and are relatively random. However, it is not unknown for damage to be concentrated in particular regions of the brain. In *cortical atherosclerotic dementia* (CAD) the damage is largely in the cortex,[12] whilst in *subcortical arteriosclerotic dementia* (SAD) damage is principally in the subcortical regions. As might be predicted, CAD is associated with greater intellectual impairment and SAD with movement disorders (see Holtz, 2011; Tomimoto, 2011). Two common forms of SAD are *lacunar strokes* and *Binswanger's disease*, which have similar symptoms though their origins are in damage to different subcortical areas.

The causes of VaD are not fully known. Not surprisingly, patients often have a history of cardiovascular problems, fatty diets and smoking, and there may also be some familial tendency to VaD or stroke (Funkenstein, 1988; Holtz, 2011). However, these are only risk factors, and finding a definitive set of causes appears to be as remote as for AD (see Stephan and Brayne, 2008). The illness is extremely rare before the age of 55. A common method of testing for VaD is the *Hachinski Ischaemic Score* (IS), after its inventor (Hachinski *et al.*, 1975). This awards points to the patient based upon the number of symptoms they display, with particularly salient symptoms being weighted to reflect their greater importance.

Because infarcts often occur randomly, the course of the illness is often difficult to predict, and symptoms can vary greatly between patients; although as with AD, memory is often an early victim. Also as with AD, the simple quantity of brain tissue destroyed by VaD bears little relationship to the symptoms produced (see Metter and Wilson, 1993). Because infarcts can occur relatively randomly, in some instances the damage they inflict can by chance mimic the effects of dementias of other aetiologies, and thus misdiagnosis and reported cases of VaD closely mimicking another type of dementia are common in the literature (e.g. Alzheimer's Society, 2007).

Although at a single point in time VaD is hard to distinguish from other dementias, over a period of months VaD *usually* progresses in

---

12 That is, the wrinkly top surface of the brain, principally involved in higher mental functions. 'Subcortical' refers to parts of the brain underneath this top surface, generally concerned with controlling movement and other bodily functions.

a different way from other dementias. Patients with most types of dementia decline at a fairly steady rate, so that it is difficult to say precisely when a particular skill is lost or becomes appreciably worse. In contrast, VaD patients *generally* show a stepwise decline – in other words, there will be a sudden drop in function, followed by no change or even some recovery of function; then there will be another sudden drop, and so forth. This is not an infallible diagnostic tool, since some patients (especially Binswanger's disease patients) display a steady decline.[13] However, the majority of texts cite stepwise decline as a cardinal feature of VaD.

Other dementias

Although AD and VaD between them account for most cases of dementia, as mentioned above there are nearly 50 other known causes. Of these, the following are perhaps the most often encountered.

Frontotemporal dementia, as its name implies, first affects the frontal and temporal regions of the cortex (see Mariani *et al.*, 2006). Frontotemporal dementias are very rare. There is an ongoing debate about how many subtypes there are (e.g. Whitwell *et al.*, 2009). However, the commonest subtype is generally agreed to be *Pick's disease* (named after its discoverer), also known as *behavioural variant frontotemporal dementia*. Almost uniquely amongst the dementias, this is not commonly a disease of later life, with the average age of onset in the late 40s. Atrophy begins and is concentrated in the frontal lobes. At a cellular level, neurons often degenerate into *Pick's bodies*, which have a characteristic swollen appearance, (though some patients can have the same *general* pattern of atrophy as Pick's disease, but lack Pick's bodies). The patient usually first presents with problems expected of frontal-lobe damage, such as loss of planning skills, ability to think in the abstract, and so forth. It may also incorporate compulsive sexual behaviour, often without regard for social propriety. As the disease progresses, dementing symptoms akin to AD begin to manifest themselves. Often language is more impaired than memory, but this is not an infallible rule.

---

13 Note there is also a danger of 'seek and ye shall find'. Both my mother and paternal grandmother had VaD and in both cases I found myself looking for proof of stepwise decline that in hindsight was nowhere near as clear-cut as I imagined at the time.

Another form of frontotemporal dementia is *semantic dementia*, also known as *temporal variant frontotemporal dementia*. The initial symptoms result from atrophy beginning in the temporal lobes. Atrophy in the left temporal lobe causes language skills to deteriorate, whilst atrophy in the right temporal lobe causes loss of facial recognition and the ability to recognise emotions. Atrophy on one side of the brain eventually leads to atrophy on the other side. Symptoms then develop further in a manner akin to Pick's disease.

Creutzfeldt-Jakob disease (CJD) is a very rare illness, affecting approximately one in a million people. The illness typically manifests itself first as a movement disorder before intellectual deterioration begins. The illness is atypical of dementias in two main respects – first, death is usually swifter (often about one year after onset of symptoms), and second, it is known that it is contracted via an infection. CJD is of especial interest because a new variant of the disease (vCJD[14]) was discovered in the 1990s. There is strong evidence that the infection source may be beef contaminated with *bovine spongiform encephalopathy* (BSE), an infective agent that produces symptoms similar to CJD in cattle. Stories in the news media in the early 1990s were often dramatic in their predictions of the number of victims vCJD would claim. However, so far an epidemic has not happened. By 2010, only 17 new cases of BSE were reported worldwide, indicating the disease had practically been eradicated. So far, there have been circa 170 deaths from vCJD, with a mean age of victim of 28 years. Susceptibility to the disease seems to be dependent upon the genotype of the victim. The genes in this instance are only two – M and V, meaning that an individual is either MM, VV or MV. All people who have so far contracted vCJD have been MM, which is the gene variant of circa 37 per cent of the population. We know that in kuru, most people who contract that disease are also MM, but a smaller proportion with MV contract the disease later in life (Collinge *et al.*, 2008). This can lead to inevitable speculation that we might begin to see cases of vCJD in people with the MV variant and perhaps ultimately with the VV variant as well (Coghlan, 2011). However, there are grounds for doubting this. First, MV cases of kuru are relatively rare relative to cases of MM. Since MM cases of vCJD are rare within the population,

---

14 Otherwise known as *new variant CJD* or nvCJD.

this might mean that MV cases will be incredibly scarce, and VV cases simply not arise. Certainly no MV cases of vCJD have yet been found (Coghlan, 2011). Second, if vCJD is going to be a persistent problem, then we should expect a rising or at least consistent number of cases. But the available evidence shows a rise, peak and fall of cases, far more consistent with a brief outbreak. Of course continued vigilance is required, and the rarity of vCJD does not in any way lessen the sympathy that should be extended to the bereaved families of victims. But an attitude of sensible caution, rather than scaremongering stories is arguably the sensible approach.

Huntington's disease (a.k.a. Huntington's chorea) is not considered to be a dementia by all commentators. Like CJD it is relatively rare, but it tends to cluster in families, indicating a strong genetic component. Also like CJD, the early symptoms of the illness are disturbances of movement, often taking the form of writhing and twitching. Subsequently, patients develop dementing symptoms, although the decline can also mimic schizophrenia (Kermis, 1986). Patients with Huntington's disease tend to last longer than patients with other dementias, typical life expectancy after the appearance of the first symptoms being circa 15 years. The illness can strike at any age, but onset in middle age is commonest.

Parkinson's disease (PD) is also chiefly characterised by movement disorders, including a characteristic shuffling gait and tremors. However, there is a higher than average risk that PD patients will also develop dementia (c. 10–15%: Lezak, 1995). It should be noted that many AD patients develop PD-like symptoms as their illness progresses. The most salient difference between PD and AD patients is that linguistic skills are usually considerably better preserved (or even unaffected) in PD (LaRue, 1992).

Dementia with Lewy bodies (DLB) is also known as *Lewy body dementia*. *Lewy bodies* are tiny balls of protein that were first found inside the basal ganglia[15] of patients with Parkinson's disease. Lewy bodies are hard to detect, but improvements in measurement techniques in recent years have led to the discovery that Lewy bodies are in brain cells other than those in the basal ganglia in some demented patients. Some researchers and clinicians argue that patients with Lewy bodies

15 A subcortical area of the brain involved in the control of movement.

outside the basal ganglia should be classified as having DLB, which they regard as a distinct type of dementia (e.g. Alzheimer's Society, 2007; Woods, 2011). However, others argue that Parkinson's disease and DLB are essentially the same (see Nestor, 2010; Revuelta and Lippa, 2009). Onset of DLB is relatively rapid and hallucinations are a common (but not universal) symptom. Movement problems similar to Parkinson's disease might be present. Cognitive skills can be impaired, but memory impairment is rarely a notable early symptom (Woods, 2011).

Dementia can also appear as a symptom of other illnesses, such as *normal pressure hydrocephalus* (where cerebrospinal fluid gets trapped in the brain instead of draining away, putting destructive pressure on the brain tissue), brain tumours and AIDS; and also as a result of long-term exposure to toxic chemicals and chronic alcohol abuse.

Illnesses that can be confused with dementia

An assortment of conditions can give the appearance of dementia but in fact have other causes. The two commonest of these are both treatable, unlike the dementias, and for this reason are sometimes called the *reversible dementias*. The first of these is *pseudodementia*. This can arise in some older people who suffer severe depression. In becoming depressed, the patient loses motivation and this is reflected in very poor scores on tests of memory and intellect. This, and their general lack of interest in their surroundings, can provide an excellent imitation of dementia. There are several key differences between pseudodementia and the genuine article. First, pseudodemented patients are usually well orientated in time and space; for example, they know where they are, what day of the week it is, why they are being tested, and so forth. Second, they are also typically aware that they are performing badly on memory and intellectual tests. Third, pseudodemented patients' intellectual performance typically fluctuates in tandem with their level of depression, and improves as their depression is treated (LaRue, 1992).

However, it would be misleading to suppose that depression and 'genuine' dementia have no connection. Between 20 and 30 per cent of patients with dementia also have some symptoms of depression (e.g. Carlson, Sherwin and Chertkow, 2000) and depression is a very common symptom prior to developing dementia (Vinkers *et al.*, 2004).

For this reason, some researchers and clinicians are unwilling to use the term 'pseudodementia' because often there is a real dementia present.

The other major impersonator of dementia is *delirium*, also known as *acute confusional state*. Delirium is typically rapid in onset (usually a matter of hours or days). The age groups most at risk are children and older adults. There are many possible causes, including fever, infection, (legally prescribed) drug intoxication, stroke and inadequate diet (see Lin *et al.*, 2010). Most cases of delirium are cured by treating the underlying causes. Delirious patients display poor intellectual and memory skills, and also tend to be either excessively languid or agitated/anxious or a mixture of both. It is also possible for the patient to exhibit no 'obvious' behavioural symptoms. However, generally, rambling or incoherent speech is also a common feature. To this extent, a patient with delirium can resemble, for example, a demented patient, a depressed patient or a very anxious patient, and misdiagnosis is relatively common (see Foreman and Milisen, 2004). This can have serious consequences. For example, a delirious patient may have a serious underlying physical condition that needs urgent treatment; mistaking this for a severe anxiety attack, for example, and sedating the patient could be life-threatening. However, a major difference between delirium and dementia, other than the rapid onset of the former, is that many delirious patients suffer from *illusions* (distorted perceptions of the world around them). Illusions are relatively rare in dementia, in spite of some popular misconceptions on this subject. In addition, attention span in delirium is limited, whereas (surprisingly) it is often reasonably well preserved in demented patients. Various diagnostic tests, which act as a checklist of symptoms (e.g. the *Delirium Rating Scale*) are available (see Wong *et al.*, 2010 for a review). Note, however, that delirium can, and does, occur in demented patients (see Marengoni, Calíbrese and Cossi, 2004) and because of their weakened cognitive state, might be more easily contracted and be of greater severity (Voyer *et al.*, 2011).

A person-centred approach

It is entirely right and proper that we should be concerned about dementia. It is a nasty illness with horrible consequences for both patient and loved ones. Even if one is not moved by that thought, then the huge financial bill that the illness presents should be enough to attract the attention of even the flintiest of hearts. However, we can overplay the arguments to the disadvantage of the very people we are trying to help. By presenting dementia as something that changes a patient's mental state, we are losing sight of the fact that the person with dementia is still trying to make sense of the world and to enjoy living in it. Kitwood (1993, 1997) argued that the person with dementia is more than just a patient with a disease, but a rich mixture of many influences. This led him to create the following equation:

$$D = P + B + H + NI + SP$$

Where D is the demented patient as they present themselves. This presentation is made up principally of their personality (P), their life experiences up to that point, or biography (B), their physical health (H), their level of neurological impairment from the dementia (NI), and social psychology (SP). These phrases are reasonably self-explanatory except for the last one. 'Social psychology' means what is often termed *malignant social psychology*, where the surroundings the demented person finds themself in are intimidating and strip the person of a sense of personal identity. Anyone who has ever visited a badly run residential home will know instantly what this means. But it is not just the obviously badly run institutions that are at fault. Bullying and sadistic staff are mercifully rare, but just as damaging can be care homes that, whilst consciously doing their best for the residents, strip away dignity and independence by doing everything for the residents, not allowing them any leeway in their behaviours so that things are kept neat and tidy.

The central message of Kitwood's work is that dementia care should be person-centred. A measure of this is *dementia care mapping*, which involves analysing patients with dementia to see how they react not only to their own treatment, but also to the general activities on the ward.[16] The observations are then fed back in an attempt to amend behaviours to create a better environment. Some behaviours can appear surprisingly trivial. For example, care practitioners are often unaware that things they take for granted, such as chatting to each other as they enter a room or ward, and not greeting or involving patients, can be

---

16 More precisely, pairs of observers code patient behaviour every five minutes for six hours, making note of level of well-being, and documenting any events that occur in the patients' vicinity.

isolating and upsetting. Dementia care mapping and a person-centred approach to care of people with dementia have a lot of supporters (see Baldwin and Capstick, 2007; Kelly, 2010). However, there have been criticisms of the scoring rationale in the dementia care mapping procedure (Douglass *et al.*, 2010) and validation (Edvardsson and Innes, 2010). However, as a practical tool, Kitwood's model has proven very effective in most instances (see Ballard and Aarsland, 2009).

Dementia – a summary

Dementia is a progressive loss of memory, intellectual and linguistic skills, usually accompanied by radical changes in personality and sometimes in motor skills. Symptoms vary markedly between patients, but generally the different dementias are distinguishable by their patterns of development. Several illnesses can be confused with dementia because of a superficial similarity of symptoms, but these can usually be easily identified. At a physical level, dementias often differ in patterns and type of atrophy, but, as has been seen, the correlation between damage and psychological symptoms is far from watertight. Almost all intellectual functions decline in dementia. Although there are some interesting qualitative differences in functioning, it should be noted that these are usually only found in patients in the very early stages of the illness – as the disease progresses, patients usually lack sufficient psychological skills to comprehend or perform the tasks presented to them. It must also be remembered that in dementia, like many other illnesses, it is not only the patient who suffers, and that the disease can be a great source of stress and burden to caregivers.

In closing this section, it is worth noting that the severity and awfulness of dementia's symptoms can lead to an exaggerated view of its prevalence and lead to views that 'all is lost' if a person develops the disease. It is very important to stress that most people who develop dementia will experience only the early stages of it before they die. And a person who develops dementia is still a person, with rights to dignity, self-worth and enjoyment.

Learning disabilities

Research on learning disabilities in later life[17] is relatively scarce (Holland, 2000), and responsibility for service provision for older adults with learning disabilities is (if you will pardon the phrase) something of a grey area (Benbow et al., 2011). Some specific conditions are already reasonably well documented (e.g. there is a considerable literature on cognitive skills in people with Down syndrome in later life, because of the potential relevance to Alzheimer's disease – see McCallion and McCarron, 2004), but others are not. For example, Stuart-Hamilton and Morgan (2011) found that in the previous decade there had been more than 20,000 papers written on autism spectrum disorder; of these, under ten had looked at older people.

Where studies have been conducted, a key finding is that older people with learning disabilities have significantly higher levels of anxiety and depression than the general population (e.g. Patel, Goldberg and Moss, 1993), a conclusion echoed in subsequent studies (e.g. Smiley, 2005). A note of caution is sounded by Perez-Achaiga, Nelson and Hassiotis (2009). They conducted a review of studies of depression in older adults with learning disabilities, and found that some studies had used diagnostic tools that were fit for purpose, others were less reliable. This creates a potential problem – if a test is not properly standardised (and thus norms are unknown), there is a danger that a condition will be either under- or over-diagnosed.

An especially worrying point is that many of those identified as having depression were not at the time of testing being treated for it. Patel et al. (1993) noted that caregivers had often noted symptoms of depression but had not realised their significance. Within the mainstream older population, depression is known to lower intellectual functioning. In extreme cases this can lead to pseudodementia, as noted earlier in the chapter. In the case of people with learning disabilities, the effect could be very profound. Tsiouris and Patti (1997) conducted a study of pseudodementia in older people with Down syndrome. The paper in question addressed the efficacy of drug treatment of depression in people with Down syndrome. The paper

---

17 This section is on learning disabilities in older people. For the important topic of older parents of adult children with learning disability, see Davys and Haigh (2008).

noted that in four of 37 cases studied, the individuals in question had pseudodementia.

In addition to pseudodementia, people with learning disabilities might contract 'true' dementia (Kerr, 2007). It is known that people with Down syndrome have a greatly elevated risk of developing dementia (McCallion and McCarron, 2004). Strydom *et al.* (2009) argued that in adults over 60 with learning disability but *without* Down syndrome, dementia was between two and three times more prevalent than in the general population. Whether this is 'true' dementia might be questioned. It is possible that some people with learning disabilities have experienced nothing more than age-typical decline, but because they already had a low level of cognitive skills, this has made them *functionally* resemble patients with dementia. Studies of neuroimaging in older adults with learning disabilities and dementia have so far been somewhat inconclusive (see Gangadharan and Bhaumik, 2006). Whether older people with learning disabilities develop 'true' dementia at a higher rate or simply come to functionally resemble people with dementia is for the moment a moot point. However, it has been observed that the behavioural changes in people with learning disabilities diagnosed with dementia are similar to those in people without a learning disability (Duggan, Lewis and Morgan, 1996).

It should also be noted that diagnosis of dementia in people with learning disabilities is difficult. Because a person with learning disabilities is already performing at a low level on cognitive tasks, discriminating between this and a demented state can be problematic (Bell, Turnbull and Kidd, 2009; Nagdee and O'Brien, 2009; Torr, 2009). Although there are measures available to assess dementing change in people with learning disabilities (see Kirk, Hick and Laraway, 2006), many are not necessarily appropriate (see Perkins and Small, 2006). Added to this is the problem that cognitive changes in people with learning disabilities are often discounted or overlooked (Hassiotis *et al.*, 2003).

It should be noted that not everyone with learning disabilities is going to develop depression or dementia. When no problems of great magnitude appear, the evidence points to neurotypical and learning-disabled older people experiencing very similar patterns of ageing (Oliver, Adams and Kaisy, 2008).

Depression

Depression is a condition that almost all people experience in a relatively mild form many times in their lives. In most cases, the feeling of melancholy is in reaction to a specific event, disperses in a few days, and would not typically be considered a mental illness. Depression meriting clinical attention is long-lasting, and severe enough to interfere with normal functioning. It is important to stress that clinical depression is not solely 'feeling down' – the patient is in effect incapacitated by the condition. In addition to experiencing a depressed mood, he or she is typically lacking in both mental and physical energy to an extreme degree, has irrational feelings of worthlessness and/or guilt, and may have preoccupations with dying and suicide (generally, older patients have a greater preponderance of physical symptoms – see Caine *et al.*, 1994). Depression of this magnitude is far less common in later life than in any other age group (Luijendijk *et al.*, 2008). However, there are exceptions – people in institutionalised care,[18] people with dementia and caregivers of people with dementia all have a very elevated risk of developing depression (Woods, 2011). Also, older adults might be less likely to report symptoms of depression (Bryant, 2010). In addition, isolated *symptoms* of depression are far more frequent (Kasl-Godley, Gatz and Fiske, 1998; Smyer and Qualls, 1999). The latter finding is probably due to older people being exposed to a higher proportion of depressing events, such as bereavement, painful illness, and so on. It is also worth noting that, older depressed people carry the unique risk of developing pseudodementia (see page 169).

Causes of depression in later life are often attributed (unsurprisingly) to stressful and negative events. For example, bereavement is known to cause depressive symptoms, though these in most instances are relatively short-lasting. Sleep disturbance is a known factor in depression, independent of physical illness (Cho *et al.*, 2008). Again, illness and medical treatment side-effects can cause or exacerbate depression in some patients (see Sadavoy *et al.*, 1995). Numerous other factors have been linked with depression. So, even allowing

---

18 Contrary to the popular myth that it is the institution that makes people depressed, the available evidence is that most depressed people are depressed *before* they enter a care home or similar (Woods, 2011). This does not mean that institutionalised care necessarily always helps matters, however.

for confounding variables, depression has been shown to have a wide variety of causes. It is also important to note that depression can be caused by single or multiple factors. Harris *et al.* (2003) found that level of disability, health, socio-economic status, feeling of control and social support all were separate predictors of depression. There is little age difference in responsivity to treatment, with the majority of both younger and older depressed patients recovering (Kasl-Godley *et al.*, 1998; see also Andreescu *et al.*, 2008), though recurrence of symptoms is higher in late-onset depression (Woods, 2011).

Anxiety

The term 'anxiety', rather like 'depression', is something that most people can understand from their own experience. Practically everyone has at some time felt anxious about a situation they have found themselves in. The level of anxiety experienced by a person seeking clinical treatment is far greater than this, and is often identified by the term *anxiety disorder*. This refers to a long-lasting state of anxiety characterised by symptoms such as extreme restlessness, insomnia and fatigue, producing distress and impairment of function. It can manifest itself in many forms, including *phobias* (an irrational or inappropriately high fear of an item or event, such as open spaces, spiders, and so on), *generalised anxiety* (according to Wetherell, Le Roux and Gatz, 2003, characterised in older adults by a perpetual or frequent feeling of uncontrollable anxiety, sleep disturbance, and muscle rigidity), *obsessive-compulsive disorder* (a condition in which the patient is compelled to repeat the same act to relieve anxiety feelings, e.g. repeatedly washing the hands to remove anxiety-invoking dirt), and *panic disorder* (characterised by repeated *panic attacks*, e.g. sudden attacks of overwhelming apprehension, shortness of breath, feeling of loss of control).

Anxiety is relatively rare in older adults in comparison with the younger population (Smyer and Qualls, 1999), but this does not mean it is not a cause for concern, since within any one age group it is one of the commonest mental illnesses (Scogin, 1998), and is often found in tandem with depression and dementia (see Scogin, 1998). It is also possible that older adults under-report symptoms of anxiety (Bryant, 2010).

Substance abuse

The term 'substance abuse' refers to the use of either illegal substances or licit substances with an addictive quality (such as alcohol) in excessive quantities to the point where everyday functioning is severely affected. The stereotype of older people militates against an image of them as addicts, but health authorities are becoming increasingly concerned at the prospect of a significant proportion of older adults suffering from one or more addictive behaviours (Blow and Oslin, 2003; Stewart and Oslin, 2001). Often in the past healthcare providers were arguably under-trained to recognise and deal with these problems.

The idea of 'addiction' immediately brings to mind alcohol and drug abuse, but it can also include gambling. In the USA in particular, casinos are widespread and offer not only gambling but a social experience, with organised visits (often sponsored or encouraged by the casinos – see McNeilly and Burke, 2001) by seniors groups a common feature. This means that gambling presents both an attractive and an unattractive face. On the negative side, McNeilly and Burke (2002) report case studies of older adults who had developed gambling problems. A slightly more recent study found that circa 3 per cent of older American adults are gambling at a level probably meriting treatment (Wiebe and Cox, 2005). Also, the more available gambling is, the greater the risk that an older person will develop a gambling habit that places them at least in the at-risk (of developing an addiction) category (Preston, Shapiro and Keene, 2007).[19] However, on the positive side, researchers have reported that, for some older individuals, participating in gambling (visits to casinos, etc.) is a key social activity with no notably negative effects (e.g. Vander Bilt et al., 2004). However, it is easy to overlook that the social side of gambling can, like other addictive behaviours, such as alcohol consumption, mask a serious problem. A study by Southwell, Boreham and Laffan (2008) of electronic gaming machine use in licensed gambling venues in Queensland, Australia, found that older people used the clubs as a social meeting place. Many had no partner and had physical disabilities. However, 27 per cent of those interviewed said that they had drawn on savings to fund their gambling, and the group as a whole had a

---

19 Preston et al. studied a group of people who had retired to Las Vegas – not perhaps the wisest of moves if one wishes to avoid gambling.

low annual income. It does not help matters that older adults with mild cognitive impairment are very poor at making risk judgements in gambling tasks (Zamarian, Weiss and Delazer, 2011).

Even someone with very egalitarian views of ageing would find it hard to imagine older people using psychoactive drugs, but in fact they are heavy consumers of (legitimately prescribed) hypnotic (i.e. sleep inducing) and sedative drugs. Simoni-Wastila and Yang (2006) estimated that one in four of older Americans take drugs that could (at least in theory) be abused and that about 11 per cent actually do so. Misuse (accidental or deliberate) of these drugs is one of the commonest causes for admission to the casualty department/ emergency room of a US hospital (Midlov, Eriksson and Kragh, 2009). In many instances, the reason for this is that the ageing body cannot adequately metabolise the drug in question even when on the dosage schedule prescribed by the doctor, leading to serious health problems, such as delirium. However, an appreciable proportion of older adults are taking prescription sedatives and similar, and have become dependent on them (Midlov *et al.*, 2009). The problem is exacerbated by the fact that patients may be unaware of the risks associated with many psychoactive drugs, reasoning that if a medical professional has prescribed them, then 'they must be all right', and thus, deterioration in, for example, alertness and cognitive abilities is ignored.

However, drug use in older adults is not simply confined to misuse of legal drugs, but involves use of illicit drugs as well. Whilst absolute numbers are not on a par with young adults, nonetheless older drug addicts can be found (see Rosenberg, 1997). It might be intuitively assumed that older addicts form a rump of younger adults who through some medical miracle have survived into old age. Certainly there are such people, and the available evidence suggests that those who have used drugs throughout their lives will not give up their habit with any ease. The concept that older people grow out of drug habits is very wide of the mark (Chait, Fahmy and Caceres, 2010). For example, Levy and Anderson (2005) found that the older drug users they studied (aged 50–68 years) would only give up use of illicit injection drugs for two things – serious illness or death. Such behaviour is likely to lead to imprisonment, either for drug use or for crimes committed to pay for the habit. Arndt, Turvey and Flaum (2002), in a study of US prison inmates, found that 71 per cent of older (defined here as

55 years and over) prisoners had a substance-abuse problem (drugs and/or alcohol) and a third had never received any treatment at all for it. For those older drug users who avoid prison, they may nonetheless find themselves marginalised by the drug-using community, which is predominantly composed of much younger adults (Anderson and Levy, 2003).

This problem is likely to get worse. The ageing 'baby boomers' generation will bring with it a higher amount of drug abuse, not only because of an increase in absolute numbers but also because abuse has not abated amongst drug users of that cohort, as has been the case with earlier generations (Johnson and Sung, 2009). Gfroerer *et al.* (2003) estimated that, in the USA alone, the number of older adults requiring treatment for substance abuse will rise from the 2001 figure of 1.7 million to 4.4 million by 2020. Using more recent data, Han *et al.* (2009) raised the projected figure to 5.7 million.[20]

It is also worth noting that not all drug habits start in youth. For example, Lofwall *et al.* (2005) found that the older drug users in their study (a group of 41 adults aged 50–66 years) had begun using opioid drugs later in life. But this is probably not a case of middle-aged adults suddenly succumbing after a lifetime of drug-free living. Lofwall *et al.* found that the participants had a prior history of other forms of substance abuse and psychiatric problems. Roe *et al.* (2010) reported similar findings, noting that early deaths of friends and family members (leading to isolation) were contributory factors in some cases. Roe *et al.* also noted that there was no single gateway drug that seemed to have led older adults into abuse. Research by Rosen (2004) explains the likely course of events. His study found that amongst older (aged over 50) methadone users, there was a willingness to try other illicit drugs if they were available within their social network. Accordingly, one addictive behaviour can lead to another.

Another common form of substance abuse is excessive alcohol consumption. Generally, it is assumed that alcohol consumption declines in later life. In part, this may be explained by the macabre (but alas accurate) argument that heavier drinkers are likely to die before they reach old age, either through the effects of alcohol or because in general they have led unhealthier lives, thereby accounting for at

---

20 Based on an annual average of 2.8 million illicit drug users aged 50+ in 2002–2006.

least some of these statistics. Nonetheless, over-drinking is still an appreciable problem in later life. It is estimated that circa 5 per cent of older American adults living independently have an alcohol problem (Emlet, Hawks and Callahan, 2001). Hajat *et al.* (2004) report similar data for UK older adults (c. 5% of men and c. 2.5% of older women). In general, studies find that older men are more prone to alcohol abuse than women (e.g. Hallgren, Hogberg and Andreasson, 2010). Emlet *et al.* (2001) found that men were three times more likely to drink than women. Note, however, that precise figures can vary between studies, depending upon the particular culture tested and measurement method used, and may also to some extent be dependent on cohort effects.

Regardless of what percentage of the population have a problem with alcohol, the health risks for alcoholics and heavy drinkers are greater (O'Connell *et al.*, 2003; Weyerer *et al.*, 2009). However, there is a danger that a 'killjoy' attitude can be extrapolated from this, implying that *all* alcohol consumption must have a negative effect in older people. In fact, when drinking variables are controlled for, older adults have fewer behavioural problems than younger drinkers (Livingston and Room, 2009). In many instances, the association between alcohol consumption and illness and injury in later life is not clear-cut (Reid *et al.*, 2002). Indeed, it appears that alcohol consumption can be beneficial for health. McCaul *et al.* (2010) conducted a ten-year longitudinal study and found that moderate daily alcohol intake (up to four units/day for men, two for women) significantly lowered the mortality risk compared with people who did not drink every week. However, it should be noted that those individuals who regularly drank, but abstained from alcohol for one or two days a week had even better mortality rates. This raises the possibility that it is having a relaxed happy lifestyle that matters rather than consuming alcohol *per se*.

Before leaving this section, it is perhaps worth inserting a reality check. Although substance-abuse problems are a serious matter and are undoubtedly growing, they still affect only a small minority of older adults. This should not lessen our level of concern for these people, but it is also worth noting that, amongst healthy older adults, substance abuse is at its lowest for any adult age group (Satre *et al.*, 2004).

Schizophrenia

The final illness to be considered in this chapter is *schizophrenia*. The term means 'cloven mind' in the sense of a broken or fragmented self, rather than the popular misconception of a 'split personality'. In essence, it is a profound disorder of thought, perception and language in the absence of intellectual disability, characterised by a severe distortion of perception of reality and concomitant changes in emotions and behaviour. There are various forms of the illness, each with a distinct set of symptoms. The commonest of these symptoms include irrational beliefs about the way the world functions, often with a central theme that the patient is being persecuted. There may also be hallucinations (such as 'voices in the head'). Language can often be best described as 'surreal', with unusual expressions and ideas, and invented words.

Most commonly, schizophrenia first appears in early adulthood (*early-onset schizophrenia* or EOS), but about a quarter of cases arise in middle age or later (*late-onset schizophrenia* or LOS),[21] and some studies have estimated about a tenth of schizophrenic patients first show symptoms in their 60s or older (see e.g. Bartels and Mueser, 1999). Thus, older schizophrenic patients can be divided into EOS and LOS groups, depending upon the length of time they have had the illness. It would be misleading to create the impression that LOS suddenly appears without warning. Studies often report that LOS patients have led fairly reclusive, undemanding lives, with few social contacts. They have typically been protected either consciously or tacitly by parents or friends, and it is often the death or incapacitation of the latter that triggers the illness (see Quin *et al.*, 2009). In other words, LOS may have been an illness waiting to happen.

There would appear to be little difference in the symptoms found in EOS and LOS (Sponheim *et al.*, 2010). Some early research noted that a disproportionate number of schizophrenic patients develop dementia or at least dementing symptoms (see Arnold and Trojanowski, 1996), but more recent studies have generally failed to find Alzheimer-like atrophy in the brains of older schizophrenic patients (Arnold *et al.*, 1998).

---

21 Some researchers reserve the label of LOS for cases beginning between 40 and 59 years, with cases older than this being labelled very late onset schizophrenia-like psychosis.

Summary

Dementia is not unique to old age, but it is far commoner. Although there are many types of dementia, most are extremely rare, and the majority of patients have Alzheimer's disease, vascular dementia, frontotemporal dementia or Dementia with Lewy bodies. Distinguishing between the dementia types is often very difficult, compounded by the fact that a significant proportion of patients have two types of dementia co-existing. Furthermore, pseudodementia and delirium can also be confused with dementia, and the borderline between dementia and mild cognitive impairment is far from clear. However, as Kitwood's research demonstrated, people with dementia should not be seen as shut off from the everyday world.

It is very important to remember that mental health in later life should not be seen solely in terms of dementia. An assortment of conditions, such as learning disability, depression, anxiety and addiction are all present in later life and each creates problems that are affected by the age of the person. However, it should be recalled that mental illness in older adults is often lower than for the population as a whole. The problems faced by older patients can of course be grave, but, in many instances, evidence points to these not being appreciably worse in themselves than those faced by younger patients with the same illnesses. Of course, contracting a mental illness in later life does not absolve the patient from becoming ill with common age-related physical complaints such as arthritis or hearing impairment, and of course it may be anticipated that these will exacerbate the problem.

Suggested further reading

Woods (1999, 2011) provides an excellent introduction to this area. So do Smyer and Qualls (1999). *Dementia UK* (Alzheimer's Society, 2007) is a good general guide to the prevalence of the dementias and their financial and care costs in the UK. A good general introduction to dementia for the layperson is Graham and Warner (2009). There is a good guide to developmental disability and ageing by O'Brien and Rosenbloom (2009). Tallis and Fillit (2003) is an embarrassment of riches on all matters connected with mental illness in later life as well as physical health. However, some chapters are perhaps a little 'technical' for some readers. More accessible perhaps is Manthorpe and

Iliffe's (2005) book on depression in later life, which also takes a more applied approach that some readers may find useful. Leentjens and van der Mast (2005) provide a useful overview of studies of delirium.

References

Abas, M., Punpuing, S., Jirapramukpitak, T., Guest, P. and Tangchoniatip, K. (2009) Rural-urban migration and depression in ageing family members left behind. *British Journal of Psychiatry, 195,* 54–60.

Abel, T. and Werner, M. (2003) HIV risk behaviour of older persons. *European Journal of Public Health, 13,* 350–2.

Aboderin, I. (2004) Decline in material family support for older people in urban Ghana, Africa: Understanding processes and causes of change. *The Journals of Gerontology Series B: Psychological Sciences and Social Sciences, 59,* 128–37.

Abrams, L., Farrell, M. and Margolin, S. (2010) Older adults' detection of misspellings during reading. *The Journals of Gerontology Series B: Psychological Sciences and Social Sciences, 65,* 680–3.

Adams, C. (1991) Qualitative age differences in memory for text: A life-span developmental perspective. *Psychology and Aging, 6,* 323–36.

Adams, C., Smith, M.C., Pasupathi, M. and Vitolo, L. (2002) Social context effects on story recall in older and younger women: Does the listener make a difference? *The Journals of Gerontology Series B: Psychological Sciences and Social Sciences, 57,* 28–40.

Adams-Price, C. (1992) Eyewitness memory and aging: Predictors of accuracy in recall and person recognition. *Psychology and Aging, 7,* 602–8.

Adkins, G., Martin, P. and Poon, L. (1996) Personality traits and states as predictors of subjective well-being in centenarians, octogenarians and sexagenarians. *Psychology and Aging, 11,* 408–16.

Adrian, J., Postal, V., Moessinger, M., Rascle, N. and Charles, A. (2011) Personality traits and executive functions related to on-road driving performance among older drivers. *Accident Analysis and Prevention, 43,* 1652–9.

Aiken, L.R. (1989) *Later Life.* Hillsdale, NJ: Lawrence Erlbaum.

Aitchison, J. (2007) *The Articulate Mammal: An Introduction to Psycholinguistics.* London: Routledge.

Akiyama, H., Antonucci, T., Takahashi, K. and Langfahl, E.S. (2003) Negative interactions in close relationships across the life span. *The Journals of Gerontology Series B: Psychological Sciences and Social Sciences, 58,* 70–9.

Albert, M.S. (1988) Cognitive function. In M.S. Albert and M.B. Moss (eds) *Geriatric Neuropsychology*. New York, NY: Guilford.

Albert, M.S., Duffy, F.H. and Naeser, M.A. (1987) Nonlinear changes in cognition and their non-psychological correlation. *Canadian Journal of Psychology, 41*, 141–57.

Allemand, M., Zimprich, D. and Hendriks, A. (2008) Age differences in five personality domains across the life span. *Developmental Psychology, 44*, 758–70.

Alpaugh, P.K. and Birren, J.R. (1977) Variables affecting creative contributions across the adult life span. *Human Development, 20*, 240–8.

Alsenany, S. (2009) Student nurses' attitudes and knowledge towards the care of older people in Saudi Arabia. *Generations Review, 19*, 1–9.

Altgassen, M., Kliegel, M., Brandimonte, M. and Filippello, P. (2010) Are older adults more social than younger adults? Social importance increases older adults' prospective memory performance. *Aging, Neuropsychology and Cognition, 17*, 312–28.

Alzheimer's Society (2007) *Dementia UK*. London: Alzheimer's Society.

American Psychiatric Association (2013) *Diagnostic and Statistical Manual of Mental Disorders* (5th edn). Arlington, VA: American Psychiatric Association.

Anderson, T.L. and Levy, J.A. (2003) Marginality among older injectors in today's illicit drug culture: Assessing the impact of ageing. *Addiction, 98*, 761–70.

Andreescu, C., Mulsant, B., Houck, P., Whyte, E. *et al.* (2008) Empirically derived decision trees for the treatment of late-life depression. *American Journal of Psychiatry, 165*, 855–62.

Ardelt, M. (1998) Social crisis and individual growth: The long-term effects of the Great Depression. *Journal of Aging Studies, 12*, 291–314.

Ardelt, M. (2010) Are older adults wiser than college students? A comparison of two age cohorts. *Journal of Adult Development, 17*, 193–207.

Ardelt, M. and Jacobs, S. (2009) Wisdom, integrity, and life satisfaction in very old age. In M. Smith and N. DeFrates-Densch (eds) *Handbook of Research on Adult Learning and Human Development*. New York, NY: Routledge.

Arenberg, D. (1982) Changes with age in problem solving. In F.M. Craik and A.S. Trehub (eds) *Aging and Cognitive Processes*. New York, NY: Plenum.

Arias-Castillo, L., Ceballos-Osorio, J., Ochoa, J. and Reyes-Ortiz, C. (2009) Correlates of sexuality in men and women aged 52–90 years attending a university medical health service in Colombia. *Journal of Sexual Medicine, 6*, 3008–18.

Arndt, S., Turvey, C.L. and Flaum, M. (2002) Older offenders, substance abuse and treatment. *American Journal of Geriatric Psychiatry, 10*, 733–40.

Arnold, S.E. and Trojanowski, J.Q. (1996) Cognitive impairment in elderly schizophrenia: A dementia (still) lacking distinctive histopathology. *Schizophrenia Bulletin, 22*, 5–9.

Arnold, S.E., Trojanowski, J.Q., Gur, R.E., Blackwell, P., Han, L. and Choi, C. (1998) Absence of neurodegeneration and neural injury in the cerebral cortex in a sample of elderly patients with schizophrenia. *Archives of General Psychiatry, 55*, 225–32.

Austad, S.N. (2006) Why women live longer than men: Sex differences in longevity. *Gender Medicine, 3*, 79–92.

Ayalon, L. and King-Kallimanis, B. (2010) Trading years for perfect health: Results from the health and retirement study *Journal of Aging and Health, 22*, 1184–97.

Bäckman, L. and Nyberg, L. (2010) Dopamine, cognition, and human aging: New evidence and ideas. In L. Bäckman and L. Nyberg (eds) *Memory, Aging and the Brain: A Festschrift in Honour of Lars-Göran Nilsson*. New York, NY: Psychology Press.

Baddeley, A., Eysenck, M. and Anderson, M. (2009) *Memory*. New York, NY: Psychology Press.

Baddeley, A.D. (1983) *Your Memory: A User's Guide*. London: Penguin.

Baddeley, A.D. (1986) *Working Memory*. Oxford: Oxford Scientific Publications.

Baddeley, A.D. and Hitch, G. (1974) Working memory. In G.H. Bower (ed.) *Attention and Performance VI*. New York, NY: Academic Press.

Bailey, H., Dunlosky, J. and Hertzog, C. (2009) Does differential strategy use account for age-related deficits in working memory performance? *Psychology and Aging, 24*, 82–92.

Baldwin, C. and Capstick, A. (eds) (2007) *Tom Kitwood on Dementia: A Reader and Critical Commentary*. Maidenhead: McGraw Hill/Open University Press.

Ballard, C. and Aarsland, D. (2009) Person-centred care and care mapping in dementia. *The Lancet Neurology, 8*, 302–3.

Baltes, M. (1996) *The Many Faces of Dependency in Old Age*. New York, NY: Cambridge University Press.

Baltes, M. and Wahl, H.W. (1996) Patterns of communication in old age: The dependence-support and independence-ignore script. *Health Communication, 8*, 217–31.

Baltes, P.B. and Baltes, M.M. (1990) Psychological perspectives on successful aging: The model of selective optimization with compensation. In P.B. Baltes and M.M. Baltes (eds) *Successful Aging: Perspectives from the Behavioral Sciences*. Cambridge: Cambridge University Press.

Baltes, P.B. and Staudinger, U.M. (2000) Wisdom: A metaheuristic (pragmatic) to orchestrate mind and virtue toward excellence. *American Psychologist, 55*, 122–36.

Banning, M. (2007) Medication review for the older person. *Reviews in Clinical Gerontology, 17*, 25–32.

Barefoot, J.C. Beckham, J.C., Haney, T.L., Siegler, I.C. and Lipkus, I.M. (1993) Age differences in hostility among middle-aged and older adults. *Psychology and Aging, 8*, 3–9.

Barnes, L.L., Mendes de Leon, C.F., Bienias, J.L. and Evans, D.A. (2004) A longitudinal study of black–white differences in social resources. *The Journals of Gerontology Series B: Psychological Sciences and Social Sciences, 59*, 146–53.

Baron, A. and Banaji, M. (2006) The development of implicit attitudes: Evidence of race evaluations from ages 6 to 10 and adulthood. *Psychological Science, 17*, 1, 53–58.

Bartels, S.J. and Mueser, K.T. (1999) Severe mental illness in older adults: Schizophrenia and other late-life psychoses. In M.A. Smyer and S.H. Qualls (eds) *Aging and Mental Health* (pp.182–207). Oxford: Blackwell.

Bartlett, F.C. (1932) *Remembering*. Cambridge: Cambridge University Press.

Basso, M.R., Schefft, B.K. and Hamsher, K. (2005) Aging and remote memory declines: Preliminary findings. *Aging Neuropsychology and Cognition, 12*, 175–86.

Baum, S.R. (1993) Processing of center-embedded and right-branching relative clause sentences by normal elderly individuals. *Applied Psycholinguistics, 14*, 75–88.

Beardsall, L. (1998) Development of the Cambridge Contextual Reading Test for improving the estimation of premorbid verbal intelligence in older persons with dementia. *British Journal of Clinical Psychology, 37*, 229–40.

Becker, G., Beyene, Y., Newsom, E. and Mayen, N. (2003) Creating continuity through mutual assistance: Intergenerational reciprocity in four ethnic groups. *The Journals of Gerontology Series B: Psychological Sciences and Social Sciences, 58*, 151–9.

Beckman, A., Parker, M. and Thorslund, M. (2005) Can elderly people take their medicine? *Patient Education and Counselling, 59*, 186–91.

Bekris, L., Galloway, N., Millard, S., Lockhart, D. *et al.* (2011) Amyloid precursor protein (APP) processing genes and cerebrospinal fluid APP cleavage product levels in Alzheimer's disease. *Neurobiology of Aging, 32*, 13–23.

Bell, D., Turnbull, A. and Kidd, W. (2009) Differential diagnosis of dementia in the field of learning disabilities: A case study. *British Journal of Learning Disabilities, 37*, 56–65.

Bell, L.J. (1980) *The Large Print Book and Its User*. London: Library Association.

Belmont, J.M., Freeseman, L.J. and Mitchell, D.W. (1988) Memory and problem solving: The cases of young and elderly adults. In M.M. Gruneberg, P.E. Morris and R.N. Sykes (eds) *Practical Aspects of Memory: Current Research and Issues, Volume 2*. Chichester: Wiley.

Benbow, S., Kingston, P., Bhaumik, S., Black, S. *et al.* (2011) The interface between learning disability and old age psychiatry: Two specialities travelling alone or travelling together? *Mental Health Review Journal, 16*, 25–35.

Bengston, U.L. and Treas, J. (1980) The changing family context of mental health and aging. In J.E. Birren and B. Sloane (eds) *Handbook of Mental Health and Aging*. Englewood Cliffs, NJ: Prentice Hall.

Bennett, D.J. and McEvoy, C.L. (1999) Mediated priming in younger and older adults. *Experimental Aging Research, 25*, 141–59.

Bennett, K.M. (2002) Low level social engagement as a precursor of mortality among people in later life. *Age and Ageing, 31*, 165–8.

Bent, N., Rabbitt, P. and Metcalfe (2000) Diabetes mellitus and the rate of cognitive ageing. *British Journal of Clinical Psychology, 39*, 349–63.

Berg, L. (1988) Mild senile dementia of the Alzheimer type: Diagnostic criteria and natural history. *Mount Sinai Journal of Medicine, 55*, 87–96.

Berntsen, D. and Rubin, D.C. (2002) Emotionally charged autobiographical memories across the life span: The recall of happy, sad, traumatic and involuntary memories. *Psychology and Aging, 17*, 636–52.

Birren, J.E. and Fisher, L.M. (1995) Aging and speed of behavior: Possible consequences for psychological functioning. *Annual Review of Psychology, 46*, 329–53.

Black, H.K. and Rubinstein, R.L. (2004) Themes of suffering in later life. *The Journals of Gerontology Series B: Psychological Sciences and Social Sciences, 59*, 17–24.

Blackburn, J.A. and Papalia, D.E. (1992) The study of adult cognition from a Piagetian perspective. In R.J. Sternberg and C. Berg (eds) *Intellectual Development.* Cambridge: Cambridge University Press.

Blelak, A.A.M., Hultsch, D.F., Strauss, E., MacDonald, S.W.S. and Hunter, M.A. (2010) Intraindividual variability is related to cognitive change in older adults: Evidence for within-person coupling. *Psychology and Aging, 25*, 575–86.

Blessed, G., Tomlinson, B.E. and Roth, M. (1968) The association between quantitative measures of dementia and senile changes in the cerebral grey matter of elderly subjects. *British Journal of Psychiatry, 114*, 797–811.

Blow, F.C. and Oslin, D.W. (2003) Late-life addictions. *Geriatric Psychiatry, 22*, 111–43.

Boekamp, J.R., Strauss, M.E. and Adams, N. (1995) Estimating premorbid intelligence in African-American and White elderly veterans using the American version of the National Adult Reading Test. *Journal of Clinical and Experimental Neuropsychology, 17*, 645–53.

Bohnen, N.I., Kaufer, D.I., Hendrickson, R., Ivanco, L.S. *et al.* (2005) Cognitive correlates of alterations in acetylcholinesterase in Alzheimer's disease. *Neuroscience Letters, 380*, 127–32.

Bookwala, J., Harralson, T.L. and Parmelee, P.A. (2003) Effects of pain on functioning and well-being in older adults with osteoarthritis of the knee. *Psychology and Aging, 18*, 844–50.

Bopp, K.L. and Verhaeghen, P. (2005) Aging and verbal memory span: A meta-analysis. *The Journals of Gerontology Series B: Psychological Sciences and Social Sciences, 60*, 223–33.

Bouchard Ryan, E., Anas A.P., Beamer, M. and Bajorek, S. (2003) Coping with age-related vision loss in everyday reading activities. *Educational Gerontology, 29*, 37–54.

Bowles, N.L. and Poon, L.W. (1981) The effect of age on speed of lexical access. *Experimental Aging Research, 7*, 417–25.

Bowles, N.L. and Poon, L.W. (1985) Aging and retrieval of words in semantic memory. *Journal of Gerontology, 40*, 71–7.

Bowles, R.P. and Salthouse, T.A. (2003) Assessing the age-related effects of proactive interference on working memory tasks using the Rasch model. *Psychology and Aging, 18*, 608–15.

Bowling, A. and Stenner, P. (2011) Which measure of quality of life performs best in older age? A comparison of the OPQOL, CASP-19 and WHOQOL-OLD. *Journal of Epidemiology and Community Health, 65*, 273–80.

Braskie, M., Klunder, A., Hayashi, K., Protas, H. *et al.* (2010) Plaque and tangle imaging and cognition in normal aging and Alzheimer's disease. *Neurobiology of Aging, 31*, 1669–78.

Brébion, G., Smith, M.J. and Ehrlich, M.F. (1997) Working memory and aging: Deficit or strategy differences. *Aging, Neuropsychology and Cognition, 4*, 58–73.

Brickell, K., Leverenz, J., Steinbart, E., Rumbaugh, M. and Schallenberg, G. (2007) Clinicopathological concordance and discordance in three monozygotic twin pairs with familial Alzheimer's disease. *Journal of Neurology, Neurosurgery and Psychiatry, 78*, 1050–55.

Brinley, J.F. (1965) Cognitive sets, speed and accuracy in the elderly. In A.T. Welford and J.E. Birren (eds) *Behavior, Aging and the Nervous System*. New York, NY: Springer.

Bromley, D.B. (1958) Some effects of age on short-term learning and memory. *Journal of Gerontology, 13*, 398–406.

Bromley, D.B. (1988) *Human Ageing. An Introduction to Gerontology* (3rd edn). Harmondsworth: Penguin.

Brown, R. (2010) Broadening the search for safe treatments in dementia agitation: A possible role for low-dose opioids? *International Journal of Geriatric Psychiatry, 25*, 1085–6.

Brown, R. and McNeill, D. (1966) The 'tip-of-the-tongue' phenomenon. *Journal of Verbal Learning and Verbal Behavior, 5*, 325–37.

Brown, S. and Kawamura, S. (2010) Relationship quality among cohabitors and marrieds in older adulthood. *Social Science Research, 39*, 777–86.

Brown, S.L., Roebuck Bulanda, J. and Lee, G.R. (2005) The significance of nonmarital cohabitation: Marital status and mental health benefits among middle-aged and older adults. *The Journals of Gerontology Series B: Psychological Sciences and Social Sciences, 60*, 21–9.

Bryant, C. (2010) Anxiety and depression in old age: Challenges in recognition and diagnosis. *International Psychogeriatrics, 22*, 511–13.

Bucks, R., Scott, M.I., Pearsall, T. and Ashworth, D.L. (1996) The short NART: Utility in a memory disorders clinic. *British Journal of Clinical Psychology, 35*, 133–141.

Bunce, D.J., Barrowclough, A. and Morris, I. (1996) The moderating influence of physical fitness on age gradients in vigilance and serial choice responding tasks. *Psychology and Aging, 11*, 671–82.

Burke, D.M., Worthley, J. and Martin, J. (1988) I'll never forget what's-her-name: Aging and tip of the tongue experiences in everyday life. In M.M. Gruneberg, P.E. Morris and R.N. Sykes (eds) *Practical Aspects of Memory: Current Research and Issues*. Chichester: Wiley.

Burns, A. (1995) Cause of death in dementia. In E. Murphy and G. Alexopoulos (ed.) *Geriatric Psychiatry: Key Research Topics for Clinicians* (pp.95–101). Chichester: Wiley.

Burns, A. (2006) *Severe Dementia*. New York, NY: Wiley.

Burns, A., Allen, H., Tomenson, B., Duignan, D. and Byrne, J. (2009) Bright light therapy for agitation in dementia: A randomized controlled trial. *International Psychogeriatrics, 21,* 711–21.

Butler, R.N. (1967) *Creativity in Old Age.* New York, NY: Plenum.

Byrd, M. (1985) Age differences in the ability to recall and summarise textual information. *Experimental Aging Research, 11,* 87–91.

Cabeza, R. (2002) Hemispheric asymmetry reduction in old adults: The HAROLD model. *Psychology and Aging, 17,* 85–100.

Caine, E.D., Lyness, J.M., King, D.A. and Connors, B.A. (1994) Clinical and etiological heterogeneity of mood disorders in elderly patients. In L.S. Schneider, C.F. Reynolds, B.D. Lebowitz and A.J. Friedhoff (eds) *Diagnosis and Treatment of Depression in Late Life* (pp.25–53). Washington, DC: American Psychological Association.

Camp, C.J. (1988) Utilisation of world knowledge systems. In L.W. Poon, D.G. Rubin and B.A. Wilson (eds) *Everyday Cognition in Adulthood and Later Life.* Cambridge: Cambridge University Press.

Capone, J., Della Sala, S., Spinnler, H. and Venneri, A. (2003) Upper and lower face and ideomotor apraxia in patients with Alzheimer's disease. *Behavioural Neurology, 14,* 1–8.

Carlson, L.E., Sherwin, B.B. and Chertkow, H.M. (2000) Relationships between mood and estradiol (E2) levels in Alzheimer's disease (AD) patients. *The Journals of Gerontology Series B: Psychological Sciences and Social Sciences, 55,* 47–53.

Carp, J., Gmeindl, L. and Reuter-Lorenz, P. (2010) Age differences in the neural representation of working memory revealed by multi-voxel pattern analysis. *Frontiers in Human Neuroscience, 4,* 217–30.

Carreon, D. and Noymer, A. (2011) Health-related quality of life in older adults: Testing the double jeopardy hypothesis. *Journal of Aging Studies, 25,* 371–9.

Carretti, B., Borella, E. and De Beni, R. (2007) Does strategic memory training improve the working memory performance of younger and older adults? *Experimental Psychology, 54,* 311–20.

Caspi, A., Roberts, B.W. and Shiner, R.L. (2005) Personality development: Stability and change. *Annual Review of Psychology, 56,* 453–84.

Castelo-Branco, C., Palacios, S., Ferrer-Barriendos, J. and Alberich, X. (2010) Do patients lie? An open interview vs. a blind questionnaire on sexuality. *Journal of Sexual Medicine, 7,* 873–80.

Cerella, J. (1985) Information processing rate in the elderly. *Psychological Bulletin, 98,* 67–83.

Cerella, J. (1990) Aging and information-processing rate. In J.E. Birren and K.W. Schaie (eds) *Handbook of the Psychology of Aging* (3rd edn). San Diego, CA: Academic Press.

Cerella, J. and Fozard, J.L. (1984) Lexical access and age. *Developmental Psychology, 20,* 235–43.

Cervera, T., Soier, M., Dasi, C. and Ruiz, J. (2009) Speech recognition and working memory capacity in young-elderly listeners: Effects of hearing sensitivity. *Canadian Journal of Experimental Psychology, 63*, 216–26.

Chait, R., Fahmy, S. and Caceres, J. (2010) Cocaine abuse in older adults: An underscreened cohort. *Journal of the American Geriatrics Society, 58*, 391–2.

Chapman, B., Duberstein, P., Sorensen, S., Lyness, J. and Emery, L. (2006) Personality and perceived health in older adults: The five factor model in primary care. *The Journals of Gerontology Series B: Psychological Sciences and Social Sciences, 61*, 362–5.

Chapman, B., Lyness, J, and Duberstein, P. (2007) Personality and medical illness burden among older adults in primary care. *Psychosomatic Medicine, 69*, 277–82.

Chapman, B., Shah, M., Friedman, B., Drayer, R. *et al.* (2009) Personality traits predict emergency department utilization over 3 years in older patients. *American Journal of Geriatric Psychiatry, 17*, 526–35.

Charlton, R.A., Barrick, T.R., Markus, H.S. and Morris, R.G. (2010) The relationship between episodic long-term memory and white matter integrity in normal aging. *Neuropsychologia, 48*, 114–22.

Charlton, R.A., Landau, S., Schiavone, F., Barrick, T. *et al.* (2008) A structural equation modeling investigation of age-related variance in executive function and DTI measured white matter damage. *Neurobiology of Aging, 29*, 1547–55.

Charness, N. (1979) Components of skill in bridge. *Canadian Journal of Psychology, 133*, 1–16.

Charness, N. (1981) Aging and skilled problem solving. *Journal of Experimental Psychology: General, 110*, 21–38.

Charness, N., Kelley, C.L., Bosman, E.A. and Mottram, M. (2001) Word-processing training and retraining: Effects of adult age, experience and interface. *Psychology and Aging, 16*, 110–27.

Chen, S. (2008) Reading practices and profiles of older adults in Taiwan. *Educational Gerontology, 34*, 428–42.

Chertkow, H., Massoud, F., Nasreddine, Z., Belleville, S. *et al.* (2009) Diagnosis and treatment of dementia: 3. Mild cognitive impairment and cognitive impairment without dementia. *Focus, 7*, 64–78.

Chipperfield, J.G. and Havens, B. (2001) Gender differences in the relationship between marital status transitions and life satisfaction in later life. *The Journals of Gerontology Series B: Psychological Sciences and Social Sciences, 56*, 176–86.

Cho, H., Lavretsky, H., Olmstead, R., Levin, M. and Oxman, M. (2008) Sleep disturbance and depression recurrence in community-dwelling older adults: A prospective study. *American Journal of Psychiatry, 165*, 1543–50.

Christianson, K., Williams, C., Zacks, R. and Ferreira, F. (2006) Younger and older adults' 'good enough' interpretations of garden-path sentences. *Discourse Processes, 42*, 205–38.

Clark, L., Gatz, M., Zheng, L., Chen, Y. *et al.* (2009) Longitudinal verbal fluency in normal aging, preclinical, and prevalent Alzheimer's disease. *American Journal of Alzheimer's Disease and Other Dementias, 24*, 461–8.

Clarke, P. and Smith, J. (2011) Aging in a cultural context: Cross-national differences in disability and the moderating role of personal control among older adults in the United States and England. *The Journals of Gerontology Series B: Psychological Sciences and Social Sciences, 66,* 457–67.

Cockburn, J. and Smith, P.T. (1988) Effects of age and intelligence on everyday memory tasks. In M.M. Gruneberg, P.E. Morris and R.N. Sykes (eds) *Practical Aspects of Memory: Current Research and Issues.* Chichester: Wiley.

Coghlan, A. (2011) Curtain falls on mad cow disease. *New Scientist, 209,* 6–7.

Cohen, G. (1988) Age differences in memory for texts: Production deficiency of processing limitations? In D.M. Burke and L.L. Light (eds) *Language, Memory and Aging.* New York, NY: Cambridge University Press.

Cohen, G. (1989) *Memory in the Real World.* Hove: Lawrence Erlbaum.

Cohen, G. and Faulkner, D. (1988) Life span changes in autobiographical memory. In M.M. Gruneberg, P.E. Morris and R.N. Sykes (eds) *Practical Aspects of Memory: Current Research and Issues, Volume 2.* Chichester: Wiley.

Cohen, G. and Faulkner, D. (1989) The effects of aging on perceived and generated memories. In L.W. Poon, D.C. Rubin and B.A. Wilson (eds) *Everyday Cognition in Later Life.* Cambridge: Cambridge University Press.

Cohen-Mansfield, J. (2007) Temporal patterns of agitation in dementia. *American Journal of Geriatric Psychiatry, 15,* 395–405.

Coleman, P.G. and O'Hanlon, A. (2004) *Ageing and Development: Theories and Research.* London: Arnold.

Collinge, J., Whitfield, J., McKintosh, E., Frosh, A. *et al.* (2008) A clinical study of kuru patients with long incubation periods at the end of the epidemic in Papua New Guinea. *Philosophical Transactions of the Royal Society B: Biological Sciences, 363,* 3725–39.

Cong, Y.S., Wright, W.E. and Shay, J.W. (2002) Human telomerase and its regulation. *Microbiology and Molecular Biology Review, 66,* 407–25.

Connor, L.T., Spiro, A., Obler, L.K. and Albert, M.L. (2004) Change in object naming ability during adulthood. *The Journals of Gerontology Series B: Psychological Sciences and Social Sciences, 59,* 203–9.

Continuous Mortality Investigation (2006a) *The Graduation of the CMI 1999-2002 Mortality Experience: Final '00' Series Mortality Tables – Assured Lives.* Working Paper 21 (a).

Continuous Mortality Investigation (2006b) *The Graduation of the CMI 1999-2002 Mortality Experience: Final '00' Series Mortality Tables – Annuitants and Pensioner.* Working Paper 22 (b).

Conway, S.C. and O'Carroll, R.E. (1997) An evaluation of the Cambridge Contextual Reading Test (CCRT) in Alzheimer's disease. *British Journal of Clinical Psychology, 36,* 623–5.

Cordingly, L. and Webb, C. (1997) Independence and aging. *Reviews in Clinical Gerontology, 7,* 137–46.

Cornman, J.C., Lynch, S.M., Goldman, N., Weinstein, M. and Lin, H.S. (2004) Stability and change in the perceived social support of older Taiwanese adults. *The Journals of Gerontology Series B: Psychological Sciences and Social Sciences 59*, 350–7.

Corrada, M., Brookmeyer, R., Paganini-Hill, A., Berlau, D. and Kawas, C. (2010) Dementia incidence continues to increase with age in the oldest old: The 90+ study. *Annals of Neurology, 67*, 114–21.

Cosentino, S., Manly, J. and Mungas, D. (2007) Do reading tests measure the same construct in multiethnic and multilingual older persons? *Journal of the International Neuropsychological Society, 13*, 228–36.

Costa, P.T. and McCrae, R.R. (1980) Still stable after all these years: Personality as a key to some issues of adulthood and old age. In P.B. Baltes and G.G. Brim (eds) *Life-span Development and Behaviour, Volume 3*. New York, NY: Academic Press.

Costa, P.T. and McCrae, R.R. (1982) An approach to the attribution of aging: Period and cohort effects. *Psychological Bulletin, 92*, 238–50.

Cottle, N. and Glover, R. (2007) Combating ageism: Change in student knowledge and attitudes regarding aging. *Educational Gerontology, 33*, 501–12.

Coupland, N., Coupland, J. and Giles, H. (1991) *Language, Society and the Elderly*. Oxford: Blackwell.

Coxon, P. and Valentine, T. (1997) The effects of the age of eyewitnesses on the accuracy and suggestibility of their testimony. *Applied Cognitive Psychology, 11*, 415–30.

Craik, F.I.M. (1977) Age differences in human memory. In J.E. Birren and K.W. Schaie (eds) *Handbook of the Psychology of Aging*. New York, NY: Van Nostrand Reinhold.

Craik, F.I.M. and Jennings, J.M. (1992) Human memory. In F.I.M. Craik and T.A. Salthouse (eds) *The Handbook of Aging and Cognition*. Hillsdale, NJ: Lawrence Erlbaum.

Craik, F.I.M. and Rabinowitz, J.C. (1984) Age differences in the acquisition and use of verbal information. In H. Bouma and D. Bouwhuis (eds) *Attention and Performance X: Control of Language Processes*. Hillsdale, NJ: Erlbaum, 471–99.

Craik, F.I.M. and Salthouse, T.A. (eds) (2008) *The Handbook of Aging and Cognition* (3rd edn). New York, NY: Psychology Press.

Craik, F.I.M., Anderson, N.D., Kerr, S.A. and Li, K.Z.H. (1995) Memory changes in normal ageing. In A.D. Baddeley, B.A. Wilson and F.N. Watts (eds) *Handbook of Memory Disorders* (pp.211–42). Chichester: Wiley.

Cramer, P. (2003) Personality change in later adulthood is predicted by defense mechanism use in early adulthood. *Journal of Research in Personality, 37*, 76–104.

Crawford, J.R., Stewart, L.E., Garthwaite, P.H., Parker, D.M. and Bessan, J.A.O. (1988) The relationship between demographic variables and NART performance in normal subjects. *British Journal of Clinical Psychology, 27*, 181–2.

Crook, T.H. and West, R.L. (1990) Name recall performance across the adult life span. *British Journal of Psychology, 81*, 335–49.

Crowley, K., Mayer, P. and Stuart-Hamilton, I. (2009) Changes in reliance on reading and spelling subskills across the lifespan. *Educational Gerontology, 35*, 503–22.

Cruz-Jentoft, A.J., Franco, A., Sommer, P., Baeyens, J.P. *et al.* (2008) European silver paper on the future of health promotion and preventive actions, basic research, and clinical aspects of age-related disease. *Gerontechnology, 7,* 331–9.

Cumming, E. and Henry, W.E. (1961) *Growing Old.* New York, NY: Basic Books.

Cunningham, W.R. and Brookbank, J.W. (1988) *Gerontology: The Psychology, Biology and Sociology of Ageing.* New York, NY: Harper and Row.

Dahlin, E., Backman, L., Neely, A. and Nyberg, L. (2009) Training of the executive component of working memory: Subcortical areas mediate transfer effects. *Restorative Neurology and Neuroscience, 27,* 405–19.

Davies, E. and Cartwright, S. (2011) Psychological and psychosocial predictors of attitudes to working past normal retirement age. *Employee Relations, 33,* 249–68.

Davys, D. and Haigh, C. (2008) Older parents of people who have a learning disability: Perceptions of future accommodation needs. *British Journal of Learning Disabilities, 36,* 66–72.

De Beni, R., Borella, E. and Carretti, B. (2007) Reading comprehension in aging: The role of working memory and metacomprehension. *Aging, Neuropsychology and Cognition, 14,* 189–212.

De Bot, K. and Makoni, S. (2005) *Language and Aging in Multilingual Contexts.* Clevedon: Cromwell Press.

De Jong Gierveld, J., Marjolein van Groenou, B., Hoogendoorn, A. and Smit, J. (2009) Quality of marriages in later life and emotional and social loneliness. *The Journals of Gerontology Series B: Psychological Sciences and Social Sciences, 64,* 497–506.

de Magalhaes, J.P. (2011) The biology of ageing: A primer. In I. Stuart-Hamilton (ed.) *An Introduction to Gerontology.* Cambridge: Cambridge University Press.

de Vaus, D., Wells, Y., Kendig, H. and Quine, S. (2007) Does gradual retirement have better outcomes than abrupt retirement? Results from an Australian panel study. *Ageing and Society, 27,* 667–82.

Deary, I.J. (2001) *Intelligence: A Very Short Introduction.* Oxford: Oxford University Press.

Deary, I.J. and Der, G. (2005) Reaction time, age, and cognitive ability: Longitudinal findings from age 16 to 63 years in representative population samples. *Aging, Neuropsychology, and Cognition, 12,* 187–215.

Deary, I.J., Johnson, W. and Starr, J. (2010) Are processing speed tasks biomarkers of cognitive aging? *Psychology and Aging, 25,* 219–28.

Deary, I.J., Whalley, L.J., Lemmon, H., Crawford, J.R. and Starr, J.M. (2000) The stability of individual differences in mental ability from childhood to old age: Follow-up of the 1932 Scottish Mental Survey. *Intelligence, 28,* 49–55.

Dehon, H. and Brédart, S. (2004) False memories: Young and older adults think of semantic associates at the same rate, but young adults are more successful at source monitoring. *Psychology and Aging, 19,* 191–7.

DeLamater, J.D. and Sill, M. (2005) Sexual desire in later life. *Journal of Sex Research, 42,* 138–49.

Delbaere, K., Crombez, G., Vanderstraeten, G., Willems, T. and Cambier, D. (2004) Fear-related avoidance of activities, falls and physical frailty. A prospective community-based cohort study. *Age and Aging, 33,* 368–73.

Dellenbach, M. and Zimprich, D. (2008) Typical intellectual engagement and cognition in old age. *Aging, Neuropsychology and Cognition, 15,* 208–31.

Dennerstein, L., Alexander, J.L. and Kotz, K. (2003) The menopause and sexual functioning: A review of the population-based studies. *Annual Review of Sex Research, 14,* 64–83.

Denney, D.R. and Denney, N.W. (1974) Modelling effects on the questioning strategies of the elderly. *Developmental Psychology, 10,* 458.

Denney, N.W. (1974) Evidence for developmental changes in categorization criteria for children and adults. *Human Development, 17,* 41–53.

DePaola, S.J., Griffin, M., Young, J.R. and Neimeyer, R.A. (2003) Death anxiety and attitudes toward the elderly among older adults: The role of gender and ethnicity. *Death Studies, 27,* 335–54.

Dijkstra, K. and Misirlisoy, M. (2009) Recognition accuracy for original and altered verbal memory reports in older adults. *Quarterly Journal of Experimental Psychology, 62,* 248–56.

Dixon, R.A., Kurzman, D. and Friesen, I.C. (1993) Handwriting performance in younger and older adults: Age, familiarity and practice effects. *Psychology and Aging, 8,* 360–70.

Dodge, H., Chang, C., Kamboh, I. and Ganguli, M. (2011) Risk of Alzheimer's disease incidence attributable to vascular disease in the population. *Alzheimer's and Dementia, 7,* 356–60.

Douglass, C., Keddie, A., Brooker, D. and Surr, C. (2010) Cross-cultural comparison of the perceptions and experiences of dementia care mapping 'mappers' in the United States and the United Kingdom. *Journal of Aging and Health, 22,* 567–88.

Druley, J.A., Stephens, M.A.P., Martire, L.M., Ennis, N. and Wojno, W.C. (2003) Emotional congruence in older couples coping with wives' osteoarthritis: Exacerbating effects of pain behavior. *Psychology and Aging, 18,* 406–14.

Duberstein, P., Chapman, B., Tindle, H., Sink, K. *et al.* (2011) Personality and risk for Alzheimer's disease in adults 72 years of age and older: A 6-year follow-up. *Psychology and Aging, 26,* 351–62.

Duerson, M., Thomas, J., Chang, J. and Stevens, C.B. (1992) Medical students' knowledge and misconceptions about aging: Responses to Palmore's Facts on Aging quizzes. *The Gerontologist, 32,* 171–174.

Duggan, L., Lewis, M. and Morgan, J. (1996) Behavioural changes in people with learning disability and dementia: A descriptive study. *Journal of Intellectual Disability Research, 40,* 311–21.

Duñabeitia, J.A., Marín, A., Avilés, A., Perea, M. and Carreiras, M. (2009) Constituent priming effects: Evidence for preserved morphological processing in healthy old readers. *European Journal of Cognitive Psychology, 21,* 283–302.

Dunning, T. (2009) Aging, activities, and the internet. *Activities, Adaptation and Aging, 33,* 120–1.

Earles, J.L., Kersten, A.W., Mas, B.B. and Miccio, D.M. (2004) Aging and memory for self-performed tasks: Effects of task difficulty and time pressure. *The Journals of Gerontology Series B: Psychological Sciences and Social Sciences, 59*, 285–93.

Edvardsson, D. and Innes, A. (2010) Measuring person-centered care: A critical comparative review of published tools. *The Gerontologist, 50*, 834–46.

Egolf, B., Lasker, J., Wolf, S. and Potvin, L. (1992) The Roseto effect: A 50-year comparison of mortality rates. *American Journal of Public Health, 82*, 1089–92.

Eichenbaum, H. (2003) How does the hippocampus contribute to memory? *Trends in Cognitive Science, 7*, 427–9.

Eisdorfer, C., Cohen, D. and Paveza, G.J. (1992) An empirical evaluation of the Global Deterioration Scale for staging Alzheimer's disease. *American Journal of Psychiatry, 149*, 190–4.

Elias, J. and Ryan, A. (2011) A review and commentary on the factors that influence expressions of sexuality by older people in care homes. *Journal of Clinical Nursing, 20*, 11–20.

Ellison, C., Burdette, A. and Hill, T. (2009) Blessed assurance: Religion, anxiety and tranquility among US adults. *Social Science Research, 38*, 656–67.

Elmstahl, S., Sommer, M. and Hagberg, B. (1996) A 3-year follow-up of stroke patients: Relationships between activities of daily living and personality characteristics. *Archives of Gerontology and Geriatrics, 22*, 233–44.

Elwood, P.C., Gallacher, J.E.J., Hopkinson, C.A., Pickering, J. *et al.* (1999) Smoking, drinking and other life style factors and cognitive function in men in the Caerphilly cohort. *Journal of Epidemiology and Community Health, 53*, 9–15.

Elwood, P.C., Pickering, J., Bayer, A. and Gallacher, J.E.J. (2002) Vascular disease and cognitive function in older men in the Caerphilly cohort. *Age and Ageing, 31*, 43–8.

Emlet, C.A. (2004) HIV/AIDS and aging: A diverse population of vulnerable older adults. *Journal of Human Behavior in the Social Environment, 9*, 45–63.

Emlet, C.A., Hawks, H. and Callahan, J. (2001) Alcohol use and abuse in a population of community dwelling, frail older adults. *Journal of Gerontological Social Work, 35*, 21–33.

Erikson, E.H. (1982) *The Life Cycle Completed: A Review*. New York, NY: Norton.

Erten-Lyons, D., Woltjer, R., Dodge, H., Nixon, R. *et al.* (2009) Factors associated with resistance to dementia despite high Alzheimer disease pathology. *Neurology, 72*, 354–60.

Eysenck, H.J. (1952) The effects of psychotherapy: An evaluation. *Journal of Consulting Psychology, 16*, 319–24.

Eysenck. H.J. (1987) Personality and ageing: An exploratory analysis. *Journal of Social Behaviour and Personality, 3*, 11–21.

Eysenck, H.J. and Eysenck, M.W. (1985) *Personality and Individual Differences: A Natural Science Approach*. New York, NY: Plenum.

Farias, S., Mungas, D., Hinton, L. and Haan, M. (2011) Demographic, neuropsychological, and functional predictors of rate of longitudinal cognitive decline in Hispanic older adults. *American Journal of Geriatric Psychiatry, 19*, 440–50.

Fay, S., Isingrini, M. and Clarys, D. (2005) Effects of depth-of-processing and ageing on word-stem and word-fragment implicit memory tasks: Test of the lexical-processing hypothesis. *European Journal of Cognitive Psychology, 17, 6*, 785–802.

Ferrario, C., Freeman, F., Nellett, G. and Scheel, J. (2008) Changing nursing students' attitudes about aging: An argument for the successful aging paradigm. *Educational Gerontology, 34*, 51–66.

Ferraro, F.R. and Moody, J. (1996) Consistent and inconsistent performance in young and elderly adults. *Developmental Neuropsychology, 12*, 429–41.

Ferraro, K.F. and Su, Y. (1999) Financial strain, social relations, and psychological distress among older people: A cross-cultural analysis. *The Journals of Gerontology Series B: Psychological Sciences and Social Sciences, 54B*, S3–S15.

Ferstl, E. (2006) Text comprehension in middle aged adults: Is there anything wrong? *Aging, Neuropsychology and Cognition, 13*, 62–85.

Field, D. (1981) Retrospective reports by healthy intelligent people of personal events of their adult lives. *International Journal of Behavioral Development, 4*, 443–52.

Field, D. and Millsap, R.E. (1991) Personality in advanced old age: Continuity or change? *The Journals of Gerontology Series B: Psychological Sciences and Social Sciences, 46*, 299–308.

Filoteo, J.V. and Maddox, W.T. (2004) A quantitative model-based approach to examining aging effects on information-integration category learning. *Psychology and Aging, 19*, 171–82.

Fingerman, K.L. and Birditt, K.S. (2003) Do age differences in close and problematic family ties reflect the pool of available relatives? *The Journals of Gerontology Series B: Psychological Sciences and Social Sciences, 58*, 80–7.

Fiori, K., Consedine, N. and Magai, C. (2008) The adaptive and maladaptive faces of dependency in later life: Links to physical and psychological health outcomes. *Aging* and *Mental Health, 12*, 700–12.

Fjell, A.M. and Walhovd, K.B. (2010) Structural brain changes in aging: Courses, causes and cognitive consequences. *Reviews in the Neurosciences, 21*, 187–221.

Flood, M. and Clark, R. (2009) Exploring knowledge and attitudes toward aging among nursing and nonnursing students. *Educational Gerontology, 35*, 587–95.

Fonseca, A. (2007) Determinants of successful retirement in a Portuguese population. *Reviews in Clinical Gerontology, 17*, 219–24.

Foos, P.W. and Boone, D. (2008) Adult age differences in divergent thinking: It's just a matter of time. *Educational Gerontology, 34*, 587–94.

Foreman, M.D. and Milisen, K. (2004) Improving recognition of delirium in the elderly. *Primary Psychiatry, 11*, 46–50.

Fraboni, M., Saltstone, R. and Hughes, S. (1990) The Fraboni Scale of Ageism (FSA): An attempt at a more precise measure of ageism. *Canadian Journal on Aging, 9*, 56–66.

Freund, A.M. and Baltes, P.B. (2007) Toward a theory of successful aging: Selection, optimization, and compensation. In R. Fernandez-Ballesteros (ed.) *Geropsychology: European Perspectives for an Aging World.* Ashland, OH: Hogrefe and Huber.

Fries, J.F. (2000) Compression of morbidity in the elderly. *Vaccine, 18,* 1584–9.

Fung, H.H., Lai, P. and Ng, R. (2001) Age differences in social preferences among Taiwanese and mainland Chinese: The role of perceived time. *Psychology and Aging, 16,* 351–6.

Fung, H.H., Stoeber, F., Yeung, D. and Lang, F. (2008) Cultural specificity of socioemotional selectivity: Age differences in social network composition among Germans and Hong Kong Chinese. *The Journals of Gerontology Series B: Psychological Sciences and Social Sciences, 63,* 156–64.

Funkenstein, H.H. (1988) Cerebrovascular disorders. In M.S. Albert and M.B. Moss (eds) *Geriatric Neuropsychology.* New York, NY: Guilford.

Gallo, W.T., Bradley, E.H., Siegel, M. and Kasla, S.V. (2000) Health effects of involuntary job loss among older workers: Findings from the health and retirement survey. *The Journals of Gerontology Series B: Psychological Sciences and Social Sciences, 55,* 131–40.

Gangadharan, S. and Bhaumik, S. (2006) A retrospective study of the use of neuroimaging in the assessment of dementia in adults with learning disability. *British Journal of Developmental Disabilities, 52,* 97–104.

Garre-Olmo, J., Genís Batlle, D., del Mar Fernández, M., Marquez Daniel, F. *et al.* (2010) Incidence and subtypes of early-onset dementia in a geographically defined general population. *Neurology, 75,* 1249–55.

Gfroerer, J., Penne, M., Pemberton, M. and Folsom, R. (2003) Substance abuse treatment need among older adults in 2020: The impact of the aging baby-boom cohort. *Drug and Alcohol Dependence, 69,* 127–35.

Ghiselli, E.E. (1957) The relationship between intelligence and age among superior adults. *Journal of Genetic Psychology, 90,* 131–42.

Giannakopoulos, P., Gold, G., Duc, M., Michel, J. *et al.* (1999) Neuroanatomic correlates of visual agnosia in Alzheimer's disease: A clinicopathologic study. *Neurology, 52,* 71–7.

Gibson, H.B. (1992) *The Emotional and Sexual Lives of Older People.* London: Chapman and Hall.

Gibson, H.B. (1997) *Love in Later Life.* London: Peter Owen.

Gilchrist, A., Cowan, N. and Naveh-Benjamin, M. (2008) Working memory capacity for spoken sentences decreases with adult ageing: Recall of fewer but not smaller chunks in older adults. *Memory, 16,* 773–87.

Giles, L.C., Glonek, G.F., Luszcz, M.A. and Andrews, G.R. (2005) Effect of social networks on 10 year survival in very old Australians: The Australian longitudinal study of aging. *Journal of Epidemiological and Community Health, 59,* 574–9.

Gilleard, C.J. (1997) Education and Alzheimer's disease: A review of recent international epidemiological studies. *Aging and Mental Health, 1,* 33–46.

Godschalk, M.F., Sison, A. and Mulligan, T. (1997) Management of erectile dysfunction by the geriatrician. *Journal of the American Geriatrics Society, 45*, 1240–6.

Goffman, E. (1959) *The Presentation of Self in Everyday Life.* New York, NY: Doubleday.

Gold, G., Giannakopoulos, P., Herrmann, F., Bouras, C. and Kovari, E. (2007) Identification of Alzheimer and vascular lesion thresholds for mixed dementia. *Brain, 130*, 2830–6.

Gomez, V., Krings, F., Bangerter, A. and Grob, A. (2009) The influence of personality and life events on subjective well-being from a life span perspective. *Journal of Research in Personality, 43*, 345–54.

Goncalves, D., Guedes, J., Fonseca, A., Pinto, F. *et al.* (2011) Attitudes, knowledge, and interest: Preparing university students to work in an aging world. *International Journal of Psychogeriatrics, 23*, 315–21.

Gott, M. (2004) Are older people at risk of sexually transmitted infections? A new look at the evidence. *Reviews in Clinical Gerontology, 14*, 5–13.

Gott, M. and Hinchliff, S. (2003) How important is sex in later life? The views of older people. *Social Science and Medicine, 56*, 1617–28.

Gould, O.N. and Dixon, R.A. (1993) How we spent our vacation: Collaborative storytelling by young and old adults. *Psychology and Aging, 8*, 10–17.

Graham, N. and Warner, J. (2009) *Understanding Alzheimer's Disease and Other Dementias.* London: Family Doctor Books.

Greenwald, A. and Banaji, M. (1995) Implicit social cognition: Attitudes, self esteem and stereotypes. *Psychological Review, 102*, 1, 4–27.

Gregory, T., Nettlebeck, T. and Wilson, C. (2010) Openness to experience, intelligence, and successful ageing. *Personality and Individual Differences, 48*, 895–99.

Griffiths, C. and Fitzpatrick, J. (2001) Geographical inequalities in life expectancy in the United Kingdom, 1995–97. *Health Statistics Quarterly, 9*, 16–27.

Guo, X., Erber, J.T. and Szuchman, L.T. (1999) Age and forgetfulness: Can stereotypes be modified? *Educational Gerontology, 25*, 457–66.

Gurung, R.A.R., Taylor, S.E. and Seeman, T.E. (2003) Accounting for changes in social support among married older adults: Insights from the MacArthur Studies of Successful Aging. *Psychology and Aging, 18*, 487–96.

Haan, N. (1972) Personality development from adolescence to adulthood in the Oakland growth and guidance studies. *Seminars in Psychiatry, 4*, 399–414.

Haase, E.R. (1977) Diseases presenting as dementia. In C.E. Wells (ed.) *Dementia.* Philadelphia, PA: Davis.

Hachinski, V.C., Iliff, L.D., Zilkha, E., Du Boulay, G.H. *et al.* (1975) Cerebral blood flow in dementia. *Archives of Neurology, 32*, 632–7.

Hajat, S., Haines, A., Bulpitt, C. and Fletcher, A. (2004) Patterns and determinants of alcohol consumption in people aged 75 years and older: Results from the MRC trial of assessment and management of older people in the community. *Age and Ageing, 33*, 170–7.

Hallgren, M., Hogberg, P. and Andreasson, S. (2010) Alcohol consumption and harm among elderly Europeans: Falling between the cracks. *European Journal of Public Health, 20*, 616–8.

Hamm, V.P. and Hasher, L. (1992) Age and the availability of inferences. *Psychology and Aging, 7*, 56–64.

Han, B., Gfroerer, J., Colliver, J. and Penne, M. (2009) Substance use disorder among older adults in the United States in 2020. *Addiction, 104*, 88–96.

Hardy, D., Chan, W., Liu, C., Cormier, J. *et al.* (2011) Racial disparities in the use of hospice services according to geographic residence and socioeconomic status in an elderly cohort with nonsmall cell lung cancer. *Cancer, 117*, 1504–15.

Harris, L.A. and Dollinger, S. (2001) Participation in a course on aging: Knowledge, attitudes and anxiety about aging in oneself and others. *Educational Gerontology, 27*, 657–67.

Harris, T., Cook, D.G., Victor, C., Rink, E. *et al.* (2003) Predictors of depressive symptoms in older people – a survey of two general practice populations. *Age and Ageing, 32*, 510–18.

Hasegawa, S., Matsunuma, S., Omori, M. and Miyao, M. (2006) Aging effects on the visibility of graphic text on mobile phones. *Gerontechnology, 4*, 200–8.

Hasher, L., Zacks, R.T. and May, C.P. (1999) Inhibitory control, circadian arousal, and age. In D. Gopher and A. Koriat (eds) *Attention and Performance XVII, Cognitive Regulation of Performance: Interaction of Theory and Application* (pp.653–75). Cambridge, MA: MIT Press.

Hassiotis, A., Strydom, A., Allen, K. and Walker, Z. (2003) A memory clinic for older people with intellectual disabilities. *Aging and Mental Health, 7*, 418–23.

Hawkins, H.L., Kramer, A.F. and Capaldi, D. (1992) Aging, exercise and attention. *Psychology and Aging, 7*, 643–53.

Hayflick, L.H. (1994) *How and Why We Age.* New York, NY: Random House.

Hayflick, L.H. (1997) Mortality and immortality at the cellular level: A review. *Biochemistry, 62*, 1180–90.

Heaphy, B., Yip, A.K.T. and Thompson, D. (2004) Ageing in a non-heterosexual context. *Ageing and Society, 24*, 881–902.

Helmes, E. and Gee, S. (2003) Attitudes of Australian therapists towards older clients: Educational and training imperatives. *Educational Gerontology, 29*, 657–70.

Hendricks, J. (1999) Creativity over the life course – a call for a rational perspective. *International Journal of Aging and Human Development, 48*, 85–111.

Hertzog, C. (1991) Aging, information processing speed and intelligence. *Annual Review of Gerontology and Geriatrics, Volume 11* (pp.55–79). New York, NY: Springer.

Hertzog, C. and Jopp, D.S. (2010) Resilience in the face of cognitive aging: Experience, adaptation and compensation. In P.S. Fry and C.L.M. Keyes (eds) *New Frontiers in Resilient Aging: Life-strengths and Well-being in Late Life.* New York, NY: Cambridge University Press.

Hertzog, C. and Nesselroade, J.R. (2003) Assessing psychological change in adulthood: An overview of methodological issues. *Psychology and Aging, 18,* 639–57.

Hicks-Moore, S. and Robinson, B. (2008) Favorite music and hand massage: Two interventions to decrease agitation in residents with dementia. *Dementia, 7,* 95–108.

Hickson, J. and Housley, W. (1997) Creativity in later life. *Educational Gerontology, 23,* 539–47.

Hofer, S.M., Christensen, H., Mackinnon, A.J., Korten, A.E. *et al.* (2002) Change in cognitive functioning associated with ApoE genotype in a community sample of older adults. *Psychology and Aging, 17,* 194–208.

Holahan, C.K. and Chapman. J.R. (2002) Longitudinal predictors of proactive goals and activity participation at age 80. *The Journals of Gerontology Series B: Psychological Sciences and Social Sciences, 57,* 418–25.

Holland, A. (2000) Ageing and learning disability. *British Journal of Psychiatry, 176,* 26–31.

Holland, C. and Rabbitt, P. (1989) Subjective and objective measures of vision and hearing loss in elderly drivers and pedestrians. Talk at ESRC/General Accident Insurance Company Symposium on Road Traffic Accidents. University of Reading, 5 July.

Holland, C. and Rabbitt, P. (1990) Autobiographical and text recall in the elderly. *Quarterly Journal of Experimental Psychology, 42A,* 441–70.

Holliday, R. (2007) *Aging: The Paradox of Life.* Dordrecht: Springer.

Holtz, J. (2011) *Applied Clinical Neuropsychology: An Introduction.* New York, NY: Springer.

Holtzman, R.E., Rebok, G.W., Saczynski, J.S., Kouzis, A.C., Doyle, K.W. and Eaton, W.W. (2004) Social network characteristics and cognition in middle-aged and older adults. *The Journals of Gerontology Series B: Psychological Sciences and Social Sciences, 59,* 278–84.

Hooper, F.H., Fitzgerald, J. and Papalia, D. (1971) Piagetian theory and the aging process: Extensions and speculations. *Aging and Human Development, 2,* 3–20.

Hopkins, C., Roster, C. and Wood, C. (2006) Making the transition to retirement: Appraisals, post-transition lifestyle, and changes in consumption patterns. *Journal of Consumer Marketing, 23,* 89–101.

Hoppmann, C., Gerstorf, D. and Hibbert, A. (2011) Spousal associations between functional limitation and depressive symptom trajectories: Longitudinal findings from the Study of Asset and Health Dynamics Among the Oldest (AHEAD). *Health Psychology, 30,* 153–62.

Hosokawa, A. and Hosokawa, T. (2006) Cross-cultural study on age-group differences in the recall of the literal and interpretive meanings of narrative text. *Japanese Psychological Research, 48,* 77–90.

Hough, M.S. (2006) Incidence of word finding deficits in normal aging. *Folia Phoniatrica et Logopaedica, 59,* 10–19.

House, J.S., Kessler, R.C., Herzog, A.R., Mero, R.P., Kinney, A.M. and Breslow, M.J. (1992) Social stratification, age and health. In K.W. Schaie, D. Blazer and J. House (eds) *Aging, Health Behavior and Health Outcomes* (pp.1–37). Hillsdale, NJ: Lawrence Erlbaum.

Hoyer, W.J. and Ingolfsdottir, D. (2003) Age, skill and contextual cuing in target detection. *Psychology and Aging, 18,* 210–18.

Hoyer, W.J. and Roodin, P.A. (2003) *Adult Development and Aging* (5th edn). Boston, MA: McGraw-Hill.

Hoyte, K., Brownell, H. and Wingfield, A. (2009) Components of speech prosody and their use in detection of syntactic structure by older adults. *Experimental Aging Research, 35,* 129–51.

Hudson, L. (1987) Creativity. In R.L. Gregory and O. Zangwill (eds) *The Oxford Companion to the Mind.* Oxford: Oxford University Press.

Hult, C., Stattin, M., Janiert, U. and Jarvholm, B. (2010) Timing of retirement and mortality: A cohort study of Swedish construction workers. *Social Science and Medicine, 70,* 1480–6.

Hybertson, E.D., Perdue, J. and Hybertson, D. (1982) Age differences in information acquisition strategies. *Experimental Aging Research, 8,* 109–113.

Hyman, B.T., Arriagada, P.V., Van Housen, G.W. and Damasio, A.R. (1993) Memory impairment in Alzheimer's disease: An anatomical perspective. In R.W. Parks, R.F. Zec and R.S. Wilson (eds) *Neuropsychology of Alzheimer's Disease and Other Dementias* (pp.138–50). New York, NY: Oxford University Press.

Idler, E.L., Kasl, S.V. and Hays, J.C. (2001) Patterns of religious practice and belief in the last year of life. *The Journals of Gerontology Series B: Psychological Sciences and Social Sciences, 56,* 326–34.

Ingersoll-Dayton, B. and Saengtienchai, C. (1999) Respect for the elderly in Asia: Stability and change. *International Journal of Aging and Human Development, 48,* 113–30.

Iwasa, H., Masui, Y., Gondo, Y., Yoshida, Y. *et al.* (2009) Personality and participation in mass health checkups among Japanese community-dwelling elderly. *Journal of Psychosomatic Research, 66,* 155–9.

Jackson, G.R. and Owsley, C. (2003) Visual dysfunction, neurodegenerative diseases, and aging. *Neurologic Clinics, 21,* 709–28.

Jackson, J.L., Bogers, H. and Kersthold, J. (1988) Do memory aids aid the elderly in their day to day remembering? In M.M. Gruneberg, P.E. Morris and R.N. Sykes (eds) *Practical Aspects of Memory: Current Research and Issues, Volume 2.* Chichester: Wiley.

Jacobs, R. and Kane, M. (2011) Psychosocial predictors of self-esteem in a multi-ethnic sample of women over 50 at risk for HIV. *Journal of Women and Aging, 23,* 23–39.

James, C. (1983) *Falling Towards England.* London: Jonathan Cape.

James, J. and Haley, W. (1995) Age and health bias in practising clinical psychologists. *Psychology and Ageing, 10,* 610–16.

James, L.E. (2004) Meeting Mr. Farmer versus meeting a farmer: Specific effects of aging on learning proper names. *Psychology and Aging, 19*, 515–22.

James, L.E. (2006) Specific effects of aging on proper name retrieval: Now you see them, now you don't. *The Journals of Gerontology Series B: Psychological Sciences and Social Sciences, 61*, 180–3.

Jelenec, P. and Steffens, M. (2002) Implicit attitudes towards elderly women and men. *Current Research in Social Psychology, 7*, 275–91.

Jeong, H. and Kim, H. (2009) Aging and text comprehension: Interpretation and domain knowledge advantage. *Educational Gerontology, 35*, 906–28.

Jerant, A., Chapman, B., Duberstein, P., Robbins, J. and Franks, P. (2011) Personality and medication non-adherence among older adults enrolled in a six-year trial. *British Journal of Health Psychology, 16*, 151–69.

Johnson, P. and Sung, H. (2009) Substance abuse among aging baby boomers: Health and treatment implications. *Journal of Addictions Nursing, 20*, 124–6.

Kahn, R.L., Goldfarb, A.I., Pollack, M. and Peck, A. (1960) Brief objective measures for determination of mental status in the aged. *American Journal of Psychiatry, 117*, 326–8.

Karpel, M.E., Hoyer, W.J. and Toglia, M.P. (2001) Accuracy and qualities of real and suggested memories: Nonspecific age differences. *The Journals of Gerontology Series B: Psychological Sciences and Social Sciences, 56*, 103–10.

Kasl-Godley, J.E., Gatz, M. and Fiske, A. (1998) Depression and depressive symptoms in old age. In I.H. Nordhus, G.R. VandenBos, S. Berg and P. Fromholt (eds) *Clinical Geropsychology* (pp.211–7). Washington, DC: American Psychological Association.

Kaufman, A.S. and Horn, J.L. (1996) Age changes on tests of fluid and crystallised ability for women and men on the Adolescent and Adult Intelligence Test (KAIT) at ages 17–94 years. *Archives of Clinical Neuropsychology, 11*, 97–121.

Kelly, F. (2010) Recognising and supporting self in dementia: A new way to facilitate a person-centred approach to dementia care. *Ageing and Society, 30*, 103–24.

Kemper, S. (1986) Limitation of complex syntactic construction by elderly adults. *Applied Psycholinguistics, 7*, 277–87.

Kemper, S. (1987) Life-span changes in syntactic complexity. *Journal of Gerontology, 42*, 323–8.

Kemper, S. (1992) Adults' sentence fragments: Who, what, when, where and why. *Communication Research, 19*, 444–58.

Kemper, S. and Anagnopoulos, C. (1993) Adult use of discourse constraints on syntactic processing. In J. Cerella, J. Rybash, W. Hoyer and M.L. Commons (eds) *Adult Information Processing: Limits on Loss* (pp.489–507). San Diego, CA: Academic Press.

Kemper, S. and Rush, S.J. (1988) Speech and writing across the life span. In M.M. Gruneberg, P.E. Morris and R.N. Sykes (eds) *Practical Aspects of Memory: Current Research and Issues*. Chichester: Wiley.

Kemper, S. and Sumner, A. (2001) The structure of verbal abilities in young and older adults. *Psychology and Aging, 16*, 312–22.

Kemper, S., Crow, A. and Kemtes, K. (2004) Eye-fixation patterns of high- and low-span young and older adults: Down the garden path and back again. *Psychology and Aging, 19,* 157–70.

Kemper, S., Herman, R. and Lian, C. (2003) The costs of doing two things at once for younger and older adults: Talking while walking, finger tapping and ignoring speech of noise. *Psychology and Aging, 18,* 181–92.

Kemper, S., Schmalzried, R., Hoffman, L. and Herman, R. (2010) Aging and the vulnerability of speech to dual task demands. *Psychology and Aging, 25,* 949–62.

Kemper, S., Thompson, M. and Marquis, J. (2001) Longitudinal change in language production: Effects of aging and dementia on grammatical complexity and propositional content. *Psychology and Aging, 16,* 600–14.

Kennedy, G.J. (2010) Now neuroscience explains age-related changes in cognition: Implications for the early diagnosis of dementia. *Primary Psychiatry, 17,* 30–3.

Keranen, A., Savolainen, M., Reponen, A., Kujari, M. *et al.* (2009) The effect of eating behaviour on weight loss and maintenance during a lifestyle intervention. *Preventive Medicine, 49,* 32–8.

Kermis, M.D. (1983) *The Psychology of Human Aging: Theory, Research and Practice.* Boston, MA: Allyn and Bacon.

Kermis, M.D. (1986) *Mental Health in Later Life. The Adaptive Process.* Boston, MA: Jones and Bartlett.

Kerr, D. (2007) *Understanding Learning Disability and Dementia.* London: Jessica Kingsley Publishers.

Kim, S. and Yu, X. (2010) The mediating effect of self-efficacy on the relationship between health literacy and health status in Korean older adults: A short report. *Aging and Mental Health, 14,* 870–3.

Kirby, S.E., Coleman. P.G. and Daley, D. (2004) Spirituality and well-being in frail and nonfrail older adults. *The Journals of Gerontology Series B: Psychological Sciences and Social Sciences, 59,* 123–9.

Kirk, L.J., Hick, R. and Laraway, A. (2006) Assessing dementia in people with learning disabilities: The relationship between two screening measures. *Journal of Intellectual Disabilities, 10,* 357–64.

Kitwood, T. (1993) Towards a theory of dementia care: the interpersonal process, *Ageing and Society, 13,* 51–67.

Kitwood, T. (1997) *Dementia Reconsidered: The Person Comes First.* Buckingham: Open University Press.

Kleemeier, R.W. (1962) Intellectual changes in the senium. *Proceedings of the Social Statistics Section of the American Statistical Association, 1,* 290–5.

Knapp, J.L., Beaver, L.M. and Reed, T.D. (2002) Perceptions of the elderly among ministers and ministry students: Implications for seminary curricula. *Educational Gerontology, 28,* 313–24.

Koedam, E., Pijnenburg, Y., Deeg, D., Baak, M. *et al.* (2008) Early-onset dementia is associated with higher mortality. *Dementia and Geriatric Cognitive Disorders, 26,* 147–52.

Koepsell, T., Kurland, B., Harel, O., Johnson, E. *et al.* (2008) Education, cognitive function, and severity of neuropathology in Alzheimer disease. *Neurology, 70,* 1732–9.

Kossioni, A. and Bellou, O. (2011) Eating habits in older people in Greece: The role of age, dental status and chewing difficulties. *Archives of Gerontology and Geriatrics, 52,* 197–201.

Kott, A. (2011) Drug use and loneliness are linked to unprotected sex in older adults with HIV. *Perspectives on Sexual and Reproductive Health, 43,* 69–74.

Kozora, E. and Cullum, C.M. (1995) Generative naming in normal aging: Total output and qualitative changes using phonemic and semantic constraints. *Clinical Neuropsychologist, 9,* 313–20.

Krause, N. (2002) Church-based social support and health in old age: Exploring variations by race. *The Journals of Gerontology Series B: Psychological Sciences and Social Sciences, 57,* 332–47.

Krause, N., Shaw, B.A. and Cairney, J. (2004) A descriptive epidemiology of lifetime trauma and the physical health status of older adults. *Psychology and Aging, 19,* 637–48.

Krauss Whitbourne, S. and Whitbourne, S. (2011) *Adult Development and Ageing: Biopsychosocial Perspectives* (4th edn). Hoboken, NJ: Wiley.

Kumar, A. and Foster, T.C. (2007) Neurophysiology of old neurons and synapses. In D.R. Riddle (ed.) *Brain Aging: Models, Methods, and Mechanisms.* Boca Raton, FL: CRC Press.

Kwong See, S.T., Hoffman, H.G. and Wood, T.L. (2001) Perceptions of an old female eyewitness: Is the older eyewitness believable? *Psychology and Aging, 16,* 346–50.

Kynette, D. and Kemper, S. (1986) Aging and the loss of grammatical form: A cross-sectional study of language performance. *Language and Communication, 6,* 65–72.

Lachman, M., Agrigoroaei, S., Murphy, C. and Tun, P. (2010) Frequent cognitive activity compensates for education differences in episodic memory. *American Journal of Geriatric Psychiatry, 18,* 4–10.

Lahar, C.J., Tun, P.A. and Wingfield, A. (2004) Sentence–final word completion norms for young, middle-aged and older adults. *The Journals of Gerontology Series B: Psychological Sciences and Social Sciences, 59,* 7–10.

LaRue, A. (1992) *Aging and Neuropsychological Assessment.* New York, NY: Plenum.

Laslett, P. (1976) Societal development and aging. In R.H. Binstock and E. Shanas (eds) *Handbook of Aging and the Social Sciences.* New York, NY: Reinhold.

Latimer, J. (1963) The status of aging in intelligence. *Journal of Genetic Psychology, 102,* 175–88.

Lauver, S.C. and Johnson, J.L. (1997) The role of neuroticism and social support in older adults with chronic pain behavior. *Personality and Individual Differences, 23,* 165–7.

Laver, G.D. and Burke, D.M. (1993) Why do semantic priming effects increase in old age? A meta-analysis. *Psychology and Aging, 8,* 34–43.

LaVole, D., Mertz, H. and Richmond, T. (2007) False memory susceptibility in older adults: Implications for the elderly eyewitness. In M. Toglia, J. Read, D. Ross and R. Lindsay (eds) *The Handbook of Eyewitness Psychology, Volume 1: Memory for Events*. Mahwah, NJ: Lawrence Erlbaum.

Law, R. and O'Carroll, R.E. (1998) A comparison of three measures of estimating premorbid intellectual level in dementia of the Alzheimer type. *International Journal of Geriatric Psychiatry, 13,* 727–30.

Lawrence, M.W. and Arrowood, A.J. (1982) Classification style differences in the elderly. In F.I.M. Craik and S. Trehub (eds) *Aging and Cognitive Processes*. New York, NY: Plenum.

Leader, D. and Corfield, D. (2007) *Why Do People Get Ill?* London: Hamish Hamilton.

Lee, E. (2007) Religion and spirituality as predictors of well-being among Chinese American and Korean American older adults. *Journal of Religion, Spirituality and Aging, 19,* 77–100.

Lee, Y. and Kim, S. (2008) Effects of indoor gardening on sleep, agitation, and cognition in dementia patients – a pilot study. *International Journal of Geriatric Psychiatry, 23,* 485–9.

Leentjens, A.F.G. and van der Mast, R.C. (2005) Delirium in elderly people: An update. *Current Opinion in Psychiatry, 18,* 325–30.

Lemaire, P. (2010) Cognitive strategy variations during aging. *Current Directions in Psychological Science, 19,* 363–9.

Lennartsson, C. and Silverstein, M. (2001) Does engagement with life enhance survival of elderly people in Sweden? The role of social and leisure activities. *The Journals of Gerontology Series B: Psychological Sciences and Social Sciences, 56,* 335–42.

Levinson, D. (1980) Conception of the adult life course. In N. Smelser and E. Erikson (eds) *Themes of Work and Love in Adulthood*. Cambridge, MA: Harvard University Press.

Levy, B.R. (1999) The inner self of the Japanese elderly: A defense against negative stereotypes of aging. *International Journal of Aging and Human Development, 48,* 131–44.

Levy, B.R., Hausdorff, J.M., Hencke, R. and Wei, J.Y. (2000) Reducing cardiovascular stress with positive self-stereotypes of aging. *The Journals of Gerontology Series B: Psychological Sciences and Social Sciences, 55,* 205–13.

Levy, J.A. and Anderson, T. (2005) The drug career of the older injector. *Addiction Research and Theory, 13,* 245–58.

Lezak, M.D. (1995) *Neuropsychological Assessment*. New York, NY: Oxford University Press.

Li, F., Fisher, K.J., Harmer, P. and McAuley, E. (2005) Falls self-efficacy as a mediator of fear of falling in an exercise intervention for older adults. *The Journals of Gerontology Series B: Psychological Sciences and Social Sciences, 60,* 34–40.

Li, F., Fisher, K.J., Harmer, P., McAuley, E. and Wilson, N.L. (2003) Fear of falling in elderly persons: Association with falls, functional ability and quality of life. *The Journals of Gerontology Series B: Psychological Sciences and Social Sciences, 58,* 283–90.

Light, L.L. and Anderson, P.A. (1985) Working memory capacity, age and memory for discourse. *Journal of Gerontology, 40,* 737–47.

Light, L.L. and Burke, D. (eds) (1988) *Language, Memory and Aging.* New York, NY: Cambridge University Press.

Lin, R., Heacock, L., Bhargave, G. and Fogel, J. (2010) Clinical associations of delirium in hospitalized older adult patients and the role of admission presentation. *International Journal of Geriatric Psychiatry, 25,* 1022–9.

Lindenberger, U., Brehmer, Y., Kliegl, R. and Baltes, P. (2008) Benefits of graphic design expertise in old age: Compensatory effects of a graphical lexicon? In C. Lange-Küttner and A.Vintner (eds) *Drawing and the Non-Verbal Mind: A Life-Span Perspective.* New York, NY: Cambridge University Press.

Lindenberger, U., Marsiske, M. and Baltes, P.B. (2000) Memorizing while walking: Increase in dual-task costs from young adulthood to old age. *Psychology and Aging, 15,* 417–36.

Lindenberger, U., Mayr, U. and Kliegl, R. (1993) Speed and intelligence in old age. *Psychology and Aging, 8,* 207–20.

Litwin, H. and Shiovitz-Ezra, S. (2006) The association between activity and wellbeing in later life: What really matters? *Ageing and Society, 26,* 225–42.

Livingston, M. and Room, R. (2009) Variations by age and sex in alcohol-related problematic behaviour per drinking volume and heavier drinking occasion. *Drug and Alcohol Dependence, 101,* 169–75.

Lofwall, M.R., Brooner, R.K., Bigelow, G.E., Kindbom, K. and Strain, E.C. (2005) Characteristics of older opioid maintenance patients. *Journal of Substance Abuse Treatment, 28,* 265–72.

Long, L.L. and Shaw, R.J. (2000) Adult age differences in vocabulary acquisition. *Educational Gerontology, 26,* 651–64.

Lövdén, M., Bodammer, N., Kuhn, S., Kaufmann, J. *et al.* (2010) Experience-dependent plasticity of white-matter microstructure extends into old age. *Neuropsychologia, 48,* 3878–83.

Lovie, K.J. and Whittaker, S. (1998) Relative size magnification versus relative distance magnification: Effect on the reading performance of adults with normal and low vision. *Journal of Visual Impairment and Blindness, 92,* 433–46.

Lucas, R. and Donnellan, M. (2009) Age differences in personality: Evidence from a nationally representative Australian sample. *Developmental Psychology, 45,* 1353–63.

Luijendijk, H., van den Berg, J., Dekker, M., van Tuijl, H. *et al.* (2008) Incidence and recurrence of late-life depression. *Archives of General Psychiatry, 65,* 1394–1401.

Lun, M. (2011) Student knowledge and attitudes toward older people and their impact on pursuing aging careers. *Educational Gerontology, 37,* 1–11.

Luo, L. and Craik, F. (2008) Aging and memory: A cognitive approach. *Canadian Journal of Psychiatry, 53,* 346–53.

Luo, Y. and Waite, L.J. (2005) The impact of childhood and adult SES on physical, mental and cognitive well-being in later life. *The Journals of Gerontology Series B: Psychological Sciences and Social Sciences, 60,* 93–101.

Lynn, T.N., Duncan, R., Naughton, J.P., Brandt, E.N. *et al.* (1967) Prevalence of evidence of prior myocardial infarction, hypertension, diabetes and obesity in three neighboring communities in Pennsylvania. *American Journal of Medical Science, 254, 4,* 385–391.

Maas, M.S. and Kuypers, J.A. (1974) *From Thirty to Seventy.* San Francisco, CA: Jossey-Bass.

Mace, J. (2004) Involuntary autobiographical memories are highly dependent on abstract cuing: The Proustian view is incorrect. *Applied Cognitive Psychology, 18,* 893–9.

MacKay, D.G. and Abrams, L. (1998) Age-linked declines in retrieving orthographic knowledge: Empirical, practical and theoretical implications. *Psychology and Aging, 13,* 647–62.

MacKay, D.G., Abrams, L. and Pedroza, M.J. (1999) Aging on the input versus output side: Theoretical implications of age-linked assymetries between detecting versus retrieving orthographic information. *Psychology and Aging, 14,* 3–17.

Madden, D.J. (1992) Four to ten milliseconds per year: Age-related slowing of visual word identification. *The Journals of Gerontology, 47,* 59–68.

Maddox, G.I. (1970a) Persistence of life style among the elderly. In E. Palmore (ed.) *Normal Aging.* Durham, NC: Duke University Press.

Maddox, G.I. (1970b) Themes and issues in sociological theories of human aging. *Human Development, 13,* 17–27.

Maddox, W., Pacheco, J., Reeves, M., Zhu, B. and Schnyer, D. (2010) Rule-based and information-integration category learning in normal aging. *Neuropsychologia, 48,* 2998–3008.

Magai, C., Cohen, C., Milburn, N., Thorpe, B., McPherson, R. and Peralta, D. (2001) Attachment styles in older European American and African American adults. *The Journals of Gerontology Series B: Psychological Sciences and Social Sciences, 56,* 28–45.

Mahay, J. and Lewin, A. (2007) Age and the desire to marry. *Journal of Family Issues, 28,* 706–23.

Mahley, R. and Huang, Y. (2009) Alzheimer disease: Multiple causes, multiple effects of apolipoprotein E4, and multiple therapeutic approaches. *Annals of Neurology, 65,* 623–5.

Mak, W. and Carpenter, B. (2007) Humor comprehension in older adults. *Journal of the International Neuropsychological Society, 13,* 606–14.

Mandel, R.G. and Johnson, N.S. (1984) A developmental analysis of story recall and comprehension in adulthood. *Journal of Verbal Learning and Verbal Behavior, 23,* 643–59.

Manthorpe, J. and Iliffe, S. (2005) *Depression in Later Life.* London: Jessica Kingsley Publishers.

Manton, K.G., Gu, X. and Lowrimore, G. (2008) Cohort changes in active life expectancy in the U.S. elderly population: Experience from the 1982–2004 National Long-Term Care Survey. *The Journals of Gerontology Series B: Psychological Sciences and Social Sciences, 63,* 269–81.

Marengoni, A., Calíbrese, A.P. and Cossi, S. (2004) Hospital admissions for acute onset of behavioral symptoms in demented patients: What do they want to say? *International Psychogeriatrics, 16*, 491–3.

Mariani, C., Defendi, S., Mailland, E. and Pomati, S. (2006) Frontotemporal dementia. *Neurological Sciences, 27*, S35–S36.

Marmot, M. and Feeney, A. (1997) General explanations for social inequalities in health. *IARC Scientific Publications, 138*, 207–28.

Martin, C.E. (1981) Factors affecting sexual functioning in 60–79 year old married males. *Archives of Sexual Behavior, 10*, 339–420.

Mast, B., Zimmerman, J. and Rowe, S. (2009) What do we know about the aging brain? Implications for learning in late life. In M. Smith and N. DeFrates-Dentsch (eds) *Handbook of Research on Adult Learning and Development*. New York: Routledge.

Masters, W.H. and Johnson, V.E. (1966) *Human Sexual Response*. Boston, MA: Little, Brown.

Masunaga, H. and Horn, J. (2001) Expertise and age-related changes in components of intelligence. *Psychology and Aging, 16*, 293–311.

Maylor, E.A. (1990a) Age and prospective memory. *Quarterly Journal of Experimental Psychology, 42A*, 471–93.

Maylor, E.A. (1990b) Age, blocking and tip of the tongue state. *British Journal of Psychology, 81*, 123–34.

Maylor, E.A. and Rabbitt, P.M.A. (1994) Applying Brinley plots to individuals: Effect of aging on performance distributions in two speeded tasks. *Psychology and Aging, 9*, 224–30.

McArdle, J.J., Hamgami, F., Jones, K., Jolesz, F. *et al.* (2004) Structural modeling of dynamic changes in memory and brain structure using longitudinal data from the normative aging study. *The Journals of Gerontology Series B: Psychological Sciences and Social Sciences, 59*, 294–304.

McCallion, P. and McCarron, M. (2004) Ageing and intellectual disabilities: A review of the recent literature. *Current Opinion in Psychiatry, 17*, 349–52.

McCaul, K., Almeida, O., Hankey, G., Jamrozik, K. *et al.* (2010) Alcohol use and mortality in older men and women. *Addiction, 105*, 1391–400.

McCrae, R.R., Arenberg, D. and Costa, P.T. (1987) Declines in divergent thinking with age: Cross-sectional, longitudinal and cross-sequential analyses. *Psychology and Aging, 2*, 130–7.

McDonald, L. (2011) Retirement. In I. Stuart-Hamilton (ed.) *Introduction to Gerontology*. Cambridge: Cambridge University Press.

McDonald, L. and Stuart-Hamilton, I. (1996) Older and more moral? Age related changes in performance on Piagetian moral reasoning tasks. *Age and Ageing, 25*, 402–4.

McDonald, L. and Stuart-Hamilton, I. (2000) The meaning of life: Animism in the classificatory skills of older adults. *International Journal of Aging and Human Development, 51*, 231–42.

McDonald, L. and Stuart-Hamilton, I. (2002) Egocentrism in older adults – Piaget's three mountains task revisited. *Educational Gerontology, 28*, 35–43.

McGinnis, D. (2009) Text comprehension products and processes in young, young-old and old-old adults. *The Journals of Gerontology Series B: Psychological Sciences and Social Sciences, 64*, 202–11.

McGinnis, D. and Zelinski, E.M. (2000) Understanding unfamiliar words: The influence of processing resources, vocabulary knowledge and age. *Psychology and Aging, 15*, 335–50.

McGinnis, D. and Zelinski, E.M. (2003) Understanding unfamiliar words in young, young-old and old-old adults: Inferential processing and the abstraction-deficit hypothesis. *Psychology and Aging, 18*, 497–509.

McIntyre, J.S. and Craik, F.I.M. (1987) Age differences in memory for item and source information. *Canadian Journal of Psychology, 41*, 175–92.

McKinnon, M., Nica, E., Sengdy, P., Kovacevic, N. *et al.* (2008) Autobiographical memory and patterns of brain atrophy in frontotemporal lobar degeneration. *Journal of Cognitive Neuroscience, 20*, 1839–53.

McMamish-Svensson, C., Samuelsson, G., Hagberg, G. and Dehlin, O. (1999) Social relationships and health as predictors of life satisfaction in advanced old age: Results from a Swedish longitudinal study. *International Journal of Aging and Human Development, 48*, 301–45.

McMurtray, A., Clark, D., Christine, D. and Mendez, M. (2006) Early-onset dementia: Frequency and causes compared to late-onset dementia. *Dementia and Geriatric Cognitive Disorders, 21*, 59–64.

McMurtray, A., Ringman, J., Chao, S., Lichet, E. *et al.* (2006) Family history of dementia in early-onset versus very late-onset Alzheimer's disease. *International Journal of Geriatric Psychiatry, 21*, 597–8.

McNeilly, D.P. and Burke, W.J. (2001) Gambling as a social activity of older adults. *International Journal of Aging and Human Development, 52*, 19–28.

McNeilly, D.P. and Burke, W.J. (2002) Disposable time and disposable income: Problem casino gambling behavior in older adults. *Journal of Clinical Geropsychology, 8*, 75–85.

Medawar, P.B. (1952) *An Unsolved Problem of Biology.* London: H.K. Lewis.

Mein, G., Martikainen, P., Stansfeld, S.A., Brunner, E.J., Fuhrer, R. and Marmot, M.G. (2000) Predictors of early retirement in British civil servants. *Age and Ageing, 29*, 529–36.

Metter, E.J. and Wilson, R.S. (1993) Vascular dementias. In R.W. Parks, R.F. Zec and R.S. Wilson (eds) *Neuropsychology of Alzheimer's Disease and Other Dementias* (pp.416–37). New York, NY: Oxford University Press.

Meyer, B.J.F. (1987) Reading comprehension and aging. In K.W. Schaie (ed.) *Annual Review of Gerontology and Geriatrics, Volume 7* (pp.93–115). New York, NY: Springer.

Midlov, P., Eriksson, T. and Kragh, A. (2009) *Drug-Related Problems in the Elderly.* Dordrecht: Springer.

Miller, L.J., Myers, A., Prinzi, L. and Mittenberg, W. (2009) Changes in intellectual functioning associated with normal aging. *Archives of Clincial Neuropsychology*, 24, 681–88.

Miller, L.S. (1987) Forensic examination of arthritic impaired writings. *Journal of Police Science and Administration*, 15, 51–5.

Milne, G.G. (1956) Deterioration and over-learning. *Australian Journal of Psychology*, 8, 163–72.

Mitchell, D.B. and Schmitt, F.A. (2006) Short and long term implicit memory in aging and Alzheimer's disease. *Aging, Neuropsychology and Cognition*, 13, 611–35.

Mitchell, K.J., Johnson, M.K., Raye, C.L., Mather, M. and D'Esposito, M. (2000) Aging and reflective processes of working memory: Binding and test load deficits. *Psychology and Aging*, 15, 527–41.

Miyoshi, K. (2009) What is 'early onset dementia'? *Psychogeriatrics*, 9, 67–72.

Mockler, D., Riordan, J. and Sharma, T. (1996) A comparison of the NART (restandardized) and the NART-R (revised). *British Journal of Clinical Psychology*, 35, 567–72.

Mondragon-Rodriguez, S., Basurto-Islas, G., Lee, H., Perry, G. *et al.* (2010) Causes versus effects: The increasing complexities of Alzheimer's disease pathogenesis. *Expert Review of Neurotherapeutics*, 10, 683–91.

Morrone, I., Declercq, C., Novella, J. and Besche, C. (2010) Aging and inhibition processes: The case of metaphor treatment. *Psychology and Aging*, 25, 697–701.

Moscovitch, M. (1982) A neuropsychological approach to memory and perception in normal and pathological aging. In F.I.M. Craik and S. Trehub (eds) *Aging and Cognitive Processes*. New York, NY: Plenum.

Mroczek, D.K. and Kolarz, C.M (1998) The effect of age on positive and negative affect: A developmental perspective on happiness. *Journal of Personality and Social Psychology*, 75, 1333–49.

Mroczek, D.K. and Spiro, A. (2003) Modeling intraindividual change in personality traits: Findings from the Normative Aging Study. *The Journals of Gerontology Series B: Psychological Sciences and Social Sciences*, 58, 153–65.

Mroczek, D.K., Spiro, A. and Turiano, N. (2009) Do health behaviors explain the effect of neuroticism on mortality? Longitudinal findings from the VA Normative Aging Study. *Journal of Research in Personality*, 43, 653–9.

Mullan, P. (2002) *The Imaginary Time Bomb: Why an Ageing Population is Not a Social Problem*. New York, NY: I.B. Tauris.

Murayama, N., Iseki, E., Endo, T., Nagashima, K. *et al.* (2009) Risk factors for delusion of theft in patients with Alzheimer's disease showing mild dementia in Japan. *Aging and Mental Health*, 13, 563–8.

Murphy, E.A. (1978) Genetics of longevity in man. In E.L. Schneider (ed.) *The Genetics of Aging*. New York, NY: Plenum.

Myerson, J., Ferraro, F.R., Hale, S. and Lima, S.D. (1992) General slowing in semantic priming and word recognition. *Psychology and Aging*, 7, 257–70.

Myerson, J., Hale, S., Chen, J. and Lawrence, B. (1997) General lexical slowing and the semantic priming effect: The roles of age and ability. *Acta Psychologica, 96*, 83–101.

Nagdee, M. and O'Brien, G. (2009) Dementia in developmental disability. In G. O'Brien and L. Rosenbloom (eds) *Developmental Disability and Ageing* (pp.10–30). London: MacKeith Press.

Nash, P., Stuart-Hamilton, I. and Mayer, P. (2009) The effects of specific education and direct experience on implicit and explicit measures of ageism. *Journal of Nutrition Health and Ageing, 13*, 683.

National Center for Injury Prevention and Control (2006) *CDC Injury Fact Book.* Atlanta, GA: Centers for Disease Control and Prevention.

National Endowment for the Arts (2007) *To Read or Not to Read.* Washington, DC: National Endowment for the Arts.

Naveh-Benjamin, M., Guez, J., Kilb, A. and Reedy, S. (2004) The associative memory deficit of older adults: Further support using face-name associations. *Psychology and Aging, 19*, 541–6.

Nay, R., McAuliffe, L. and Bauer, M. (2007) Sexuality: From stigma, stereotypes and secrecy to coming out, communication and choice. *International Journal of Older People Nursing, 2*, 76–80.

Nelson, H.E. and McKenna, P. (1973) The use of current reading ability in the assessment of dementia. *British Journal of Social and Clinical Psychology, 14*, 259–67.

Nelson, H.E. and O'Connell, A. (1978) Dementia: The estimation of premorbid intelligence levels using the New Adult Reading Test. *Cortex, 14*, 234–44.

Nestor, P. (2010) Dementia in Lewy body syndromes: A battle between hearts and minds. *Neurology, 74*, 872–3.

Neupert, S., Mroczek, D. and Spiro, A. (2008) Neuroticism moderates the daily reaction between stressors and memory failures. *Psychology and Aging, 23*, 287–96.

Nielsen, T., Vogel, A., Phung, T., Gade, A. and Waldemar, G. (2011) Over- and under-diagnosis of dementia in ethnic minorities: A nationwide register-based study. *International Journal of Geriatric Psychiatry, 26*, 1128.

O'Brien, G. and Rosenbloom, L. (2009) *Developmental Disability and Ageing.* Chichester: Wiley.

O'Brien, R. and Wong, P. (2011) Amyloid precursor protein processing and Alzheimer's disease. *Annual Review of Neuroscience, 34*, 185–204.

O'Connell, H., Chin, A.V., Cunningham, C. and Lawlor, B. (2003) Alcohol use disorders in elderly people – redefining an age old problem in old age. *British Medical Journal, 327*, 664–7.

Obler, L.K., Fein, D., Nicholas, M. and Albert, M.L. (1991) Auditory comprehension and aging: Decline in syntactic processing. *Applied Psycholinguistics, 12*, 433–52.

OECD (2004) *Ageing and Employment Policies: United Kingdom.* London: OECD.

Oeppen, J. and Vaupel, J.W. (2002) Broken limits to life expectancy. *Science, 296*, 1029–31.

Office for National Statistics (2010a) *Mid-year Population Estimates.* London: HMSO.

Office for National Statistics (2010b) *Life Expectancy at Birth and at Age 65 by Local Areas in the United Kingdom, 2007–9.* London: HMSO.

Office for National Statistics (2011) *Death Registrations Summary Tables, England and Wales, 2010.* London: HMSO.

Oishi, S., Whitchurch, E., Miao, F., Kurtz, J. and Park, J. (2009) 'Would I be happier if I moved?' Retirement status and cultural variations in the anticipated and actual levels of happiness. *Journal of Positive Psychology, 4,* 437–46.

Ojha, H. and Pramanick, M. (2010) Do personality characteristics change with advancement of age? *Journal of the Indian Academy of Applied Psychology, 36,* 55–68.

Okamoto, K. and Tanaka, Y. (2004) Subjective usefulness and 6-year mortality risks among elderly persons in Japan. *The Journals of Gerontology Series B: Psychological Sciences and Social Sciences, 59,* 246–9.

Okun, M., Pugliese, J. and Rook, K. (2007) Unpacking the relation between extraversion and volunteering in later life: The role of social capital. *Personality and Individual Differences, 42,* 1467–77.

Old, S.R. and Naveh-Benjamin, M. (2008) Age-related changes in memory: Experimental approaches. In S. Hofer and D. Alwin (eds) *Handbook of Cognitive Aging: Interdisciplinary Perspectives.* Thousand Oaks, CA: Sage.

Oliver, C., Adams, D. and Kaisy, S. (2008) Ageing, dementia and people with intellectual disability. In R. Woods, and L. Clare (eds) *Handbook of the Clinical Psychology of Ageing* (2nd edn, pp.341–9). New York, NY: Wiley.

Orbuch, T.L., House, J.S., Mero, R.P. and Webster, P.S. (1996) Marital quality over the life course. *Social Psychology Quarterly, 59,* 162–71.

Ostir, G.V., Ottenbacher, K.J. and Markides, K.S. (2004) Onset of frailty in older adults and the protective role of positive affect. *Psychology and Aging, 19,* 402–8.

Ostwald, S. and Dyer, C. (2011) Fostering resilience, promoting health and preventing disease in older adults. In I. Stuart-Hamilton (ed.) *An Introduction to Gerontology.* Cambridge: Cambridge University Press.

Oyer, H.J. and Deal, L.V. (1989) Temporal aspects of speech and the aging process. *Folia-Phoniatrica, 37,* 109–112.

Palacios, S., Tobar, A.C. and Menendez, C. (2002) Sexuality in the climacteric years. *Maturitas, 43,* 69–77.

Papalia, D.E. (1972) The status of several conservation abilities across the life-span. *Human Development, 15,* 229–43.

Park, D.C. and Reuter-Lorenz, P.A. (2009) The adaptive brain: Aging and neurocognitive scaffolding. *Annual Review of Psychology, 60,* 173–96.

Park, N. (2009) The relationship of social engagement to psychological well-being of older adults in assisted living facilities. *Journal of Applied Gerontology, 28,* 461–81.

Park, Y., Song, M., Cho, B., Lim, J. *et al.* (2011) The effects of an integrated health education and exercise program in community-dwelling older adults with hypertension: A randomized controlled trial. *Patient Education and Counselling, 82,* 133–7.

Parry, R. and Stuart-Hamilton, I. (2009) Animism begins at forty: Evidence that animism and other naïve beliefs are established before the onset of old age. *Educational Gerontology, 36*, 1043–50.

Pasupathi, M. and Carstensen, L.L. (2003) Age and emotional experience during mutual reminiscing. *Psychology and Aging, 18*, 430–42.

Patel, D., Goldberg, D. and Moss, S. (1993) Psychiatric morbidity in older people with moderate and severe learning disability. II: The prevalence study. *British Journal of Psychiatry, 163*, 481–91.

Paukert, A., Phillips, L., Cully, J., Loboprabhu, S. *et al.* (2009) Integration of religion into cognitive-behavioral therapy for geriatric anxiety and depression. *Journal of Psychiatric Practice, 15*, 103–12.

Peake, M.D. and Thompson, S. (2003) Ageism in the management of lung cancer. *Age and Ageing, 32*, 171–7.

Pearman, A., Andreoletti, C. and Isaacowitz, D. (2010) Sadness prediction and response: Effects of age and agreeableness. *Aging and Mental Health, 14*, 355–63.

Peck, R.C. (1968) Psychological developments in the second half of life. In B.L. Neugarten (ed.) *Middle Age and Aging: A Reader in Social Psychology.* Chicago, IL: University of Chicago Press.

Perez-Achaiga, N., Nelson, S. and Hassiotis, A. (2009) Instruments for the detection of depressive symptoms in people with intellectual disabilities: A systematic approach. *Journal of Intellectual Disabilities, 13*, 55–76.

Perfect, T.J. (1994) What can Brinley plots tell us about cognitive aging? *Journal of Gerontology: Psychological Sciences, 49*, 60–4.

Perfect, T.J. and Maylor, E.A. (eds) (2000) *Models of Cognitive Aging.* Oxford: Oxford University Press.

Perkins, E.A. and Small, B.J. (2006) Aspects of cognitive functioning in adults with intellectual disabilities. *Journal of Policy and Practice in Intellectual Disabilities, 3*, 181–94.

Perlmutter, M. (1978) What is memory aging the aging of? *Developmental Psychology, 14*, 330–45.

Perlmutter, M. and Hall, E. (1992) *Adult Development and Aging.* New York, NY: Wiley.

Perlow, E. (2010) Accessibility: Global gateway to health literacy. *Health Promotion Practice, 11*, 123–31.

Persad, C.C., Abeles, N., Zacks, R.T. and Denburg, N.L. (2002) Inhibitory changes after age 60 and their relationship to measures of attention and memory. *The Journals of Gerontology Series B: Psychological Sciences and Social Sciences, 57*, 223–32.

Peterson, L. and Litaker, D. (2010) County-level poverty is equally associated with unmet health care needs in rural and urban settings. *Journal of Rural Health, 26*, 373–82.

Petros, T., Tabar, L., Cooney, T. and Chabot, R.J. (1983) Adult age differences in sensitivity to semantic structure of prose. *Developmental Psychology, 19*, 907–14.

Pevey, C., Jones, T. and Yarber, A. (2009) How religion comforts the dying: A qualitative inquiry. *Omega: Journal of Death and Dying, 58*, 41–59.

Pew Research Center (2010) *Americans spending more time following the news.* Washington, DC: Pew Research Center. Available at http://people-press.org/reports/pdf/652.pdf, accessed on 1 September 2013.

Phillips, L.H. (1999) Age and individual differences in letter fluency. *Developmental Neuropsychology, 15,* 249–67.

Plancher, G., Gyselinck, V., Nicolas, S. and Piolino, P. (2010) Age effect on components of episodic memory and feature binding: A virtual reality study. *Neuropsychology, 24,* 379–90.

Plassman, B., Langa, K., McCammon, R., Fisher, G. *et al.* (2011) Incidence of dementia and cognitive impairment, not dementia in the United States. *Annals of Neurology, 70,* 418–26.

Population Reference Bureau (2010) *World Population Data Sheet.* Washington, DC: Population Reference Bureau.

Post, S.G. and Binstock, R.H. (2004) *The Fountain of Youth: Cultural, Scientific and Ethical Perspectives on a Biomedical Goal.* Oxford: Oxford University Press.

Powell, R.R. (1974) Psychological effects of exercise therapy upon institutionalized geriatric mental patients. *Journal of Gerontology, 29,* 157–61.

Preston, F., Shapiro, P. and Keene, J. (2007) Successful aging and gambling: Predictors of gambling risk among older adults in Las Vegas. *American Behavioral Scientist, 51,* 102–21.

Price, C. and Balaswamy, S. (2009) Beyond health and wealth: Predictors of women's retirement satisfaction. *International Journal of Aging and Human Development, 68,* 195–214.

Quetelet, A. (1836) *Sur L'Homme et le Développement de ses Facultés.* Brussels: Haumann.

Quin, R., Clare, L., Ryan, P. and Jackson, M. (2009) 'Not of this world': The subjective experience of late-onset psychosis. *Aging* and *Mental Health, 13,* 779–87.

Rabbitt, P. (1984) Memory impairment in the elderly. In P.E. Bebbington and R. Jacoby (eds) *Psychiatric Disorders in the Elderly* (pp.101–19). London: Mental Health Foundation.

Rabbitt, P. (1989) Secondary central effects on memory and attention of mild hearing loss in the elderly. *Acta Neurologica Scandanavica, 40A,* 167–87.

Rabbitt, P. (1996) Speed of processing and ageing. In R. Woods (ed.) *Handbook of the Clinical Psychology of Ageing* (pp.59–72). Chichester: Wiley.

Rabbitt, P. and Goward, L. (1986) Effects of age and raw IQ test scores on mean correct and mean error reaction times in serial choice tasks: A reply to Smith and Brewer. *British Journal of Psychology, 77,* 69–73.

Rabbitt, P. and Winthorpe, C. (1988) What do old people remember? The Galton paradigm reconsidered. In M.M. Gruneberg, P.E. Morris and R.N. Sykes (eds) *Practical Aspects of Memory: Current Research and Issues, Volume 2.* Chichester: Wiley.

Rabbitt, P., Diggle, P., Holland, F. and McInnes, L. (2004) Practice and drop-out effects during a 17-year longitudinal study of cognitive aging. *The Journals of Gerontology Series B: Psychological Sciences and Social Sciences, 59,* 84–97.

Rabbitt, P.M.A., Lunn, M., Wong, D. and Cobain, M. (2008) Age and ability affect practice gains in longitudinal studies of cognitive change. *The Journals of Gerontology Series B: Psychological Sciences and Social Sciences, 63B*, 235–40.

Radermacher, H., Feldman, S., Lorains, F. and Bird, S. (2010) Exploring the role of family and older people's access to food in different cultures: Will the children be there to help? *Journal of Intergenerational Relationships, 8*, 354–68.

Ranchor, A.V., Sanderman, R., Bouma, J., Buunk, B.P. and van de Heuvel, W.J. (1997) An exploration of the relation between hostility and disease. *Journal of Behavioral Medicine, 20*, 223–40.

Rapp, A. and Wild, B. (2011) Nonliteral language in Alzheimer dementia: A review. *Journal of the International Neuropsychological Society, 17*, 207–18.

Ratcliff, R., Thapar, A., Gomez, P. and McKoon, G. (2004) A diffusion model analysis of the effects of aging in the lexical-decision task. *Psychology and Aging, 19*, 278–89.

Raymer, A.M. and Berndt, R.S. (1996) Reading lexically without semantics: Evidence from patients with probable Alzheimer's disease. *Journal of the International Neuropsychological Society, 2*, 340–9.

Rayner, K., Reichie, E., Stroud, M., Williams, C. and Pollatsek, A. (2006) The effect of word frequency, word predictability, and font difficulty on the eye movements of young and older readers. *Psychology and Aging, 21*, 448–65.

Rebok, G.W. (1987) *Life-Span Cognitive Development.* New York, NY: Holt, Rinehart and Winston.

Reed, I.C. (2005) Creativity: Self-perceptions over time. *International Journal of Aging and Human Development, 60*, 1–18.

Reichard, S., Livson, F. and Peterson, P.G. (1962) *Aging and Personality: A Study of 87 Older Men.* New York, NY: Wiley.

Reid, M.C., Boutros, N.N., O'Connor, P.G., Cadariu, A. and Concato, J. (2002) The health-related effects of alcohol use in older persons: A systematic review. *Substance Abuse, 23*, 149–64.

Reisberg, B., Ferris, S.H., de Leon, M.J., Kluger, A. *et al.* (1989) The stage specific temporal course of Alzheimer's disease. In K. Iqbal, H.M. Wisniewski and B. Winblad (eds) *Alzheimer's Disease and Related Disorders.* New York, NY: Alan R. Liss.

Reuter-Lorenz, P.A. and Cappell, K.A. (2008) Neurocognitive aging and the compensation hypothesis. *Current Directions in Psychological Science, 17*, 177–82.

Reuter-Lorenz, P.A. and Lustig, C. (2005) Brain aging: Reorganizing discoveries about the aging mind. *Current Opinion in Neurobiology, 15*, 245–51.

Reuter-Lorenz, P.A. and Park, D. (2010) Human neuroscience and the aging mind: A new look at old problems. *The Journals of Gerontology Series B: Psychological Sciences and Social Sciences, 65*, 405–15.

Revuelta, G. and Lippa, C. (2009) Dementia with Lewy bodies and Parkinson's disease dementia may best be viewed as two distinct entities. *International Psychogeriatrics, 21*, 213–6.

Ribot, T. (1882) *Diseases of Memory.* London: Kegan Paul, Tench and Co.

Riegel, K.F. and Riegel, R.M. (1972) Development, drop and death. *Developmental Psychology, 6*, 306–19.

Ritchie, L. and Tuokko, H. (2010) Clinical decision trees for predicting conversion from cognitive impairment no dementia (CIND) to dementia in a longitudinal population-based study. *Archives of Clinical Neuropsychology, 26*, 16–25.

Robbins, T.W., James, M., Owen, A.M., Sahakian, B.J. *et al.* (1998) A study of performance on tests from the CANTAB battery sensitive to frontal lobe dysfunction in a large sample of normal volunteers: Implications for theories of executive functioning and cognitive aging. *Journal of the International Neuropsychological Society, 4*, 474–90.

Roberts, B.W. and DelVecchio, W.F. (2000) The rank-order consistency of personality from childhood to old age: A quantitative review of longitudinal studies. *Psychological Bulletin, 126*, 3–25.

Roberts, B.W., Walton, K. and Viechtbauer, W. (2006) Patterns of mean-level change in personality traits across the life course: A meta-analysis of longitudinal studies. *Psychological Bulletin, 132*, 1–25.

Rocca, W., Petersen, R., Knopman, D., Hebert, L. *et al.* (2011) Trends in the incidence and prevalence of Alzheimer's disease, dementia, and cognitive impairment in the United States. *Alzheimer's and Dementia, 7*, 80–93.

Roe, B., Beynon, C., Pickering, L. and Duffy, P. (2010) Experiences of drug use and ageing: Health, quality of life, relationship and service implications. *Journal of Advanced Nursing, 66*, 1968–79.

Roe, C., Xiong, C., Grant, E., Miller, P. and Morris, J. (2008) Education and reported onset of symptoms among individuals with Alzheimer disease. *Archives of Neurology, 65*, 108–11.

Roe, C., Xiong, C., Miller, P. and Morris, J. (2007) Education and Alzheimer disease without dementia: Support for the cognitive reserve hypothesis. *Neurology, 68*, 223–8.

Roediger, H. and Geraci, L. (2007) Aging and the misinformation effect: A neuropsychological analysis. *Journal of Experimental Psychology: Learning, Memory and Cognition, 33*, 321–34.

Rook, K.S. (2003) Exposure and reactivity to negative social exchanges: A preliminary investigation using daily diary data. *The Journals of Gerontology Series B: Psychological Sciences and Social Sciences, 58*, 100–11.

Rose, M.R. (1999) Can human aging be postponed? *Scientific American, 281*, 6, 68–73.

Rosen, D. (2004) Factors associated with illegal drug use among older methadone clients. *The Gerontologist, 44*, 543–8.

Rosenberg, H. (1997) Use and abuse of illicit drugs among older people. In A. Gurnack (ed.) *Older Adults' Misuse of Alcohol, Medicines, and Other Drugs: Research and Practice Issues.* New York, NY: Springer.

Roth, D.L., Stevens, A.B., Burgio, L.D. and Burgio, K.L. (2002) Timed-event sequential analysis of agitation in nursing home residents during personal care interactions with nursing assistants. *The Journals of Gerontology Series B: Psychological Sciences and Social Sciences, 57*, 461–8.

Rubin, D.C. and Schulkind, M.D. (1997) Properties of word cues for autobiographical memory. *Psychological Reports, 81*, 47–50.

Ryff, C.D. (1991) Possible selves in adulthood and old age: A tale of shifting horizons. *Psychology and Aging, 6*, 286–95.

Sabbagh, M. and Cummings, J. (2011) Progressive cholinergic decline in Alzheimer's disease: Consideration for treatment with donepezil 23 mg in patients with moderate to severe symptomatology. *BMC Neurology, 11*, 21–7.

Sadavoy, J., Smith, I., Conn, D.K. and Richards, B. (1995) In E. Murphy and G. Alexopoulos (eds) *Geriatric Psychiatry: Key Research Topics for Clinicians* (pp.191–9). Chichester: Wiley.

Salthouse, T. (1985) *A Theory of Cognitive Aging.* Amsterdam: North-Holland.

Salthouse, T., Fristoe, N. and Rhee, S.H. (1996) How localized are age-related effects on neuropsychological measures? *Neuropsychology, 10*, 272–85.

Salthouse, T.A. (1991) *Theoretical Perspectives on Cognitive Aging.* Hillsdale, NJ: Lawrence Erlbaum.

Salthouse, T.A. (1992a) *Mechanisms of Age-Cognition Relations in Adulthood.* Hillsdale, NJ: Lawrence Erlbaum.

Salthouse, T.A. (1992b) Reasoning and spatial abilities. In F.I.M. Craik and T.A. Salthouse (eds) *The Handbook of Aging and Cognition.* Hillsdale, NJ: Lawrence Erlbaum.

Salthouse, T.A. (2006) Mental exercise and mental aging: Evaluating the validity of the 'use it or lose it' hypothesis. *Perspectives on Psychological Science, 1*, 68–87.

Salthouse, T.A. (2009) When does age-related cognitive decline begin? *Neurobiology of Aging, 30*, 507–14.

Salthouse, T.A. (2010) *Major Issues in Cognitive Aging.* New York, NY: Oxford University Press.

Salzman, C., Jeste, D., Meyer, R.E., Cohen-Mansfield, J. *et al.* (2008) Elderly patients with dementia-related symptoms of severe agitation and aggression: Consensus statement on treatment options, clinical trials methodology, and policy. *Journal of Clinical Psychiatry, 69*, 889–98.

Sanchez-Benavides, G., Gomez-Anson, B., Quintana, M., Vives, Y. *et al.* (2010) Problem-solving abilities and frontal lobe cortical thickness in health aging and mild cognitive impairment. *Journal of the International Neurological Society, 16*, 836–45.

Sanderson, W. and Scherbov, S. (2010) Remeasuring aging. *Science, 329*, 1287–8.

Satre, D.D., Knight, B.G., Dickson-Fuhrmann, E. and Jarvik, L.F. (2004) Substance abuse treatment initiation among older adults in the GET SMART program: Effects of depression and cognitive status. *Aging and Mental Health, 8*, 346–54.

Scazufca, M., Almeida, O. and Menezes, P. (2010) The role of literacy, occupation and income in dementia prevention: The Sao Paulo Aging and Health Study (SPAH). *International Psychogeriatrics, 22*, 1209–15.

Schaie, K.W. (2005) What can we learn from longitudinal studies of adult intellectual development? *Research in Human Development, 2*, 133–58.

Schaie, K.W. and Willis, S.L. (1991) *Adult Development and Aging*. New York, NY: HarperCollins.

Scheinin, N., Aalto, S., Kaprio, J., Kozkenvuo, M. *et al.* (2011) Early detection of Alzheimer disease: 11C-PiB PET in twins discordant for cognitive impairment. *Neurology, 77*, 453–60.

Scherder, E., Bogen, T., Eggermont, L., Hamers, J. and Swaab, D. (2010) The more physical inactivity, the more agitation in dementia. *International Psychogeriatrics, 22*, 1203–8.

Scherrer, K. (2009) Images of sexuality and aging in gerontological literature. *Sexuality Research and Social Policy, 6*, 5–12.

Schlagman, S., Kvavilashvili, L. and Schulz, J. (2007) Effects of age on involuntary autobiographical memories. In J. Mace (ed.) *Involuntary Memory: New Perspectives in Cognitive Psychology*. Malden, MA: Blackwell.

Schlehofer, M., Omoto, A. and Adelman, J. (2008) How do 'religion' and 'spirituality' differ? Lay definitions among older adults. *Journal for the Scientific Study of Religion, 47*, 411–25.

Schott, L., Kamarck, T., Matthews, K., Brockwell, S. and Sutton-Tyrell, K. (2009) Is brachial artery flow-mediated dilation associated with negative affect? *International Journal of Behavioral Medicine, 16*, 241–7.

Schwartz, B. and Frazier, L. (2005) Tip of the tongue states and aging: Contrasting psycholinguistic and metacognitive perspectives. *Journal of General Psychology, 132*, 377–91.

Schwartz, L.K. and Simmons, J.P. (2001) Contact quality and attitudes toward the elderly. *Educational Gerontology, 27*, 127–37.

Scogin, F.R. (1998) Anxiety in old age. In I.H. Nordhus, G.R. VandenBos, S. Berg and P. Fromholt (eds) *Clinical Geropsychology* (pp.205–209). Washington, DC: American Psychological Association.

Sener, A., Oztop, H., Dogan, N. and Guven, S. (2008) Family, close relatives, friends: Life satisfaction among older people. *Educational Gerontology, 34*, 890–906.

Serrano, J.P., Latorre, J.M., Gatz, M. and Montanes, J. (2004) Life review therapy using autobiographical retrieval practice for older adults with depressive symptomatology. *Psychology and Aging, 19*, 272–7.

Settersen, R.A. (1998) Time, age and the transition to retirement: New evidence on life-course flexibility? *International Journal of Aging and Human Development, 47*, 177–203.

Settersen, R.A. and Haegestad, G.O. (1996) What's the latest? Cultural age deadlines for family transitions. *The Gerontologist, 36*, 178–88.

Settlage, C.F. (1996) Transcending old age: Creativity, development and psychoanalysis in the life of a centenarian. *International Journal of Psycho-Analysis, 77*, 549–64.

Shafto, M. (2010) Orthographic error monitoring in old age: Lexical and sublexical availability during perception and production. *Psychology and Aging, 25*, 991–1001.

Sharpe, T.H. (2004) Introduction to sexuality in late life. *Family Journal: Counseling and Therapy for Couples and Families, 12*, 199–205.

Sharps, M.J. (1998) Age-related change in visual information processing: Toward a unified theory of aging and visual memory. *Current Psychology, 16,* 284–307.

Sheppard, L.D. and Vernon, P.A. (2008) Intelligence and speed of information-processing: A review of 50 years of research. *Personality and Individual Differences, 44,* 535–51.

Shimonaka, Y. and Nakazato, K. (2007) Creativity and factors affecting creative ability in adulthood and old age. *Japanese Journal of Educational Psychology, 55,* 231–43.

Shimonaka, Y., Nakazato, K. and Homma, A. (1996) Personality, longevity and successful aging among Tokyo metropolitan centenarians. *International Journal of Aging and Human Development, 42,* 173–87.

Shing, Y., Werkle-Bergner, M., Li, S. and Lindenberger, U. (2009) Committing memory errors with high confidence: Older adults do but children don't. *Memory, 17,* 169–79.

Shore, D. and Wyatt, R.J. (1983) Aluminium and Alzheimer's disease. *Journal of Nervous and Mental Disorders, 171,* 553–8.

Siegler, I.C., McCarty, S.M. and Logue, P.E. (1982) Wechsler Memory Scale scores, selective attention and distance from death. *Journal of Gerontology, 37,* 176–81.

Simoni-Wastila, L. and Yang, H. (2006) Psychoactive drug abuse in older adults. *American Journal of Geriatric Pharmacotherapy, 4,* 380–94.

Simons, J.S., Dodson, C.S., Bell, D. and Schacter, D.L. (2004) Specific- and partial-source memory: Effects of aging. *Psychology and Aging, 19,* 689–94.

Simonton, D.K. (1990) Creativity and wisdom in aging. In J.W. Birren and K.W. Schaie (eds) *Handbook of the Psychology of Aging* (3rd edn). San Diego, CA: Academic Press.

Singer, T., Verhaeghen, P., Ghisletta, P., Lindenberger, U. and Baltes, P.B. (2003) The fate of cognition in very old age: Six-year longitudinal findings in the Berlin Aging Study (BASE). *Psychology and Aging, 18,* 318–31.

Sliwinski, M. and Hall, C.B. (1998) Constraints on general slowing: A meta-analysis using hierarchical linear models with random coefficients. *Psychology and Aging, 13,* 164–75.

Smiler, A., Gagne, D.D. and Stine-Morrow, E.A.L. (2004) Aging, memory load and resource allocation during reading. *Psychology and Aging, 18,* 203–9.

Smiley, E. (2005) Epidemiology of mental health problems in adults with learning disability: An update. *Advances in Psychiatric Treatment, 11,* 214–22.

Smyer, M.A. and Qualls, S.H. (1999) *Aging and Mental Health.* Oxford: Blackwell.

Soederberg Miller, L.M. (2003) The effects of age and domain knowledge on text processing. *The Journals of Gerontology Series B: Psychological Sciences and Social Sciences, 58,* 217–23.

Soederberg Miller, L.M. (2009) Age differences in the effects of domain knowledge on reading efficiency. *Psychology and Aging, 24,* 63–74.

Souter, S. and Keller, C.S. (2002) Food choice in the rural dwelling older adult. *Southern Online Journal of Nursing Research, 3*, 5. Available at www.resourcenter. net/images/SNRS/Files/SOJNR_articles/iss05vol03.pdf, accessed on 1 September 2013.

Southwell, J., Boreham, P. and Laffan, W. (2008) Problem gambling and the circumstances facing older people. *Journal of Gambling Studies, 24*, 151–74.

Spiro, A., Aldwin, C.M., Ward, K.D. and Mroczek, D.K. (1995) Personality and the incidence of hypertension among older men: Longitudinal findings from the Normative Aging Study. *Health Psychology, 14*, 563–9.

Sponheim, S., Jung, R., Seidman, L., Mesholam-Gately, R. *et al.* (2010) Cognitive deficits in recent-onset and chronic schizophrenia. *Journal of Psychiatric Research, 44*, 421–8.

St John, P. and Montgomery, P. (2009) Marital status, partner satisfaction, and depressive symptoms in older men and women. *Canadian Journal of Psychiatry, 54*, 487–92.

Stalker, G. (2011) Leisure diversity as an indicator of cultural capital. *Leisure Sciences, 33*, 88–102.

Starr, J.M. and Lonie, J. (2007) The influence of pre-morbid IQ on Mini-Mental State Examination score at time of dementia presentation. *International Journal of Geriatric Psychiatry, 22*, 382–4.

Starr, J.M., Deary, I.J., Lemmon, H. and Whalley, L.J. (2000) Mental ability age 11 years and health status age 77 years. *Age and Ageing, 29*, 523–8.

Staudinger, U.M., Kessler, E. and Dorner, J. (2006) Wisdom in social context. In K.W. Schaie and L.L. Carstensen (eds) (2006) *Social Structures, Aging, and Self-Regulation in the Elderly.* New York, NY: Springer.

Staudinger, U.M., Lopez, D.F. and Baltes, P.B. (1997) The psychometric location of wisdom-related performance: Intelligence, personality and more? *Personality and Social Psychology Bulletin, 23*, 1200–14.

Stel, V.S., Smit, J.H., Plujm, S.M.F. and Lips, P. (2004) Consequences of falling in older men and women and risk factors for health service use and functional decline. *Age and Ageing, 33*, 58–65.

Stephan, B. and Brayne, C. (2008) Vascular factors and prevention of dementia. *International Review of Psychiatry, 20*, 344–56.

Stephan, Y., Fouquereau, E. and Fernandez, A. (2008a) Body satisfaction and retirement satisfaction: The meditational role of subjective health. *Aging and Mental Health, 12*, 374–81.

Stephan, Y., Fouquereau, E. and Fernandez, A. (2008b) The relation between self-determination and retirement satisfaction among active retired individuals. *International Journal of Aging and Human Development, 66*, 329–45.

Steunenberg, B., Beekman, A., Deeg, D., Bremner, M. and Kerkhof, A. (2007) Mastery and neuroticism predict recovery of depression in later life. *American Journal of Geriatric Psychiatry, 15*, 234–42.

Steunenberg, B., Twisk, J.W.R., Beekman, A.T.F., Deeg, D.J.H. and Kerkhof, A.J.F.M. (2005) Stability and change of neuroticism in aging. *The Journals of Gerontology Series B: Psychological Sciences and Social Sciences, 60*, 27–33.

Stevens, M. (1979) Famous personality test: A test for measuring remote memory. *Bulletin of the British Psychological Society, 32*, 211.

Stewart, D. and Oslin, D.W. (2001) Recognition and treatment of late-life addictions in medical settings. *Journal of Clinical Geropsychology, 7*, 145–58.

Stine-Morrow, E., Shake, M., Miles, J., Lee, K., Gao, X. and McConkie, G. (2010) Pay now or pay later: Aging and the role of boundary salience in self-regulation of conceptual integration in sentence processing. *Psychology and Aging, 25*, 168–76.

Stine-Morrow, E., Soederberg Miller, L. and Hertzog, C. (2006) Aging and self-regulated language processing. *Psychological Bulletin, 132*, 582–606.

Stine-Morrow, E., Soederberg Miller, L., Gagne, D. and Hertzog, C. (2008) Self-regulated reading in adulthood. *Psychology and Aging, 23*, 131–53.

Stopford, C., Snowden, J., Thompson, J. and Neary, D. (2008) Variability in cognitive presentation of Alzheimer's disease. *Cortex, 44*, 185–95.

Storandt, M. (1976) Speed and coding effects in relation to age and ability level. *Developmental Psychology, 2*, 177–8.

Storandt, M. (1977) Age, ability level and scoring the WAIS. *Journal of Gerontology, 32*, 175–8.

Strube, M.J., Berry, J.M., Goza, B.K. and Fennimore, D. (1985) Type A behavior, age and psychological well-being. *Journal of Personality and Social Psychology, 49*, 203–18.

Strydom, A., Hassiotis, A., King, M. and Livingston, G. (2009) The relationship of dementia prevalence in older adults with intellectual disability (ID) to age and severity of ID. *Psychological Medicine, 39*, 13–21.

Stuart-Hamilton, I. (ed.) (2011) *An Introduction to Gerontology*. Cambridge: Cambridge University Press.

Stuart-Hamilton, I. and Mahoney, B. (2003) The effect of ageing awareness training on knowledge of and attitudes towards, older adults. *Educational Psychology, 29*, 251–60.

Stuart-Hamilton, I. and McDonald, L. (1996) Age and a possible regression to childhood thinking patterns. *British Psychological Society Psychologists Special Interest Group in the Elderly Newsletter, 58*, 13–16.

Stuart-Hamilton, I. and McDonald, L. (1999) Limits to the use of *g*. Paper presented at the International Conference on Lifelong Learning, University College Worcester, July.

Stuart-Hamilton, I. and McDonald, L. (2001) Do we need intelligence? Some reflections on the importance of '*G*'. *Educational Gerontology, 27*, 399–407.

Stuart-Hamilton, I. and Morgan, H. (2011) What happens to people with autism spectrum disorders in middle age and beyond? Report of a preliminary on-line study. *Advances in Mental Health and Intellectual Disabilities, 5*, 22–8.

Stuart-Hamilton, I. and Rabbitt, P. (1997a) Age-related decline in spelling ability: A link with fluid intelligence? *Educational Gerontology, 23*, 437–41.

Stuart-Hamilton, I. and Rabbitt, P. (1997b) The decline of eye-voice span in elderly readers. *Educational Gerontology, 23*, 389–400.

Stuart-Hamilton, I., Perfect, T. and Rabbitt, P. (1988) Remembering who was who. In M.M. Gruneberg, P.E. Morris and R.N. Sykes (eds) *Practical Aspects of Memory, Volume 2.* Chichester: Wiley.

Sudore, R., Mehta, K., Simonsick, E., Harris, T. *et al.* (2006) Limited literacy in older people and disparities in health and healthcare access. *Journal of the American Geriatrics Society, 54,* 770–6.

Sullivan, A. (2010) Mortality differentials and religion in the United States: Religious affiliation and attendance. *Journal for the Scientific Study of Religion, 49,* 740–53.

Talarico, J. and Mace, J. (2010) Involuntary and voluntary memory sequencing phenomena: An interesting puzzle for the study of autobiographical memory organization and retrieval. In J. Mace (ed.) *The Act of Remembering: Toward an Understanding of How we Recall the Past.* Malden, MA: Wiley-Blackwell.

Tallis, R.C. and Fillit, H.M. (eds) (2003) *Brocklehurst's Textbook of Geriatric Medicine and Gerontology* (6th edn). London: Churchill Livingstone.

Taub, H.A. (1979) Comprehension and memory of prose materials by young and old adults. *Experimental Aging Research, 5,* 3–13.

Taylor, E. (1957) *Angel.* London: Peter Davies.

Taylor, J.K. and Burke, D.M. (2002) Asymmetric aging effects on semantic and phonological processes: Naming in the picture–word interference task. *Psychology and Aging, 17,* 662–76.

Terracciano, A., Lockenhoff, C., Zonderman, A., Ferrucci, L. and Costa, P. (2008) Personality predictors of longevity: Activity, emotional stability and conscientiousness. *Psychosomatic Medicine, 70,* 621–7.

Terracciano, A., Tanaka, T., Sutin, A., Deiana, B. et al. (2010) BDNF Val66Met is associated with introversion and interacts with 5-HTTLPR to influence neuroticism. *Neuropsychopharmacology, 35,* 1083–9.

Terry, A., Callahan, P., Brandon, W. and Webster, S. (2011) Alzheimer's disease and age-related memory decline (preclinical). *Pharmacology, Biochemistry and Behavior, 99,* 190–210.

Thane, P. (2000) *Old Age in English History.* Oxford: Oxford University Press.

Thogersen-Ntoumani, C. and Ntoumanis, N. (2006) The role of self-determined motivation in the understanding of exercise-related behaviours, cognitions and physical self-evaluations. *Journal of Sports Sciences, 24,* 393–404.

Thompson-Schill, S.L., Jondies, J., Marshietz, C., Smith, E.E. *et al.* (2002) Effects of frontal lobe damage on interference effects in working memory. *Cognitive, Affective and Behavioral Neuroscience, 2,* 109–20.

Tomijenovic, L. (2011) Aluminum and Alzheimer's disease: After a century of controversy, is there a plausible link? *Journal of Alzheimer's Disease, 23,* 567–98.

Tomimoto, H. (2011) Subcortical vascular dementia. *Neuroscience Research, 71,* 193–9.

Tomlinson, B.E., Blessed, G. and Roth, M. (1968) Observations on the brains of nondemented old people. *Journal of Neurological Science, 7,* 331–56.

Topolski, J.M., Gotham, H.J., Klinkenberg, W.D., O'Neill, D.L. and Brooks, A.R. (2002) Older adults, substance use and HIV/AIDS: Preparing for a future crisis. *Journal of Mental Health and Aging, 8,* 349–63.

Torr, J. (2009) Assessment of dementia in people with learning disabilities. *Advances in Mental Health and Learning Disabilities, 3,* 3–9.

Tran, U.S. and Formann, A.K. (2008) Piaget's water-level tasks: Performance across the lifespan with emphasis on the elderly. *Personality and Individual Differences, 45,* 232–7.

Tsiouris, J.A. and Patti, P.J. (1997) Drug treatment of depression associated with dementia or presented as 'pseudodementia' in older adults with Down syndrome. *Journal of Applied Research in Intellectual Disabilities, 10,* 312–22.

Tucker, J.S., Klein, D.J. and Elliott, M.N. (2004) Social control of health behaviors: A comparison of young, middle-aged and older adults. *The Journals of Gerontology Series B: Psychological Sciences and Social Sciences, 59,* 147–50.

Turner, R. and Crisp, R. (2010) Imagining intergroup contact reduced implicit prejudice. *British Journal of Social Psychology, 49,* 129–42.

Uekermann, J., Channon, S. and Daum, I. (2006) Humor processing, mentalizing, and executive functioning in normal aging. *Journal of the International Neuropsychological Society, 12,* 184–91.

Uekermann, J., Thoma, P. and Daum, I. (2008) Proverb interpretation changes in aging. *Brain and Cognition, 67,* 51–7.

Unger, R. (2006) Trends in active life expectancy in Germany between 1984 and 2003 – a cohort analysis with different health indicators. *Journal of Public Health, 14,* 155–63.

Vahia, I.V., Cain, A. and Depp, C.A. (2010) Cognitive interventions: Traditional and novel approaches. In C.A. Depp and D.V. Jeste (eds) *Successful Cognitive and Emotional Aging.* Arlington, VA: American Psychiatric Publishing.

van den Berg, T., Elders, L. and Burdorf, A. (2010) Influence of health and work on early retirement. *Journal of Occupational and Environmental Medicine, 52,* 576–83.

van der Vlies, A., Pijnenburg, Y., Koene, T., Klein, M. et al. (2007) Cognitive impairment in Alzheimer's disease is modified by APOE genotype. *Dementia and Geriatric Cognitive Disorders, 24,* 98–103.

van Oijen, M., de Jong, F., Hofman, A., Koudstaal, P. and Breteler, M. (2007) Subjective memory complaints, education, and risk of Alzheimer's disease. *Alzheimer's and Dementia, 3,* 92–7.

van Rooij, M., Lusardi, A. and Alessie, R. (2011) Financial literacy and retirement planning in the Netherlands. *Journal of Economic Psychology, 32,* 593–608.

van Solinge, H. and Henkens, K. (2007) Involuntary retirement: The role of restrictive circumstances, timing, and social embeddedness. *The Journals of Gerontology Series B: Psychological Sciences and Social Sciences, 62,* 295–303.

Vander Bilt, J., Dodge, H.H., Pandav, R., Shaffer, H.J. and Ganguli, M. (2004) Gambling participation and social support among older adults: A longitudinal community study. *Journal of Gambling Studies, 20,* 373–90.

Vassallo, M., Sharma, J.C., Briggs, R.S.J. and Allen, S.C. (2003) Characteristics of early fallers on elderly patient rehabilitation wards. *Age and Ageing, 32,* 338–42.

Verghese, J., Lipton, R., Katz, M., Hall, C. *et al.* (2003) Leisure activities and the risk of dementia in the elderly. *New England Journal of Medicine, 348,* 2508–16.

Verhaeghen, P. (2006) Reaction time. In G.L. Maddox (ed.) *The Encyclopedia of Aging* (4th edn). New York, NY: Springer.

Verhaeghen, P. (2011) Cognitive processes and ageing. In I. Stuart-Hamilton (ed.) *Introduction to Gerontology*. Cambridge: Cambridge University Press.

Viard, A., Piolino, P., Desgranges, B., Chetelat, G. *et al.* (2007) *Cerebral Cortex, 17,* 2453–67.

Vinkers, D.J., Gussekloo, J., Stek, M.L., Westendrop, R.G.J. *et al.* (2004) Temporal relation between depression and cognitive impairment in old age: Prospective population-based study. *British Medical Journal, 329,* 881–3.

Voyer, P., Richard, S., Doucet, L. and Carmichael, P. (2011) Factors associated with delirium severity among older persons with dementia. *Journal of Neuroscience Nursing, 43,* 62–9.

Wachelke, J. and Contarello, A. (2010) Social representations on ageing: Structural differences concerning age group and cultural context. *Revista Latinoamericana de Psicologia, 42,* 367–80.

Wait, S. (2011) Policies on ageing. In I. Stuart-Hamilton (ed.) *Introduction to Gerontology*. Cambridge: Cambridge University Press.

Waite, L., Laumann, E., Das, A. and Schumm, P. (2009) Sexuality: Measures of partnerships, practices, attitudes, and problems in National Social Life, Health, and Aging Study. *The Journals of Gerontology Series B: Psychological Sciences and Social Sciences, 64,* 156–66.

Walton, J. (2010) Evidence for participation of aluminum in neurofibrillary tangle formation and growth in Alzheimer's disease. *Journal of Alzheimer's Disease, 22,* 65–72.

Walz, T. (2002) Crones, dirty old men, sexy seniors: Representations of sexuality of older persons. *Journal of Aging and Identity, 7,* 99–112.

Ward, R. (1977) The impact of subjective age and stigma on older persons. *Journal of Gerontology, 32,* 227–32.

Ward, R. (1984) *The Aging Experience*. Cambridge: Harper and Row.

Weisberg, N. and Wilder, R. (eds) (2001) *Expressive Arts with Elders: A Resource* (2nd edn). London: Jessica Kingsley Publishers.

Wells, Y., Foreman, P., Gething, L. and Petralia, W. (2004) Nurses' attitudes toward aging and older adults: Examining attitudes and practices among health services providers in Australia. *Journal of Gerontological Nursing, 30,* 5–13.

West, R.L. (1988) Prospective memory and aging. In M.M. Gruneberg, P.E. Morris and R.N. Sykes (eds) *Practical Aspects of Memory: Current Research and Issues, Volume 2* (pp.119–225). Chichester: Wiley.

Wetherell, J.L., Le Roux, H. and Gatz, M. (2003) DSM-IV criteria for generalized anxiety disorder in older adults: Distinguishing the worried from the well. *Psychology and Aging, 18,* 622–7.

Weyerer, S., Schaufele, M., Eiffaender-Gorfer, S., Kohler, L. *et al.* (2009) At-risk alcohol drinking in primary care patients aged 75 years and older. *International Journal of Geriatric Psychiatry, 24,* 1376–85.

Whelihan, W.M., Thompson, J.A., Piatt, A.L., Caron, M.D. and Chung, T. (1997) The relation of neuropsychological measures to levels of cognitive functioning in elderly individuals: A discriminant analysis approach. *Applied Neuropsychology,* *4,* 160–4.

Whitbourne, S.K. (2010) *The Search for Fulfillment.* New York, NY: Ballantine.

Whitbourne, S.K. and Whitbourne, S.B. (2011) *Adult Development and Aging: Biopsychosocial Perspectives (*4th edn). Hoboken, NJ: Wiley.

White, K.K. and Abrams, L. (2002) Does priming specific syllables during tip-of-the-tongue states facilitate word retrieval in older adults? *Psychology and Aging,* *17,* 226–35.

White-Means, S.I. (2000) Racial patterns in disabled elderly persons' use of medical services. *The Journals of Gerontology Series B: Psychological Sciences and Social Sciences,* *55,* 76–89.

Whitfield, K.E. and Baker-Thomas, T. (1999) Individual differences in aging minorities. *International Journal of Aging and Human Development, 48,* 73–9.

Whitwell, J., Przybelski, S., Weigand, S., Ivnik, R. *et al.* (2009) Distinct anatomical subtypes of the behavioural variant of frontotemporal dementia: A cluster analysis study. *Brain, 132,* 2932–46.

Whitworth, R. and Larson, C. (1988) Differential diagnosis and staging of Alzheimer's disease with an aphasia battery. *Neuropsychiatry, Neuropsychology and Behavioral Neurology, 1,* 255–65.

Wiebe, J.M.D. and Cox, B.J. (2005) Problem and probable pathological gambling among older adults assessed by the SOGS-R. *Journal of Gambling Studies, 21,* 205–21.

Wilcox, S., Bopp, M., Oberrecht. L., Kammermann, S.K. and McElmurray, C.T. (2003) Psychosocial and perceived environmental correlates of physical activity in rural and older African American and white women. *The Journals of Gerontology Series B: Psychological Sciences and Social Sciences, 58,* 329–37.

Williams, K., Holmes, F., Kemper, S. and Marquis, J. (2003) Written language clues to cognitive changes of aging: An analysis of the letters of King James VI/I. *The Journals of Gerontology Series B: Psychological Sciences and Social Sciences, 58,* 42–4.

Willis, R. (2008) Advantageous inequality or disadvantageous equality? Ethnicity and family support among older people in Britain. *Ethnicity and Inequalities in Health and Social Care, 1,* 18–23.

Wilson, R.S., Beckett, L.A., Barnes, L.L., Schneider, J.A. *et al.* (2002) Individual differences in rates of change in cognitive abilities of older persons. *Psychology and Aging, 17,* 179–93.

Wilson, R.S., Mendes de Leon, C.F., Bienias, J.L., Evans, D.A. and Bennett, D.A. (2004) Personality and mortality in old age. *The Journals of Gerontology Series B: Psychological Sciences and Social Sciences, 59,* 110–16.

Wink, P. and Dillon, M. (2003) Religiousness, spirituality and psychosocial functioning in late adulthood: Findings from a longitudinal study. *Psychology and Aging, 18,* 916–24.

Wong, C., Holroyd-Leduc, J., Simel, D. and Strauss, S. (2010) Does this patient have delirium? Value of bedside instruments. *Journal of the American Medical Association, 304*, 779–86.

Wood, E., Whitfield, E. and Christie, A. (1995) Changes in survival in demented hospital inpatients 1957–1987. In E. Murphy and G. Alexopoulos (eds) *Geriatric Psychiatry: Key Research Topics for Clinicians* (pp.85–93). Chichester: Wiley.

Woods, R.T. (1999) Mental health problems in late life. In R.T. Woods (ed.) *Psychological Problems of Ageing* (pp.73–110). Chichester: Wiley.

Woods, R.T. (2011) The psychology of atypical ageing. In I. Stuart-Hamilton (ed.) *An Introduction to Gerontology.* Cambridge: Cambridge University Press.

Woodward, K. (1991) *Aging and its Discontents. Freud and Other Fictions.* Bloomington, IN: Indiana University Press.

World Health Organization (2004) *World Health Report 2000.* Geneva: World Health Organization.

Yan, E., Wu, A., Ho, P. and Pearson, V. (2011) Older Chinese men and women's experiences and understanding of sexuality. *Culture, Health and Sexuality, 13*, 983–99.

Yarmey, A.D. and Yarmey, M.J. (1997) Eyewitness recall and duration estimates in field settings. *Journal of Applied Social Psychology, 27*, 330–44.

Zamarian, L., Weiss, E. and Delazer, M. (2011) The impact of mild cognitive impairment on decision making in two gambling tasks. *The Journals of Gerontology, 66*, 23–31.

Zeintl, M. and Kliegel, M. (2010) Proactive and coactive interference in age-related performance in a recognition-based operation span task. *Gerontology, 56*, 421–9.

Zelinski, E.M. and Burnight, K.P. (1997) Sixteen-year longitudinal and time lag changes in memory and cognition in older adults. *Psychology and Aging, 12*, 503–13.

Zelinski, E.M. and Hyde, J.C. (1996) Old words, new meanings: Aging and sense creation. *Journal of Memory and Language, 35*, 689–707.

Zelinski, E.M. and Stewart, S.T. (1998) Individual differences in 16-year memory changes. *Psychology and Aging, 13*, 622–30.

Zhang, X.H., Sasaki, S. and Kesteloot, H. (1995) The sex ratio of mortality and its secular trends. *International Journal of Epidemiology, 24*, 720–9.

Zhang, Z. and Hayward, M.D. (2001) Childlessness and the psychological well-being of older persons. *The Journals of Gerontology Series B: Psychological Sciences and Social Sciences, 56*, 311–20.

Ziegler-Graham, K., Brookmeyer, R., Johnson, E. and Arrighi, H. (2008) Worldwide variation in the doubling time of Alzheimer's disease incidence rates. *Alzheimer's and Dementia, 4*, 316–23.

Zimprich, D. and Martin, M. (2002) Can longitudinal changes in processing speed explain longitudinal age changes in fluid intelligence? *Psychology and Aging, 17*, 690–5.

Zwaan, B.J. (1999) The evolutionary genetics of ageing and longevity. *Heredity, 82*, 589–97.

Subject Index

Note that this index identifies the pages where the topics are principally mentioned. Some topics (e.g. intelligence, longitudinal studies) are mentioned throughout the book, and giving every single reference would be overkill.

Author Index